THE NEGLECTED OLDER AMERICAN

Publication No. 898

AMERICAN LECTURE SERIES®

A Publication in
THE BANNERSTONE DIVISION OF AMERICAN LECTURES
IN SOCIAL AND REHABILITATION PSYCHOLOGY

Consulting Editors

RICHARD E. HARDY, ED.D.
Chairman, Department of Rehabilitation Counseling
Virginia Commonwealth University
Richmond, Virginia

and

JOHN G. CULL, PH.D.
Director, Regional Counselor Training Program
Department of Rehabilitation Counseling
Virginia Commonwealth University
Fishersville, Virginia

The American Lecture Series in Social and Rehabilitation Psychology offers books which are concerned with man's role in his milieu. Emphasis is placed on how this role can be made more effective in a time of social conflict and a deteriorating physical environment. The books are oriented toward descriptions of what future roles should be and are not concerned exclusively with the delineation and definition of contemporary behavior. Contributors are concerned to a considerable extent with prediction through the use of a functional view of man as opposed to a descriptive, anatomical point of view.

Books in this series are written mainly for the professional practitioner; however, academicians will find them of considerable value in both undergraduate and graduate courses in the helping services.

THE NEGLECTED
OLDER AMERICAN

Social and Rehabilitation Services

JOHN G. CULL

RICHARD E. HARDY

CHARLES C THOMAS • PUBLISHER

Springfield • Illinois • U.S.A.

Published and Distributed Thruoghout the World by

CHARLES C THOMAS • PUBLISHER

Bannerstone House

301–327 East Lawrence Avenue, Springfield, Illinois, U.S.A.

© *1973, by* CHARLES C THOMAS • PUBLISHER

ISBN 0-398-02835-4

Library of Congress Catalog Card Number: 73-2686

*With THOMAS BOOKS careful attention is given to all details of
manufacturing and design. It is the Publisher's desire to present books
that are satisfactory as to their physical qualities and artistic possibilities
and appropriate for their particular use. THOMAS BOOKS will be true
to those laws of quality that assure a good name and good will.*

Library of Congress Cataloging in Publication Data

Cull, John G
 The neglected older American.

 (American lecture series, publication no. 898. A
publication in the Bannerstone division of American
lectures in social and rehabilitation psychology)

 1. Aged—United States. I. Hardy, Richard E.,
joint author. II. Title.

HV1461.C84 362.6'0973 73-2686

ISBN 0-398-02835-4

Printed in the United States of America

CC-11

This book is dedicated to a concerned practitioner who is highly respected for her leadership role in the area of services to the older American.

Doris Anne Miller

The following books have appeared thus far in this Series:

VOCATIONAL REHABILITATION: PROFESSION AND PROCESS
John G. Cull and Richard E. Hardy

CONTEMPORARY FIELD WORK PRACTICES IN REHABILITATION
John G. Cull and Craig R. Colvin

SOCIAL AND REHABILITATION SERVICES FOR THE BLIND
Richard E. Hardy and John G. Cull

FUNDAMENTALS OF CRIMINAL BEHAVIOR AND
CORRECTIONAL SYSTEMS
John G. Cull and Richard E. Hardy

MEDICAL AND PSYCHOLOGICAL ASPECTS OF DISABILITY
A. Beatrix Cobb

DRUG DEPENDENCE AND REHABILITATION APPROACHES
Richard E. Hardy and John G. Cull

INTRODUCTION TO CORRECTION REHABILITATION
Richard E. Hardy and John G. Cull

VOLUNTEERISM: AN EMERGING PROFESSION
John G. Cull and Richard E. Hardy

APPLIED VOLUNTEERISM IN COMMUNITY DEVELOPMENT
Richard E. Hardy and John G. Cull

VOCATIONAL EVALUATION FOR REHABILITATION SERVICES
Richard E. Hardy and John G. Cull

ADJUSTMENT TO WORK: A GOAL OF REHABILITATION
John G. Cull and Richard E. Hardy

SPECIAL PROBLEMS IN REHABILITATION
A. Beatrix Cobb

CONTRIBUTORS

ALLEN R. COHEN: Director, Developmental Disabilities Program, Department Mental Hygiene and Hospitals. Formerly: a Psychologist with The Department of Pediatrics at the University of Virginia in Charlottesville. He was special education and psychological consultant with the North Carolina Department of Public Instruction and has taught at Eastern Carolina University and Western Carolina University. Mr. Cohen is a former Assistant Regional Representative of the Rehabilitation Services Administration.

JOHN G. CULL: Ph.D. Director, Regional Counselor Training Program and Professor, Department of Rehabilitation, School of Community Services, Virginia Commonwealth University, Fishersville, Virginia; Adjunct Professor in Psychology and Education, School of General Studies, University of Virginia; Technical Consultant, Rehabilitation Services Administration, U. S. Department of Health, Education and Welfare; Lecturer, Medical Department Affiliate Program, Woodrow Wilson Rehabilitation Center; Consulting Editor, American Lectures in Social and Rehabilitation Psychology, Charles C Thomas, Publisher. Formerly Rehabilitation Counselor, Texas Commission For the Blind and Texas Rehabilitation Commission; Director, Division of Research and Program Development, Virginia Department of Vocational Rehabilitation. The following are some of the books Dr. Cull has co-authored and coedited: *Vocational Rehabilitation: Profession and Process, Contemporary Fieldwork Practices in Rehabilitation, Social and Rehabilitation Services For The Blind* and *Fundamentals of Criminal Behavior And Correctional Systems.* Dr. Cull also has contributed more than fifty publications to the professional literature in psychology and rehabilitation.

HARRY A. GRACE: Professor, Department of Management, Graduate School of Business Administration, University of Southern California, Los Angeles, California.

ABBE HACKER: Director, Office of Special Services for Adults, Division of Senior Centers, New York, New York. Mr. Hacker has had extensive experience in the senior center movement, as a group worker, center director, and administrator. He is a member of the National Council on the Aging and the National Association of Social Workers. Mr. Hacker is particularly interested in the training of staff, and has conducted numerous staff development workshops, including those for the New York State Education Department and Columbia University.

RICHARD E. HARDY: Ed.D. Chairman, Department of Rehabalitation, School of Community Services, Virginia Commonwealth University, Richmond, Va.; Technical Consultant, Rehabilitation Services Administration, U.S. Department of Health, Education and Welfare; Consulting Editor, American Lectures in Social and Rehabilitation Psychology, Charles C Thomas, Publisher; and Associate Editor, Journal of Voluntary Action Research. Formerly: Rehabilitation Counselor in Virginia; Chief, Psychologist and Supervisor of Training, South Carolina Department of Vocational Rehabilitation and member South Carolina State Board of Examiners in Psychology; Rehabilitation Advisor, Rehabilitation Services Administration, U.S. Department of Health, Education and Welfare. The following are some of the books Dr. Hardy has coauthored and coedited: *Social and Rehabilitation Services For The Blind, Vocational Rehabilitation: Profession and Process, The Unfit Majority, Fundamentals of Criminal Behavior And Correctional Systems.* Dr. Hardy has contributed more than fifty publications to the professional literature in psychology and rehabilitation.

JAMES D. HODGSON: Secretary of Labor, Washington, D.C. Before joining the Nixon Administration as Under Secretary, Mr. Hodgson was corporate vice president for Lockheed Aircraft Corporation. He also served as consultant to the State of California on manpower, as community advisor to the Institute of Industrial Relations of the University of California at Los Angeles, and as a member of the Los Angeles Mayor's Labor-Management Executive Committee.

RUTH KAARLELA: Assistant Director Program for Training Rehabilitation Teachers, Institute of Blind Rehabilitation College of Education, Western Michigan University, Kalamazoo, Michigan. Formerly: Social Caseworker and Supervisor in a family service agency, teaching hospital, and agency for the blind; Teacher of Blind Children; Administrator of School for Emotionally Disturbed Children.

IRA KAYE: Chief, Community Development Branch, Community Development Division, Office of Program Development, Office of Economic Opportunity, Washington, D.C. Formerly: Chief of Rural Programs Branch OEO/CAP, Washington, D.C.; Overseas Staff US Peace Corps; Senior Attorney of War Crimes Defense Section in Yokohama, Japan.

U. VINCENT MANION: Associate Professor of Management, University of Texas on the Permian Basin. Formerly: Member of faculty of the University of Oregon. Manion is the author of several publications and has been instructing courses dealing with the unique situation of the older person in society and industry.

JOHN McDOWELL: Director for Social Welfare, Department of Social Justice, National Council of Churches. Formerly: Executive Director, Neighborhood House, Executive Director, Soho Community House, Pittsburgh, Pennsylvania; Associate Executive Secretary, National Federation of Settlements and Neighborhood Centers, New York, New York; Dean, School of Social Work, Boston University.

DONOVAN J. PERKINS: President, Health and Medical Care Foundation, Inc. Formerly: President, ModuCare Company, Inc.; Management Consulting for Health Services, California Coordinating Committee for Education of Personnel in Facilities for the Aged; Consultant to Nursing Service Advisory Committee; Respiratory Center for Poliomyelitis, Rancho Los Amigos Hospital Executive Assistant to Chief Physician.

H. CHARLES PYRON: Associate Professor of Management, College of Business Administration, Department of Personnel & Industrial Management, University of Oregon.

JANET SAINER: Director, Serve Project, Community Service Society of New York City. Delegate to the White House Conference on Aging, November 1971, and a member of the Technical Committee on Roles and Activities of the Conference; member of the Executive Board of the Mayor's Voluntary Action Council, New York City; Co-author of *"SERVE: Older Volunteers in Community Service,"* and author of numerous articles and papers on aging and volunteerism.

FREDRICK C. SWARTZ: M.D. Chairman, Committee on Aging—Counsel on Medical Services, American Medical Association. Member Technical Committee, Employment and Retirement, White House Conference on Aging 1971, member National Task Force on Geriatric Blindness, American Foundation for the Blind, Member, Accreditation Council for Long-term Care Facilities—Joint Commission for Accreditation of Hospitals.

E. GRANT YOUMANS: Ph.D. Sociologist, Economic Research Service, U.S. Department of Agriculture, and Adjunct Professor of Sociology, University of Kentucky. Formerly: member of the Kentucky Commission on Aging and consultant to the University of Miami Geriatric Clinic and to the Southern Regional Research Project on Aging. Editor *Older Rural Americans,* University of Kentucky Press. Dr. Youmans is a Fellow in the Gerontological Society and has contributed numerous articles to the professional literature on the social psychological aspects of human aging.

PREFACE

Steadily during the last couple of decades, our aging population has grown in size. However, it has remained until only recently the least vocal minority group. We as a society have remained relatively ignorant and unconcerned about the needs of the older American.

The contemporary older American developed during a period of time in our culture which accepted readily the dicta and pronouncements of authority figures. They have been inculcated with the concept that there is an inherent justice in society—you get what you deserve—all comes to he who waits. Contemporary values have changed radically. We live in an era of mass demonstrations and violence. We have become youth oriented as a result of the strident demands of youth. This shift in values has left the current generation of older Americans with a feeling of *anomie*. They are a lost generation—a generation whose day did not arrive. The role their elders played in the culture and the role they expected to mature into has become a nonfunctional role. There has been a breakdown of the social values, customs, and mores. This segment of our population is angry, bewildered, concerned, lost and is groping for a meaningful role in society.

This text is an attempt at delineating some of the needs and concerns of the older American. It is an approach at developing awareness and concern for many who are in the social sciences. We have long been deeply concerned about the apathy social scientists exhibit in regard to the older American. This is a significant reservoir of experienced, mature manpower which remains untapped. We are vitally concerned that this natural resource has been and continues to be wasted with such little concern.

We would like to express our appreciation to all the contributors who worked so hard with us to bring this effort to completion. They have demonstrated remarkable restraint in the face of our demands and our strivings for completeness. We thank each of you. Also, we would like to express our thanks to Dorothy Powell for her stenographic contribution. In the face of the hectic activity surrounding the development of this text, she remained in good humor.

JOHN G. CULL
RICHARD E. HARDY

CONTENTS

THE NEGLECTED OLDER AMERICAN

Chapter 1

CHARACTERISTIC HEALTH PROBLEMS OF THE OLDER AMERICAN

FREDERICK C. SWARTZ

TOLL OF RETIREMENT
BEGINNINGS OF GERIATRIC MEDICINE
MEDICAL RESULTS OF AGING
COMMITTEE ON AGING RECOMMENDATIONS
SUMMARY

"If one is to spin from his own visceral wisdom, he must say, first, 'I shall not be a fake;' and, second, 'What do I know, or think I know, from my own experience and not by literary osmosis?' An honest answer would be 'Not much; and I am not too sure of most of it.' "*

Let's take a look at the status of the older American.

The first scene began almost forty years ago. A child born at that time had a life expectancy of approximately fifty years. Infectious diseases were still rampant. There were few refugees from these afflictions around. One out of every three children born died of acute infectious diseases. In addition

---

* Expressed by Dean Acheson in a 1946 address.

to this, nephritis, arteriosclerosis, hypertension, and arthritis, like the Four Horsemen, ran uncontrolled over the landscape. Pneumonia "the old man's friend" took a toll as high as 65 percent some winters. The old man referred to was mostly in his fifties. When a blood transfusion was needed on the surgical side of the house, frequently it was obtained from the hypertensive on the medical side as a part of his treatment. The failing vascular tree and heart received some support from digitalis, morphine, and ammonium chloride, but mostly they gasped out their final breaths propped up in bed or on the throne. It was not a pretty picture and the inevitableness of it all seemed to transfix everyone. No one ever seemed to think that there might be another way. Most people found their interests in other departments of medicine.

The second scene, a few years later, has a rural setting. A community of 571 souls with a surrounding countryside. Catholicism was the only religion, and families ran from eight to twelve children. Pediatrics and obstetrics constituted the major part of a medical practice.

But here the family and the farm supported the oldster as long as he lived. He always had something to do. He was needed and appreciated and therefore motivated to make the effort to live on. True, he was slow to consult the physician and slower yet to accept hospitalization—this was where people died. He was his own utilization committee and daily demanded to go home to lessen the expense and to make room for others. And when it was time for him to leave the hospital, there was always a place for him to go. Family ties held the sick and well together in the care and concern for one another. There were no foster homes or nursing homes in this community.

TOLL OF RETIREMENT

After this early experience in the country practice, there was a period of time spent at the Mayo Clinic, where one saw a parade of executives of great companies, most of them in their preretirement years, getting their periodic health appraisals. One learned many things from these men because there were hardly two attitudes toward retirement that were exactly the same. Some looked forward to it with anticipation. Most resented the fact that they had to give up their life's work, and some made complete failures of the program that was forced upon them.

At the same time, one witnessed what happened to some of the great medical clinicians of the time, who were our teachers and co-workers. These men guarded the lives of the lame, the halt and the blind until after the passage of certain birthdays, and then, although nothing else happened to them, they had neither patients, nor position, nor assignment in a world that just a few days before had been so real to them. The success and failure role with retirement presented about the same percentage as in the executive group. The only real point of importance here is that their contributions never again equaled their potential capacity. It was almost like being buried alive and certainly was a wanton waste of medical manpower. In the late years, however, just as certain universities are hiring the retired Nobel prize winners, so various clinics and groups throughout the country are utilizing retired medical men of the larger clinics.

Logically, it follows that most of these people retired because chronologic years constitutes a loss in manpower, judgment and wisdom that this nation nor any other nation can long tolerate. This statement would be true many times over if we could ever raise a generation that would not have been brainwashed by the idea that at sixty-five you are over the hill, you are through, you are an amateur golfer or a simple fisherman. In our troubled times one wonders how the course of national and international happenings might be altered if the vigor of the younger would be without conflict, tempered by the wisdom and judgment of the older. Plato, in *THE RE-PUBLIC,* 370B.C., wrote: "It gives me great pleasure to converse with the aged. They have been over the road that all of us must travel and know where it is rough and difficult and where it is level and easy."

BEGINNINGS OF GERIATRIC MEDICINE

Our interest in the older patient began about eighteen years ago when the American Medical Association formed its geriatric committee. Since geriatrics was defined as a study of the diseases of the aging, it seemed very simple. All we had to do was to find out what diseases were the result of the aging process, so-called, and begin their study and conquest. Of course there were several other sets of problems at that time which have less importance today. One of the problems was to try to get the young doctor, the middle-aged doctor, and the older doctor interested in taking care of his older patients, with the same enthusiasm and expectations of success that he entertained for his younger patients. The idea popularly held at that time was that you could not do much for anyone who was made up of so many old worn-out parts. We also had the challenge to try to direct the care of the older patients into the mainstream of medicine.

At our first meeting we found that although much had been written about "aging," no one ever specified exactly what they were talking about. We were unable to find one disease entity that depended directly upon the passage of time. We found diseases usually associated with older people also appearing in the younger, and diseases usually associated with the younger also occurring in the older. We found ourselves interested in the older individual, however, because he was being set aside by society as a thing apart. He was being treated differently and we thought he needed a friend in court. As a result we went back to the American Medical Association and asked them to establish a committee on aging rather than a geriatric committee, which they did. We became interested in every phase of the oldster's life: his health, his housing, recreation, education, sex, retirement, employment, insurance, automobile safety, and many others.

It was the avowed purpose of the committee to try to get and keep the oldster in the mainstream of medicine. There used to be signs on the doors of the operating rooms at the University of Michigan forbidding certain types of operations for those who were sixty or over, and others for those who were sixty-five and over, and other limitations for those who were seventy years and over. These limitations now have been removed. Age is no bar to good medical or surgical treatment, so long as the patient presents himself as a reasonable physiologically functioning unit to the physician. Vascular disease and pulmonary disease influence the expectations of treatment more than the patient's age.

In those early days the medical school deans agreed that the oldster belonged in the mainstream of medicine. Very little interest was manifested in the formation of the departments of geriatric medicine. Doctor Joseph Freeman reported last month that there were only four major geriatric departments and fewer than twenty scholastic appointments in rosters listing 25,000 teachers in ninety-nine medical schools.

MEDICAL RESULTS OF AGING

The position of the Committee on Aging from the very first was that they could find no disease entity or physical or mental condition that resulted from the passage of time. There were no prophesied pictures or conditions that could reasonably be expected to occur in anyone after the passage of so much time.

This characterization of aging as offered by the committee was acceptable to very few people when it was first offered. It was hard to give up the old ideas that certain degenerative processes so-called, and certain stigmata: the tottery gait, the shaky hand, the forgetful mind, failing vision, hearing and voice, along with arteriosclerosis and atherosclerosis and hypertension did not result because of the passage of time.

Observations without number the last fifteen years have tended to support the basic concept of the committee. A sampling of some of these observations is now offered.

When a chronic disease surfaces all agree that the machine has been ill for many years to life. The basic determinant of chronic disease appears early and pursues its relentless course if the patient lives long enough to accommodate the complete development of the pathology.

The following quotations come from several contributors to the book entitled *Clinical Features of Older Patients* by Doctor Joseph Freeman.

Doctor Warren Andrew says, "The characteristics of an aging, muscular apparatus is the picture of an atrophy of disuse."

Doctor Frederick T. Zugibe says, "For many years arteriosclerosis was believed to be a part of old age. More recent investigations have shown the invalidity of the thesis that a man is as old as his arteries. Some septogenarians and octogenarians have been found at autopsy to have coronary arteries relatively free of plaque formation, whereas individuals who died before the age of thirty have shown occlusive artheromatous lesions. Major William Enos, of the United States Army Medical Corps revealed that about 77 percent of a group of American soldiers in their twenties, who were killed in Korea, had atheromatous deposits in the coronary arteries. These were heavy in over 40 percent. Such observations are prima facie evidence that arterioscslerosis is not an inevitable product of chronologic age alone."

Doctor Zugibe further states, "The earliest morphological alteration observed in human aortas, coronary arteries, and cerebral arteries was a primary deposition of lipids. Lipid was first observed in the aorta of fetuses but was rarely observed in the cerebral arteries before the fifteenth year. Lipid was absent in the coronary arteries of fetuses but made its advent in the first few weeks after birth."

In a book on emphysema and bronchitis, authors Petty and Nette say, "Age itself does not damage the lung."

Doctor John P. Tindall, writing in the volume titled *Working With Older People,* Department of Health, Education and Welfare, Public Health Service, says, "Changes in the dermas attributed to aging are, in reality, those of chronic sunshine exposure and short wave ultra violet light."

In the same volume, Tindall further states, "The sebaceous glands also are influenced greatly by hormones, especially the sex hormones. Smith (1959) particularly studied the aged sebaceous glands and found no significant difference in sebaceous gland secretion in the aged male as compared to the adolescent male."

Henschel and Associates studied heat intolerance in elderly persons and said, "These elderly persons were able to tolerate the work in heat stress without evidence of excessive physiologic strain."

Dan M. Gordan said, "Theoretically and practically the eye is so constructed that normally it can be expected to function efficiently even beyond its owner's lifetime. Histologic studies of the eyes taken from the aged at autopsy revealed normal findings in over one half—over 80 percent of the population over sixty-five had a vision of 20/50 or better."

Raymond Harris said, "Atheromatosis must not be confused with the aging process or considered an inevitable feature of aging. It is a separate, independent disease which, in time, may be conquered."

Herman T. Blumenthal says, "While vascular disorders constitute the leading cause of death in the aged, the prevalent view is that their genesis is essentially the same as in the younger age group, and basic measures of prevention and therapy should also be similar. In this view aging is considered as simply providing a sufficient period of time for a slowly developing progressive process that an intensification of factors responsible for the disorder accounts for the earlier occurrence in some individuals."

Jaffee says, "The total care of the elderly includes the maintenance of maximum activity, emotional security, and physical comfort. Certainly much can be offered by medical practitioners toward relief of debilitating somatic and social distresses of the elderly presented by the commonplace diseases of the lower urinary tract. There are no greater forms of personal human tragedy than the disorders of urinary control and sexual performance. Too often these losses are equated with and relegated to the ravages of old age and are denied the careful inspection and investigation so readily available to the young."

Lindeman says, "The ability to maintain within their limits fluid volumes and electrolyte concentrations in the various body compartments is necessary for survival. Older persons retain a remarkable capacity to maintain the chemical and physical composition of the body fluids within a narrow, normal range under basal conditions. However, they do require a longer period of time to return at normal blood levels to the normal range when deficits or excesses are imposed by disease or environmental stresses."

And, finally, Doctor Morris Pollard, Director of Lobund Laboratories at the University of Notre Dame, where life is being maintained as near out of contact with environmental forces as humanly possible, we have this much of a statement regarding the work which is still unfinished. "We do not know what germ-free rats ultimately will die of, since they have not been observed for long enough periods under sterile living conditions, but it appears that many changes now associated with aging are actually due to the organism's lifelong exposure to the outside world and its hardships."

Almost proof enough to indicate that the health picture seen in the older American results from chronic diseases and has nothing to do with the passage of time. Since the facets of chronic disease are vulnerable to some modification, a whole field of therapeutics is open which, in the future, has as much promise for the preservation of life as the attack on acute disease had a number of years ago.

Most readers of this chapter will have been brainwashed by the writings of Shakespeare in his Seven Ages of Man in *As You Like It,* where it is said:

"The sixth age shifts
Into the lean and slippered pantaloons,
With spectacles on nose and pouch on side;
His youthful hose, well saved, a world too wide
For his shrunk shank; and his big manly voice,
Turning again towards childish treble, pipes,
And whistles in his sound.
Last scene of all,
That ends this strange eventful history,
His second childishness,
And mere oblivion,
Sans teeth, sans eyes, sans taste, sans everything."

Also, by the tenth verse of the 90th Psalm, and the concepts of a Bismarck, that at sixty-five one's useful life is finished.

Most articles discussing the health of the older American are prefaced by the picture that resembles Whistler's Mother and start off with the unsupported, undocumented statement, "It is widely recognized that the aged are more often ill or disabled than younger persons; that, in general, they have less income, and are less well able to care for themselves, and that facilities for their care are often inadequate." If this has ever been supported by a good analytic study, it has escaped my observation. However, it is a documented fact that 75 percent of the chronically disabled are below sixty-four years of age.

Ethel Shanas, Professor of Sociology, University of Illinois, finds that the institutionalized and homebound constitute in round figures, about 18 percent of the older Americans, meaning those past sixty-five years of age. Her work also indicated that 82 percent of the oldsters were in surprisingly good health. These statistics are grossly substantiated by observations in England and in Monroe County, New York. The 1960 to 1970 Government Census report indicates that the number of persons below sixty-five increased by 12 percent in this ten-year period. The number of persons above sixty-five increased by 21 percent. The number of persons above seventy-five increased by 37 percent, while the number of people over one hundred more than doubled. The Shanas and the Census reports indicate a happier health situation for the oldster than most people have imagined. Obviously, medicine's first job is to care for and rehabilitate insofar as possible the ill among the oldsters.

COMMITTEE ON AGING RECOMMENDATIONS

For the continued improvement of the health status of the oldster, the Committee on Aging has through the years promoted the following program:

1. Periodic health appraisals
2. Daily physical exercise

3. Daily mental exercise
4. Controlled good nutrition
5. Participation in preventive medical programs such as taking advantage of certain desirable inoculations
6. The elimination of harmful habits such as tobacco and alcohol

May we emphasize again, at this point, that many of the so-called infirmities of age stem directly from lack of conditioning. Great numbers of individuals, after leaving high school or college, settle down to a routine of breadwinning which uses only a small portion of their muscular equipment. Under these circumstances it is easy to understand why the physical horizons become cramped, why the hand shakes, and why the gait becomes uncertain and tottering. This being true, if behooves the young and old to continue some type of physical development and exercise throughout life instead of neglecting these important duties after leaving school.

Forgetfulness, mental confusion, and retardation result largely from the lack of attention and failure to concentrate any loss of motivation. This can be prevented largely if we all continue to encourage some habits of study we learned in school. Some serious reading and thinking should be a part of everyone's daily life. The muscles are strengthened and the wits are sharpened only by proper exercise and mental activity. Our whole program aimed at improving the status of the oldster would fall short of accomplishment if we did not at the same time strike a blow for moderation in the use of alcohol, tobacco, and food.

Much propaganda must be directed to the already brainwashed oldster and increasing efforts must be made to prevent the brainwashing of those coming behind him. The fatal concept that debilities come with age and that at age sixty-five one is over the hill, condemns the oldster to a period of ever-narrowing horizons until the final sparks of living are the psychoneurotic concerns of the workings of his own body.

After the committee outlined this program, they realized that this regimen would produce far better results the earlier that it was started in life. The committee surmises that the next great advance against chronic disease will come when the patient is so disciplined that as younger individuals they can accept the program as offered by the Committee on Aging and practice it to its fullest. The conviction follows that this program plus high motivation for living will increase the length of life and the depth of living for the coming generation of oldsters to an immeasurable degree.

From the very beginning, our group entertained the concept of a positive health program. We realized that among the non-ill or the so-called well, there must be degrees of wellness. We did not want to spend all our attention on the care and the rehabilitation of the sick for we felt that those who were recognized as being surprisingly well could benefit by some medical attention directed their way that would improve the degree of their wellness. Maybe someday we will have a breed of physicians who are not so disease oriented and who will be adapted from the psychological and physiologic standpoint to take care of this particular problem.

Early in our work, it was realized that the health of the oldster—as for everybody—depends to a varying degree on his environment: his housing, his recreation, his religion, and, probably more than one realizes, on his employment. We have been in the past and still are deeply concerned with the policies which call for arbitrary retirement based on age alone without regard to individual desires or capabilities.

This concept has been accepted as one of the recommendations issuing from the 1971 White House Conference on Aging. Along with this and coming from the same technical committee was the recommendation that there should be no age discrimination in employment.

The problems of employment and retirement may not seem at first to have any medical aspects to them, but the medical aspects are evident when you realize that when a man becomes completely separated from his job and goes home to stay the rest of his life, it lasts about two-and-a-half years. In addition to these stark facts, the non-worker soon becomes a complete medical problem, portraying most of the real and/or imaginary symptoms that flesh is heir to. Medicine has a vital stake in the solution of this situation. It seems almost insolvable when one views the various positions taken by labor and management and in the face of an increasing unemployment figure for the nation. Somewhere, somehow, with the increased health of the aging we will have to find some way to keep them employed, motivated, and wanted.

SUMMARY

A vignette of the health this chapter points out: status of the older American in the first third of this century as compared with the health status of the oldster today finds that 82 percent are in surprisingly good health.

That no disease entity or physical or mental condition directly resulted from the passage of time.

That in this scientific age when etiology, pathology and reproducibility constitute the features necessary to the establishment of a clinical entity, many doctors keep using the term "aging" and "aging process" without defining or recognizing the criteria which make for the recognition of clinical entities.

That the older person belongs in the mainstream of medicine.

That the expected results of medical and/or surgical treatment will be influenced by the status of the vascular and pulmonary systems more than the age of the patient.

That the future health picture of the older person will depend on our ability to control and eradicate chronic disease.

That in addition to the necessary medical and rehabilitation care, a plan for positive health program is offered.

REFERENCES

Andrew, Warren: The Pathology Profile. In Freeman, Joseph T.: *Clinical Features of the Older Patient.* Springfield, Ill., Charles C Thomas, Publisher, 1965, pp. 68–75.

Zugibe, Frederick T.: The Natural History of Vascular Change. In Freeman, Joseph T.: *Clinical Features of the Older Patient.* Springfield, Ill., Charles C Thomas, Publisher, 1965, pp. 91–102.

Enos, William: The Natural History of Vascular Change. In Freeman,

Joseph T.: *Clinical Features of the Older Patient.* Springfield, Ill., Charles C Thomas, Publisher, 1965.

Tindall, John P.: Geriatric Dermatology. In Austin B. Chinn (Ed.) : *Working with Older People, Clinical Aspects of Aging,* vol. IV, pp. 3–27.

Smith, J. G.: The Aged Human Sebaceous Gland. *Arch Dermatol, 80*: 663.

Henschel, A.; Cole, M. B., and Lycszkowsky, J. O.: Heat Tolerance of Elderly Persons Living in a Subtropical Climate. *J Gerontol, 23*: 17, 1968.

Gordan, Dan M.: Eye Problems of the Aged. In Chinn, Austin B. (Ed.) : *Working with Older People, Clinical Aspects of Aging,* vol. IV, pp. 28–37.

Harris, Raymond: Special Features of Heart Disease in the Elderly Patient. In Chinn, Austin B. (Ed.) : *Working with Older People, Clinical Aspects of Aging,* vol. IV, pp. 81–102.

Blumenthal, Herman T.: Aging and Peripheral Vascular Disease. In Chinn, Austin B. (Ed.) : *Working with Older People, Clinical Aspects of Aging,* vol. IV, pp. 103–112.

Jaffee, Jack W.: Common Lower Urinary Tract Problems in Older Persons. In Chinn, Austin, B. (Ed.) : *Working with Older People, Clinical Aspects of Aging,* vol. IV, pp. 141–148.

Lindeman, Robert D.: Application of Fluid and Electrolyte Balance Principles to the Older Patient. In Chinn, Austin B. (Ed.) : *Working with Older People, Clinical Aspects of Aging,* vol. IV, pp. 229–240.

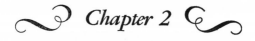

Chapter 2

PROBLEMS OF DISABILITY FOR THE OLDER AMERICAN

RUTH KAARLELA

PERSONAL MANAGEMENT
ENVIRONMENTAL MANAGEMENT
SOCIAL PROBLEMS
PSYCHOLOGICAL PROBLEMS
SUMMARY

A discussion of the problems of disability for the older person requires a frame of reference and definitions of a number of terms. Although the process of aging extends throughout the continuum of the life cycle, the concern here will be primarily upon the person who is sixty-five years of age or older.

During the course of aging, there are changes in, and/or loss of, vital cells. There are "normal" physiological and systemic changes, there are chronic pathological conditions, and there are anatomical impairments. These various conditions may be unrelated to each other, they may be interrelated, or they may be overlapping.

A disability is defined as an impairment which interferes with the everyday function of an individual. (An impairment may be defined as a malfunction.) A disability may be the consequence of "normal" aging—such as the limitations of personal physical independence which are imposed by the gradual diminution of vision, hearing, and strength. A disability may be the sequel to an "acute" illness (a sickness which lasts less than three months), such as restricted activity resulting from a cardiovascular accident. A disability may result from a chronic illness (a condition which lasts for more than three months)—such as the physical limitations which are imposed by arthritis. And, a disability may also occur through a traumatic incident such as the loss of a limb in an accident.

The following statistics illustrate the increase in incidence of impairments among aging persons in the United States (Riley and Foner, 1968, p. 206).

Type of impairment among persons 45 or over, United States, 1957 to 1958 (rate per 1,000)

Type of impairment	Age 45–64	Age 65–74	Age 75+
All impairments	212.4	376.6	615.0
Blindness	5.9	25.9	83.3
Other visual impairment	18.5	48.8	74.3
Hearing impairments	52.2	129.2	256.4
Speech defects	3.7	6.8	6.1
Paralysis	8.8	15.9	34.4
Absence, fingers, toes, only	15.9	22.6	17.4
Absence, major extremities	3.3	4.4	7.0
Impairment,[a] lower extremities	26.5	37.1	39.7
Impairment,[a] upper extremities	17.6	24.6	26.6
Impairment,[a] limbs, back, trunk, except extremities only	48.7	49.7	61.6
All other impairments	11.2	11.6	8.2

[a] Except paralysis and absence

The greatest increase in incidence of impairment after age sixty-five occurs in the sensory organs—and through paralysis. The ways in which impairments are disabling will be discussed later.

Earlier reference was made to the fact that certain chronic conditions result in disability. Although the incidence of chronic conditions is high among older people, self-reports by them indicate relatively low degree of limitation in activity (function). Only 4 to 5 percent of our older population is confined in institutions. Among the 95 percent of older people who live in the community, 19 percent report no chronic conditions. Among the remaining 81 percent who live within the community, and who report one or more chronic conditions, 32.3 percent report no limitation in activity, 7.3 percent report some limitation, but not in major activities, 25.9 percent report a degree of limitation, and only 15.5 percent report inability to carry on major activity. Major activity refers to employment or household duties.

Among the major chronic conditions which do limit activity among older people, the National Center for Health Statistics, 1965, reported the following data for persons age sixty-five and over in the United States, 1961–1963 (Riley and Foner, 1968, p. 215) as follows:

Condition	Percent of Older People
Heart conditions	21.8
Arthritis and rheumatism	20.7
Visual impairments	9.5
Hypertension (without heart involvement)	8.3
Mental and Nervous Condition	5.8
Impairments—lower extremities and hips (except paralysis and absence)	5.6

The attention by society to persons who have disabling conditions is usually expressed through services which are provided within the framework of rehabilitation. A measure of the concern of society may be the quality and/or quantity of rehabilitation services which are provided for older disabled Americans. In general, rehabilitation services for older people are limited or nonexistent. Vocational rehabilitation service through federal-state programs requires that the recipient be work-bound. Younger, less-disabled persons, therefore, have been served. One example of the allocation of services to older people is in the field of work for the blind, in which less than 10 percent of the services are provided to persons over sixty-five, but who constitute approximately 50 percent of the blind population (Scott, 1968, p. 70). Further, planning for the 1971 White House Conference on Aging did not include rehabilitation of older people in the program.

A number of factors may account for this disregard of older persons in the United States. It is generally accepted that ours is a youth-oriented, active, instrumental society and inattention to the older disabled person is consistent with our rejection of oldness. Because a number of disabilities are related to chronic, irreversible conditions, healing and helping professional personnel are less interested, inasmuch as the prognosis of a chronic condition is unlikely to be dramatically hopeful. Older disabled people do not have visibility, nor are they organized in any type of pressure group. The older person, himself, may accept disability as a norm of aging—and thereby possesses few expectations of either relief or rehabilitation.

What, then are the problems of disability among older persons? These will be discussed under four headings: 1) personal management, 2) environmental management, 3) social problems and, 4) psychological problems. Needless to say, all are intermingled.

PERSONAL MANAGEMENT

A disability may potentially interfere with the spectrum of activities which are necessary for the care of one's person— and from a mild to a severe degree. Severe visual impairments may affect skills in grooming, care and matching of clothing, management of eating skills, handling of money, and safe movement in the environment, for example. Neurological and orthopedic impairments which restrict motion in the extremities limit the ability to dress, to feed oneself, to move about freely, and, in severe cases, to attend to basic physiological needs. Certain conditions cause loss of balance or tremors, which make independent activity uncertain, unsafe or embarrassing.

The problems relating to personal management are twofold. The intake of food, and attention to physiological processes are essential for survival. When severe limitations are imposed by disability the older person may experience extreme anxiety. Also, the assistance which is required with respect to severe disabilities, places the older person in a very dependent position—which may be distressing to one who has previously been self-sufficient, and, very likely, a source of support for others. The physiological care which is essential, and the relearning of elementary skills may be humiliating to the adult.

The fact that 28 percent of our older people live alone or with non-relatives raises question about the kind of assistance which is available to the person who has problems in carrying out the every day skills of living. Some may be bereft of continuing, consistent help, and others may receive perfunctory assistance from strangers.

ENVIRONMENTAL MANAGEMENT

Each individual is surrounded by a "world." For some persons the life-space is the home and the immediate community. For others, it is the larger community. For yet others, it may be the whole country or a number of continents—and in our space age, a few persons have moved out into the universe. Whatever the *world,* individuals must be able to experience a sense of mastery of their environment in order both to survive independently and to maintain a degree of self-esteem.

Disability creates a disequilibrium with the environment. Sensory losses restrict communication and the intake of information and thereby limit awareness of the environment. Other disabilities make mobility within the environment limited or impossible. Safety factors must be considered in many cases.

Perhaps the major frustration with respect to the relationship with the environment is the loss of mobility. This may be caused by inability to walk, inability to see, or loss of balance. However, one may be able to move about physically, and yet be restricted in the environment, if a disability makes it impossible to drive a car, if one cannot afford to own a car, if one is not within reach of public transportation or if the disability is of such a nature that it is not possible to enter a public transportation vehicle. Further, there may be transportation available for the disabled person, but upon reaching his destination he may find that the building architecturally is a barrier to him. There may be too many steps, no elevators, no ramps, or a variety of obstacles which prevent access.

Limitations impaired by disability therefore create problems in a variety of ways for the older person within his environment: he may be limited in moving to a desired destination; it may be unsafe for him to go where he wishes; there may not be resources to transport him; he may not be able to maintain former social contacts; he may be unable to carry out the usual tasks of shopping and doing errands; he may be unable to keep up with the changes in his environment or to keep up-to-date with the generally changing scene.

It is important to keep in mind that not only is the older person experiencing the loss of earlier mastery and activity, but he is also experiencing the sense of entrapment which accompanies limitations in mobility.

SOCIAL PROBLEMS

Disability frequently causes cosmetic changes. Older persons are less concerned about their external appearance than are young people. However, appearance can affect social relationships—and a physically-impaired older person is more likely to be isolated from others.

The preceding discussion of mobility pointed out the problems of the disabled person's initiating and maintaining social contacts due to inability to move about. There may be problems of social interaction, also, because communication is difficult due to hearing deficiencies; one may not initiate communication because it is not possible to identify people due to visual impairment; or, perhaps one is aphasic as a result of a stroke. The combination of physical isolation (due not only to inability to move about, but also the fact that members of the family or peers may have died) plus the variety of factors which negate the opportunity to initiate social contacts, causes large numbers of older disabled people to be very lonely.

Disability affects the ability to continue other types of social roles. Older people give up employment, club activities, church activities and other leadership activities when disability occurs. Within the family, roles may change. A husband might be found caring for household tasks and administering to a chronically disabled wife—or a wife may assume the instrumental role when the husband becomes disabled.

How members of households adapt to changed roles is dependent both upon our cultural expectations as well as earlier relationships and personality needs. Certainly for the head of the household to be placed into a dependent role can be extremely frustrating and ego-shattering.

The nature of the disability may also be a factor in assignment of role. A particular condition might become the primary identification of an individual. This is particularly true of blindness, in that blindness becomes the role identification.

It is well known that the economic status of older people is poor—and that resources are extremely limited for corrective and rehabilitative services—to say nothing of resources for maintenance medications.

PSYCHOLOGICAL PROBLEMS

Disability and aging cause a number of reality problems. It is real for many older Americans that their resources are limited, that speedy recovery from a disabling condition is unlikely, that cohorts will become fewer through death, and that aging and disability are threatening conditions not only to the older people, but to those about them. Their power and influence are no longer as effective as earlier. Many find their memories to be poorer, and their reaction time slower.

Studies of aging populations generally show a correlation between a positive self-image and physical well-being. Old people take pride, not only in the number of years during which they have lived—but in their physical condition. A disability, in addition to the fact of aging, is likely to affect the self-image of the older person. This is illustrated particularly among hard-of-hearing persons who do not wish to admit that they have poor hearing—and particularly resist the use of a hearing aid.

The adjustment to the disability and the effort to make adaptations will be related to the prior life patterns of the older person, to his self-concept and to his image of the role of the older person. It will also depend of course, upon his age—whether he is "young-old"— or "old-old."

SUMMARY

The older disabled American has been neglected over the years. The concept of rehabilitation has not been extended to this group. Surveys of certain disability groups regarding resistance to particular corrective measures (Miller, 1964) indicate fear, lack of understanding, and lack of outreach as factors in resistance to rehabilitative services. Other reports describe older people as accepting service—primarily for the human contact which a service offers. Neither our society nor our older people have established a mental set toward rehabilitation. Rehabilitation goals have focused upon returning an individual to gainful employment.

If we support concepts of *equal opportunity* and *quality of life*—then it would appear imperative that as long as people live, they should have equal opportunities for maintaining as high a quality of life as is possible. Rehabilitation services must be offered to persons of all ages. The costs of institutional care are high. Older people want to remain in the community. Rehabilitation services should be extended to disabled older people—in the areas of physical restoration, personal management re-education, social work services, and psychological services. The ability to maintain one's person, or to prepare one's own lunch, or to ride to a senior citizens center, or to manipulate a talking-book machine may mean the difference between a candidate for a nursing home and a moderately-contented citizen living in his own home.

REFERENCES

Miller, I.: Resistance to Cataract Surgery. New York, American Foundation for the Blind, 1964.

Riley, M., et al.: *Aging and Society*. New York, Russell Sage Foundation, 1968.

Scott, R. A.: *The Making of Blind Men*. New York, Russell Sage Foundation, 1969.

Chapter 3

POVERTY ASPECTS OF AGING

Harry A. Grace

"The experience was eye-opening and rewarding, yet frustrating. It was eye-opening, because despite being a social worker for almost twenty years, I had never experienced the extreme poverty endemic to the rural areas of these four counties. It was frustrating because the need is so obviously great and the available resources so very inadequate. It was rewarding because I was met with an openness and honesty by the staff that is unusual, and I saw a staff that was gradually picking away at a mountain of need rather than becoming overwhelmed by the enormity of the problem."

This quotation from the narrative report of one evaluator typifies the reaction of professional persons to the conditions of poverty among older persons uncovered in a 1970–71 nationwide study sponsored by the Office of Economic Opportunity, which provides the basis for this chapter. Whether persons achieve the state of poverty as they become older, or whether persons in poverty become older is not the issue. The issue is that older persons in our nation tend to meet or exceed the guidelines of what may be defined as poverty.

In an attempt to alleviate this condition among older persons, the OEO established a program called Senior Opportunities and Services (SOS) in about one-hundred locations, thirty three of which were visited by evaluators whose reports are the basis for this chapter.

Before continuing with the purposes of the SOS program, and the design, results, and discussion of its evaluation, this concluding remark from a position statement based on having read the original report, does well to set the stage for what follows.

"Perhaps the most stimulating aspect of the narrative reports has been the observation of so many instances of high dedication and strong commitment to improving the quality of later life. . . We have many alternatives as we consider the societal stance toward older people. We can eliminate them through neglect; we can make them pathetic through mere tolerance; or we can make them proud legators of our own and future generations by our efforts to provide opportunities for the gratification of their basic human needs by whatever creative—even ingenious—means necessary as long as life lasts."

SOS PROGRAM PURPOSES

The letters, SOS, in the program's acronym fully convey the spirit of emergency underlying the manner in which this program was generated among the fifty United States, and also the spirit of endemic emergency in which America's older poor persons find themselves.

As an OEO program, one purpose was to alleviate poverty. As an older persons' program, the focus was on persons fifty-five or older, with emphasis on persons sixty-five plus. As a program within the community action agency structure of the OEO, another purpose was to encourage older persons to organize themselves and take concerted action within their communities. As a service program, the SOS was expected to provide older poor persons with both physical and social necessities.

Just as railroad tracks, which appear parallel from one perspective, also appear to cross from another perspective, so these purposes were often in conflict at the local level. In one evaluator's words, "There appear to be two opinions regarding the kind of activity most desirable. One recommends a social, entertaining, educational approach; the other recommends a creative or productive program. A new committee is giving consideration to projects of the latter nature."

Program guidelines for the SOS only guided local units, and by no means bound them. Each local program was encouraged to design and develop itself according to local interests of older poor persons, with the understanding that age was the primary criterion to be met, followed by policy-making roles for older persons, staff positions for them in the program, and integration of the SOS into the overall life of the community.

PROGRAM PENETRATION

Measures of Penetration

The problems of the elderly poor are enormous. Project Involve represents a well-conceived attempt to resolve those problems. The program is too small to produce dramatic success but, within its purview and despite its flaws, conflicts, and limitations, it has had a significant impact on the senior aides it has hired. To them it has meant a new lease on life. Project Involve has made contact with 30,000 people and rendered significant service to 2,000.

One way to view SOS penetration is in terms of the numbers of older persons who need help, and the number who receive it. This is the perspective offered by the field evaluators quoted above.

Another view focuses on the meaning of penetration as it affects individuals. This perspective appears in narrative reports such as the one from Anniston, Alabama.

> "The elderly poor in Anniston and the surrounding counties are actively sought out and encouraged to avail themselves of the program's various services. For many, these services have meant the end of hunger, illness, loneliness, and possibly the ultimate burden of human existence—despair."

Another measure of SOS penetration is the difference between the number of programs in a locality before and after an SOS program has been introduced. Our data collection system provides information on how many senior citizens programs were extant in the locality before and after the onset of the SOS and their relative importance. Table 3-I summarizes information for 30 SOS localities.

Before introduction of the SOS seven of these localities had no program or organization for older persons whatsoever. After the SOS began, four of these seven at least had an SOS program, two had an organization in addition to the SOS, and the Luzerne County, Pennsylvania SOS gave birth to nine such organizations.

Table 3-I further indicates that El Centro, California was one of six localities having at least one senior citizens organization prior to the SOS, but that since its onset eleven such programs now exist.

Eau Claire, Wisconsin now has twelve older persons organizations operative, whereas before start of the SOS that locality had four that showed specific concern for senior citizens.

All in all, thirty localities had seventy-six older persons organizations in operation before their SOS programs began. At the time of evaluation, 147 older persons programs were operative. The total gain in such programs was seventy-one. If we subtract one program per locality, thirty in all, that leaves a remainder of forty-one organizations generated in

TABLE 3-1
The Number of Organizations for Older Persons Before and After
Onset of the SOS Program[a]
(N = 30)

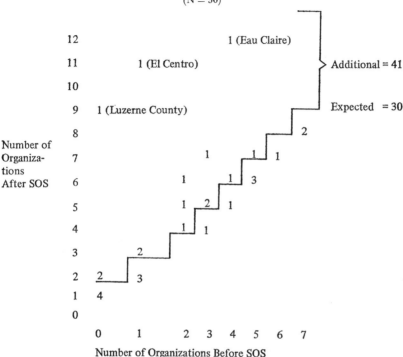

ᵃ The numbers above the lines indicate localities that generated organizations in addition to the SOS.

addition to an SOS per community. In other words, SOS leadership may have contributed to a 137 percent (i.e. 41/30) rise in organizational concern for older persons in addition to its own individual program in each community.

Yet another way to assess the impact of concern for older poor persons in a community is to examine how well various segments were aware of what the SOS mission was, and what they thought of it.

All groups contacted were knowledgeable about the nature of the program, the need to develop employment, reduce loneliness, and overcome the sense of powerlessness. All groups were cognizant of the mental health and physical health values extant in the program as it is being implemented, and all groups identified the values of employment opportunities and the ways in which the Senior Centers program is proceeding to meet employment opportunity needs within the community of the elderly. . . . Program limitations that were identified seem to spring largely from lack of finances and manpower resources for implementing programs.

No matter how one defines penetration, therefore, the SOS appears to have been successful in many localities. Of course, there have been failures to gain acceptance, failures to proliferate concern for older persons, failures to gain community-wide support. But these are specific to localities, and not the general experience.

PROGRAM EFFECTIVENESS

This section reports and analyzes the information gathered by the evaluators on the selected SOS programs. These data are measured against two sets of criteria: OEO guidelines for the SOS Program, and local program goals and emphases. The third part of this section summarizes the findings in terms of emphasis of the SOS programs on change as opposed to service.

SOS GUIDELINES

Perhaps the best way to state the guidelines is to quote from the *OEO Instruction, Guidelines for Senior Opportunities and Services Program (SOS)*, No. 6170:

All SOS programs will meet these specific program guidelines:

a. They shall have a substantial majority of program participants above the age of sixty and all above the age of fifty.

b. They shall have low income persons fifty-five years or older as a substantial majority of the professional and nonprofessional employees of the SOS component.

c. Program account shall have advisory committees or boards composed of a majority of older, poor persons and such bodies shall have substantial powers over all aspects of program conduct.

d. Program account shall incorporate a high degree of community organization activities to assure that the OEO generated service or activity can be the vehicle for increased community influence for the elderly and that the elderly will be able to affect community decisions to a greater degree in the future.

e. All program accounts shall have a direct, procedural relationship with all other CAA and community services and activties which might be utilized by the elderly, such as Neighborhood Legal Services, Concentrated Employment Programs, Neighborhood Health Centers, consumer action programs, Model Cities programs, transportation programs, etc.

f. Shall be coordinated with other community agencies and groups which are especially designed to serve the elderly including Senior Citizen centers, recreational services, senior citizen membership groups, specialized public health units, etc.

g. Utilize, to the maximum extent feasible, employment and training resources of Title I EOA and other employment and training programs.

As clearly stated as these guidelines are, it must be remembered that SOS programs were relatively new in the life of CAA's, and that the guidelines were not promulgated or enforced prior to the time of this evaluation. Most SOS's were knowledgeable about the guidelines but somewhat surprised that the evaluator applied them so strictly to measure the effectiveness of the program.

In the first part of this section, we will examine overall SOS program achievement with regard to age, sex, income, ethnicity, policy-making advisory committees, the relationship of the SOS to its CAA and local community, and training.

Age

As for age, the program is making its impact upon two groups: first, men and women in their late fifties and early sixties who have joined the program as aides, or drivers or volunteers or board members or combinations of these. The number of these persons is obviously small, but their influence certainly reaches out to others in their immediate circle of friends and acquaintances. Informally, they publicize the services being provided. These are vigorous people, and they circulate among the Senior Citizen Clubs over the area. . . . The second age group on which a large impact is made consists of persons of very advanced age who are especially in need of transportation or home services. Most of the calls made by the aides are made at the homes where the residents simply cannot get around any longer.

Tables 3-II and 3-III present information about the extent

to which SOS programs meet the age criteria. Table 3-II shows the percentages for each of five categories of age for SOS clients, staff, and directors based on information from program files. According to Table 3-II, the SOS Program meets OEO Guideline *a*: a substantial majority of program participants, 88 percent, is over sixty, and only 4 percent below age fifty. According to Guideline *b*, a majority of the staff should be fifty-five or older. Table 3-II indicates that only 49 percent of SOS Program staff meet this criterion. Furthermore, when this criterion is applied to the SOS Program Director, Table 3-II indicates that only 40 percent are fifty-five or older, with 48 percent of the directors under fifty.

TABLE 3-II

SOS Program Participants by Age Categories
(in percentages)

Age	Clients	Staff	Directors
To 49	4	18	48
50–54	3	33	12
55–59	5	10	16
60–64	16	15	4
65 up	72	24	20

On the basis of these data collected from local SOS files by our evaluators, the Program certainly serves older persons, but the staff, and the Director in particular, is not likely to meet the OEO guideline for age.

Program operations must be viewed, and assessed, within the context of the resources available and the magnitude of the task at hand. The Newport SOS program operates under the constraints of budget limitations and insufficient staff quantity for the magnitude of the tasks it has set out to accomplish. In addition, the age of the elderly staff members precludes their being able to carry out their tasks with as much vigor as younger persons. It makes good sense to employ senior citizens in terms of their being able to establish rapport and empathy with clients, but poor sense in terms of the magnitude of the job and the area to be covered. One difficulty is in reaching 30,000 potential clients with only five elderly employees working half-time. In view of these difficulties, the program's accomplishments in making three hundred contacts a month are rather remarkable.

A second table with regard to this criterion, Table 3-III, is based on the ages of clients interviewed by our evaluators. Compared with the United States population in general, the SOS Program obviously aims at the oldest of the five age groups. SOS clients interviewed were predominantly older than sixty, with a median age of seventy.

TABLE 3-III

Age of SOS Program Clients Interviewed Compared with
United States Population (in percentages)

	SOS Clients			United States Total
Age	*Male*	*Female*	*Total*	*Total*
40–49	2.5	1.0	2.0	12.3
50–54	.3	.3	.3	5.4
55–59	1.4	2.0	2.0	4.9
60–64	24.9	23.8	24.0	4.0
65 up	70.7	72.7	72.0	9.5

Source for U.S. Census Data: U.S. Bureau of the Census, *Current Population Reports, Population Estimates*, Series P-25 No. 416 (February, 1969).

In view of the data from these tables, the following descriptions of some interviewed clients approaches the norm for this evaluation, and provides some reality from which planning might proceed.

Client . . . is a seventy-six-year-old widow living with an unmarried schoolteacher daughter. The client owns a moderately productive 55-acre farm and receives $49 monthly from Social Security. She has an ulcerous leg and cannot walk—goes only from bed to chair. Without HHAP, she would need full-time nursing care. . . . One eighty-four-year-old woman neither speaks nor reads English and was a self-referral when relatives were unable to continue helping her meet everyday needs. She lives alone, receives CAA and SS assistance, has multiple physical difficulties—arthritis, emphysema, and heart trouble. The Aide spends four hours a week assisting with physical care, medical visits, shopping, and money management. . . . A seventy-eight-year-old woman, financially self-sufficient but living in a retirement home, was able to return to her own home with the help of HHAP. The Aide spends two hours a day preparing meals and doing special jobs so that this woman can live alone as she desires. . . . Another eighty-year-old, physically ill woman needs periodic help when her own full-time housekeeper is absent.

Another way in which to view age is in terms of the program's isolation or integration of older people. Evaluators were asked to examine both the program and its locality and judge the degree to which each routinely included persons of all ages in activities. Table 3-IV reports the percentage of age integration within the SOS Program and compares it with the community. Within the SOS Program, age groups are about equally likely to be integrated: in 31 percent of the programs, ages are often integrated; in 20 percent, sometimes; and in 49 percent, seldom are ages integrated. In comparison with the community at large, 24 percent of the SOS's show more age integration than is customary in the locality, 42 percent about the same degree of age integration, and 34 percent of the SOS's are less integrated regarding age than their localities. Thus, in spite of their mission aimed at older persons, SOS programs appear to separate them from other age groups only 34 percent more than is customary in the local community.

TABLE 3-IV

Age Integration Within the SOS Program and
Compared with the Community
(in percentages)

Degree	Within SOS	Degree	SOS as Compared With Community
Often	31	More	24
Sometimes	20	Same	42
Seldom	49	Less	34

In terms of the key OEO guideline for this program, age, SOS's meet or exceed the criterion for clientele, participants, or beneficiaries. Staffs and directors, however, are usually younger than OEO guidelines expect them to be, one consequence of which is discussed in the third part of this report.

Sex

Although sex was not a criterion in the OEO guidelines, it is a factor in any older persons' program. Women are known to survive longer than their male counterparts, and so constitute greater than 50 percent of the noninstitutionalized aged. SOS Program clients appear to be about two-thirds female. Among clients interviewed by our evaluators, 77 percent were women. From these data one might expect the Directors to be predominantly women; however, half of the SOS Program Directors were men.

Each evaluator was asked to judge how often men and women shared integrated activities within the SOS, and how often this prevailed in the locality. Table 3-V presents percentages for the SOS Program for these questions.

TABLE 3-V

Sex Integration Within the SOS Program and
Compared with the Community
(in percentages)

Degree	Within SOS	Degree	SOS as Compared With Community
Often	51	More	34
Sometimes	27	Same	42
Seldom	22	Less	24

At least half the SOS's demonstrate programs that often integrate men and women, 51 percent, and only 22 percent seldom integrate the sexes. Compared with the community, the SOS shows 34 percent of its programs more often integrating men and women, and another 42 percent as integrated as the community at large. Perhaps the Oklahoma City SOS does as outstanding a job in this regard as any program evaluated.

In terms of reducing the isolation of older persons, an important aspect is the relation between the sexes. It might be assumed that the SOS would cater to women; they constitute the larger surviving population and are probably more willing to engage in organized activities. To some extent this assumption holds. But the SOS programs do enable older persons to mix in their activities without regard for sex differences to an extent that equals and usually exceeds custom in the community.

Income

Originally designed for the economically poor in accord with the OEO guidelines, the Center soon found there were elderly who wanted and needed to use the Center, but whose incomes were above the specified level. The members themselves, as well as some community leaders, insisted that the Center be open to any senior citizen and wrote letters to their Congressman to that effect. They felt that any barrier—race, color, creed, or economic status—would destroy the dignity of just being a worthy human in declining years.

OEO income guidelines are more specific about SOS staff than clientele. If the average Director's income is any indication, $10,000 shared among an average of 3.2 persons, staff members tend to come from among the near-poor. Income data were not well maintained throughout the program, however, and evaluators found it difficult to get dependable information. Monticello, Phillipsburg, San Bernardino, and Santa Cruz are four of the programs that report 100 percent of their clientele below the OEO criterion for poverty. Many other SOS's are in the 80 to 99 percent category, so that the median percentage of programs below the poverty line is 86.5 percent.

Table 3-VI reports the percentages of income per person

TABLE 3-VI

Income Per Person of SOS Clients Interviewed

Income Per Person	Percentage
$ 500– 999	27
$1000–1499	27
$1500–1999	42
$2000–2499	4

sharing it for SOS clients interviewed by our evaluators. The mean income of this set of clients was $1280. However, clients in Greenville and Tallulah averaged $700 per person a year; in Monticello, San Bernardino, and Santa Cruz, $800 per person a year; and in El Centro and Pasadena, $900 per person a year.

Evaluators were also asked to judge how often the SOS integrated older persons regardless of income and how customary it was for persons of all incomes to mix in the community at large. Our reason for asking these questions was two-fold: first, we thought that some older persons would react as those in Hot Springs are reported to have done; second, Mr. Irven Eitreim, OEO Older Persons Program Specialist, felt that some programs might find it awkward to isolate older persons solely on the basis of income. Table 3-VII presents percentages of income integration within the program and between it and the community.

TABLE 3-VII

Income Integration Within the SOS Program and
Compared with the Community
(in percentages)

Degree	Within SOS	Degree	SOS as Compared With Community
Often	35	More	43
Sometimes	29	Same	46
Seldom	36	Less	11

Within 35 percent of the SOS's, older persons of all incomes mix, but in 36 percent of the SOS's there is no such mixing. When compared with the community, however, the SOS shows the same amount of income mixing among the elderly in 46 percent of the programs, and more in the SOS than in the community in 43 percent of the programs. Especially outstanding with regard to integrating older persons in the SOS without regard for income, and at variance with practices and customs in their communities, are programs in Bennington, Santa Cruz, and Tallulah. The information in this table, therefore, reinforces the hunches that led us to ask questions about income integration: 89 percent of the SOS's show the same amount or more income mixing among older persons than is true of the community.

In terms of OEO income guidelines, the SOS Program's clientele are certainly among the poor. The average income of $1280 falls even below the $1400 criterion for rural persons with only one member in the family sharing that income. Yet, in spite of this dire poverty, perhaps because of the deep values held by older persons, coupled with similar values held by SOS staff, clients are not usually isolated according to income.

> There can be no doubt that the SOS Program is serving the most needy cases in the Greenville area. The project restricted eligibility to those who were without any other sources of help. As a result, it has developed a clientele that is truly in dire need of hot food and the other benefits the program has produced. For the most part, the SOS clients are so incapacitated and dependent that there is little likelihood that they could participate in any of the other organized senior citizen activities in Greenville. . . . Without exception, the clients I visited were at the end of the road. All but a few were living in almost total isolation, really incapable of maintaining themselves with respect to housekeeping chores, cooking, shopping, and so forth. Every one of them would have been better off in some type of institutional setting but there is a good deal of resistance to the idea of going to the County Home. . . . In the context of their abject need, Meals on Wheels is a patch where there needs to be a quilt.

Ethnicity

An assumption of almost any federal program, and especially those of the OEO, is that all ethnicities will participate equally, at least in terms of their percentages in the locality. We attempted to evaluate the degree to which the SOS Program met the needs of all ethnicities, especially in comparison with their local communities.

Table 3-VIII presents age distributions of SOS clientele and the United States Census data. The Nonwhite/Non-Caucasian category is the closest definition that we could make of what the OEO defines as including all but its "Other Caucasian" category. Both evaluators and local program staff felt offended by the mere inclusion of ethnicities, a complaint prevalent in many evaluations. From the data in Table 3-VIII, we conclude that the SOS Program in age categories from fifty-five upward, clearly serves more persons outside the "Other Caucasian" category than could be expected by chance (chi square significant at the .01 level of confidence) .

TABLE 3-VIII

Nonwhite/Non-Caucasian Clients in SOS Programs and
Compared with United States Population

Ages	Percent SOS Clientele Nonwhite/Non-Caucasian	Percent U.S. Population Nonwhite/Non-Caucasian
40–49	45.2	10.7
50–54	12.5	10.1
55–59	43.8	9.3
60–64	32.5	8.5
65+	32.1	7.9
All combined	32.5	12.1

While approximately 32 percent of all SOS clients were reported as not "Other Caucasian," almost 40 percent of the clients interviewed by our evaluators fell in this category. While this difference in percentages is not significant, it is perhaps indicative of the concern that SOS Program Directors showed for all ethnicities, although 90 percent of the Directors were most likely to be classified as "Other Caucasian."

Ethnicity was also evaluated in terms of integration. Table 3-IX presents this information. Ethnicities are often integrated in 28 percent of the SOS's, sometimes integrated in 36 percent, and seldom integrated in 36 percent. On this criterion, the SOS appears rather conservative. However, when compared with ethnic integration in the locality itself, the SOS appears more ethnically integrated in 54 percent of the programs, and as integrated in 42 percent more. Tallulah appears outstanding as far as ethnic integration is concerned within its program in comparison with the customs of its locality.

TABLE 3-IX

Ethnic Integration Within the SOS Program and
Compared With the Community
(in percentages)

Degree	Within SOS	Degree	SOS as Compared With Community
Often	28	More	54
Sometimes	36	Same	42
Seldom	36	Less	4

With only 4 percent of the SOS's less integrated ethnically than their local communities, and the ethnic clientele well represented in comparison with the nation's older population, the program appears to have achieved criterion as far as ethnicity is concerned.

We say "appears to have achieved criterion" because study of the narrative reports leads one to believe that the SOS has only been able to scratch the surface of the older poor population who need help. In fact, were this evaluation to focus solely on older, poor "Other Caucasians," their needs would be so overwhelming as to require many times the budget and effort thus far expended. We can only surmise from these narrative reports that the general condition of older poor persons from ethnicities other than "Other Caucasians" is equally deplorable if not worse. Only 6 percent of SOS clients are classified as Caucasian—Mexican American; only 14 percent as Negro; and only 2 percent as, other—Filipino, (predominantly from Santa Cruz). For these reasons, we believe that although the program meets or exceeds its implied criterion of ethnic representation, the SOS has a long way to go to meet the needs of older poor persons classified outside the "Other Caucasian" category.

POLICY MAKING

A note on what the aged like and dislike; they like Social Security, the bus, Medicare (with reservations), a chance to meet and talk, to do things for themselves and their friends, to revive old memories and skills and pastimes, to reminisce. They appreciate help in finding their way around in the agencies they have to deal with—legal, medical, welfare, insurance, and the like.

But they don't like: adolescents, nutrition classes, other people's music, art classes, lectures, "culture" and other abstractions, complicated language and arguments, efforts to make them over or to elevate their tastes, or to move them from their homes or to talk to them of funerals.

OEO Guideline *c* expects an SOS to have an advisory committee composed of a majority of older poor persons with power over the program. This criterion is not being achieved as yet. We can qualify this failure to achieve policy-making stature by the phrase, "as yet," because SOS's are so embryonic that priority has been placed on political survival and delivery of services rather than policy involvement. Portsmouth is one of the exceptions.

> Clients are said to function as a "committee of the whole" for program planning. The SOS is very highly regarded in its host community. Ratings by clients were typically very favorable and its programs were classed as both important and successful almost without exception by clients and agency personnel. Many highly favorable comments about the SOS Director were voiced and she was typically seen as an effective leader for the program.

Although evaluators were asked to gather information about the role that older poor persons played in SOS policy making, little statistical evidence was forthcoming. Narrative reports, such as those cited in this section and elsewhere, lead one to believe that the clients exert a definite pressure on program development and success, but that this influence is more informal than formal.

How does policy come about? Primarily by SOS staff input, and specifically, by the SOS Program Director, certainly the most crucial person in the majority of programs. At the risk of forming a stereotype, let us attempt a composite description of the SOS Program Director.

The SOS Program Director is likely to be a forty-nine-year-old, "Other Caucasian" man or woman with a year and one-half of college education. As for his occupation prior to SOS direction, it might be nurse, insurance salesman, social worker, teacher, minister, dental assistant, home economist, housewife, secretary, civil servant, or military officer. As Program Director, the incumbent is likely to have an income between $4200 and $24,000 a year, averaging $9900, and to share that with an average of 3.2 persons, ranging from himself alone to seven in the family.

From this composite it becomes quite apparent that SOS Program Directorship cannot be readily predicted. What can be predicted, although it appears primarily in narrative reports, is that the SOS Program Director sets most of the policy, decides what procedures will be used, and often finds himself having to carry a major load of the program itself.

This does not mean that SOS's have no advisory committees, but that such committees are rarely composed of a majority of older poor persons. One-third of the programs, for instance, do not claim an advisory committee. One of these, Portsmouth, has its entire clientele as a committee of the whole.

The number of persons listed as members of the SOS staff range from a low of one in San Bernardino to highs of forty-three in Phillipsburg and forty-five in Anniston. Averaging these numbers does not make sense; the program's staff is either a handful or over twenty persons.

In terms of the OEO criterion for policy making, SOS programs do not have advisory boards composed of a majority of older poor persons. Two-thirds have advisory boards, but not necessarily of older and/or poor persons. Policy and procedure tends to be set for programs by exceptionally dynamic Directors, thirty years of age or less in La Junta and Bennington, and over seventy in Tallulah, El Centro, and San Bernardino. The variety of work that an SOS staff member can be expected to do is illustrated in the following citation.

> An example of what one senior citizen aide has recently done is appropriate to cite. [She has] helped senior citizens to dress and sell dolls, provided various activities, secured arts and crafts equipment, set up an extension club, made Christmas stockings, taken gifts to nursing homes, visited shut-ins, taken clothing to Ada Miles Rest Home. She has plans for armchair visits to take slides of travels to elderly homes, to develop a telephone exchange to keep in touch with those who live alone, to provide a movie once a month, to provide sightseeing trips. There is also a program to get older people involved with the Head Start program, to provide a "grandparent" image to the children.

Relationship to CAA and Community

The population of this four-county area is 42,700, and of this total, approximately 11,200 persons are age 55 years and older. . . . Of the

11,200 persons, some 3,900 are aged 55 to 65, and 7,300 are 65 years and older. Given these conditions, the need for senior citizens services is widespread and immediate . . . but given the independent spirit of the typical rural Nebraskan, ready acceptance of such programs is seldom easily achieved, particularly if these are "government" programs. . . . About one-half of the persons eligible for these programs live in 33 towns having populations of less than 1,000, and the remainder live in five larger communities or on farms. Most of these people have worked all their lives in agrarian pursuits, earning only adequate—but not generous—incomes. They are not affluent by any standard, but they do not consider themselves poor or poverty stricken. For these people, life has generally been hard, and while money frequently was short, food was, for the most part, sufficient and diets well-balanced. Life under these circumstances develops people who are independent, proud, conservative, self-sufficient, and suspicious of outsiders. Against this background one better understands the problems faced in organizing SOS programs in this area.

OEO Guidelines *e* and *f* expect the SOS to relate to its community and other programs, and especially to senior citizen activities. Each evaluator was asked to judge how the SOS performed in these relationships. Table 3-X presents percentages of SOS programs in terms of their community focus and their share in the community.

We defined focus in two ways: local support for the SOS, and SOS leadership *vis-à-vis* older poor persons. Table 3-X indicates that 32 percent of the SOS's showed great local sup-

TABLE 3-X

SOS Program Focus and Share in Relationships With the Community
(in percentages)

Focus			SOS Share in CAA			
Degree	Local Support For SOS	SOS as Leader	Degree	Amount	Degree	Influence
Great	32	61	More	27	Much	26
Some	43	18	Equal	40	Some	37
Little	25	21	Less	33	Little	37

port, and an additional 43 percent some local support. Yet one-fourth of the SOS's had little local support at the time of this evaluation. As far as SOS leadership in the community with regard to the status of older poor persons, evaluators rated 61 percent of the SOS's as offering great leadership, 18 percent as offering some leadership, and 21 percent as offering little leadership. When we compare local support, or its absence, with leadership by the SOS, Anniston and El Centro stand out. So, too, do Winston-Salem and Santa Cruz. Newport receives some support, but far exceeds that in the leadership it shows on behalf of older poor persons.

Two questions were asked about SOS's share in CAA: how much of its share of CAA resources does the SOS receive, and how much does the SOS influence CAA policy, procedures, programs, and strategies. Table 3-X indicates that 27 percent of the programs receive more than their share of CAA resources, 40 percent their expected share, and one-third of the SOS's less than what could be expected as their share of CAA support. Among the SOS's perceived by our evaluators to receive *much less* than their expected share of CAA resources are Oklahoma City, San Diego, Winston-Salem, and Indiana County. In spite of this condition, the Indiana County SOS has considerable influence on CAA decisions, and Winston-Salem influences its CAA more than might be expected from the resources it receives. Tallulah's SOS, while receiving its fair share of CAA resources, appears to have *very much* influence on overall CAA policy and program. For the most part, however, Table 3-X shows that only 26 percent of the SOS's have much influence on their CAA's, 37 percent have some influence, and another 37 percent having little influence on their CAA's.

Oddly enough, the Newport evaluator perceived that SOS to show *very great* leadership on behalf of older poor persons, and at the same time to have *very little* influence on CAA policy, procedures, programs, and strategies. How this condition might occur is suggested in the following citation.

A fairly good cross-section of community people was sampled (a bishop of the LDS Church, an elderly retailer, a high-school principal, a realtor, a feed-business manager, a teacher, and a meat-cutter), but the results were not encouraging. Only those who had worked with the CAA seemed to have a grasp of program goals.

In terms of OEO guidelines for SOS relationships, data on this program reflect its embryonic stature, and probably the neglect of the nation, let alone regions, states, and localities of older poor persons. We believe this neglect is reflected not only in one-quarter of the SOS's having little local support, in spite of 79 percent of them showing some or great leadership on behalf of the older poor, but also in one-third of the SOS's receiving less than their due share of CAA resources, with 37 percent having little influence on CAA decisions and actions.

Training

However elusive other information might have been, training information was most elusive. Time and again there was confusion between trainers, who reported what they had done or said or meant, and SOS staffs, who could not recall having received "training."

Statistically, this means that only nine SOS's report any training budget at all. Only nineteen report any percentage of their staff's time allocated to staff training. We asked each evaluator to list the training materials used, the topics covered in training, the qualifications of the trainers, and the kinds of events used to accomplish the goals of training.

Table 3-XI presents percentages of staff time per week

TABLE 3-XI

Time and Budget Allocated to SOS Staff Training

Time in Training		Budget for Training	
Percentage of Staff Time Per Week	*Percentage of SOS's*	*Percentage of SOS Budget*	*Percentage of SOS's*
None	26	None	67
1–5	37	1–3	18
6–10	22	4–6	11
11–15	7	More	4
16 more			

spent in training, and the percentage of SOS budget allocated to training the staff. Twenty-six percent of the SOS's spent no staff time at all in receiving training; 37 percent spent from 1 to 5 percent of staff time in training. Long Beach, with 40 percent of its staff's time spent in training, and Newport with 25 percent, rank the highest of all programs. One-third of the SOS's allocated some percentage of their budget for staff training. Of these programs, 18 percent allocated between one and three percent, 11 percent allocated between 4 and 6 percent, and one program, Eau Claire, allocated 20 percent of its SOS budget for staff training. For programs that allocated some money for training, the sums range between $400 and $5000, the average being $1466.

> Training and continuous supervision are essential in order for the aides to do their work effectively. The training program . . . was too intensive, the material given the aides too abstract, and was not immediately relevant to the concrete problems they were experiencing. Aides complained that the training was too theoretical and that they only learned when they were actually on the streets.

With regard to the focus of training, we expected materials and topics to reflect the nature of SOS clientele; that is, to be directed toward persons who were old and poor. Scoring the evidence from evaluators with these criteria for training materials (books, pamphlets, audiovisual aids) only six SOS's met the criteria: Monticello, Eau Claire, Oklahoma City, Tallulah, Troy, and La Grande. Fifteen programs met the criteria for focus on topics (concepts, ideas, skills) relevant to older poor persons. Table 3-XII indicates, therefore, that of the SOS programs, 20 percent used staff training materials, and 50 percent covered topics, that focused on older poor persons.

TABLE 3-XII

Focus and Quality of SOS Staff Training
(in percentages)

Focus		Quality	
Materials	20	Trainers	47
Topics	50	Events	30

Table 3-XII further indicates that 47 percent of the SOS programs had trainers with the educational qualifications and experience necessary to represent themselves as experts with regard to older poor persons. However, only 30 percent of the SOS's engaged in actual training events such as field trips, lectures, or role playing, directly related to characteristics of the clients for whom the SOS is intended.

Using these data that rely on reports to evaluators from SOS staff, outstanding training appears to have been conducted in Eau Claire, Oklahoma City, Tallulah, and La Grande; and good training in Monticello, Winston-Salem, Troy, and Wichita.

SOS PROGRAM EMPHASES

The *carte blanche* guidelines offered to CAA's intent on establishing SOS programs resulted in such a diversity of emphases (goals) that no two programs look alike. Moreover, in addition to OEO freedom regarding program goals, the clients themselves added their values to the challenge faced by each SOS staff.

> All of the clubs activities are encompassed in the weekly meetings, except in two cases. Two clubs are lobbying for community action in their towns: in one case for a park, in the other for a sewage system. . . . Officers have been elected for each club, and are supposed to run the meetings. Staff members usually hover near the podium, and often wind up running the meeting. The programs vary from group to group, but one common denominator seems to be bingo. People bring little gifts from home which serve as prizes for the bingo games. . . . The people enjoy the games tremendously. It seems that when staff members try to introduce new games or activities, they are not well received. . . . Sometimes films are shown at meetings; these range from travelogues to health and first aid. Guest speakers are sometimes provided. . . . Lectures on personal hygiene are given by doctors. Talks on citizenship are also given, stressing the importance of registration and voting. . . . People are passive, even at meetings. They sit quietly and accept what happens in the way of procedure and program. There is little discussion of new ideas. People seem to tolerate the procedures and goings-on to get to the bingo. . . . Not only have the older people never belonged to clubs, but clubs have never existed in their communities. Many just

cannot be persuaded to even come to one meeting. . . . These people have been farm laborers all their lives . . . they have gotten up at six in the morning and worked until sundown throughout their working lives. They come home, eat, and go to sleep. They have never cultivated any hobbies or interests.

Importance and Progress of Program Goals

Evaluators interviewed at least ten clients in each SOS, its staff, and up to ten community persons regarding (1) their perceptions of the importance of each goal, and (2) their perceptions of the SOS's progress in achieving each goal. This information was compiled in the project evaluation office for the total SOS Program; however, each narrative report focuses on the information for that individual SOS.

Table 3-XIII gives the ranking accorded to each program emphasis by clients, staff, and community persons. The numbers indicate ranks, the lower the number the higher its rank: that is, number 1 is the highest rank, and number 12 the lowest. The table has three major fields: Frequency of Mention, Rank of Interest, and Composite Rank. The Frequency of Mention field includes columns for clients, staff, and community persons. Because differences between goal importance and goal progress were not significant, only one rank is listed for each goal. The Rank of Interest field has ranks for goal importance (Imp.) and goal progress (Prog.) for each column: clients, staff, and community. The third field of Table 3-XIII is similar in display to that for the Rank of Interest, except that Composite Rank represents ranks obtained by multiplying the frequency of mention by the average score for each goal's importance and progress. We will examine this table goal by goal, and then draw some general conclusions about program emphasis in the SOS.

1. *Recreation*: Recreation ranks first in Frequency of Mention, and this accounts for its top rating in Composite Rank. The staff's ranking of recreation as least important in Rank of Interest, 12, mars an otherwise perfect sweep of first place in program emphasis as far as SOS's are concerned. On the basis of Interest, clients appear mildly dis-

TABLE 3-XIII
SOS Program Emphases Ranked by Clients, Staff, and Community Persons

Program Emphases (Goals)	Frequency of Mention			Rank of Interest						Composite Rank					
	Client	Staff	Community	Client		Staff		Community		Client		Staff		Community	
				Imp.	Prog.	Imp.	Prog.	Imp.	Prog.	Imp.	Prog.	Imp.	Prog.	Imp.	Prog.
1. Recreation	1	1	1	2+	5	12	2+	3	3+	1	1	3	1	1	1
2. Outreach	2	2	2	10	10	9+	6+	11+	9	2	2	2	2	2	5
3. Income	3	3	3	5+	6	6+	9	6+	8	3	3	1	3	3	3
4. Education	5	5	5	9	9	8	2+	6+	6	5	5	5	4	5	4
5. Health	8	4	6	7+	7+	4	6+	8+	11	8	6	4	6	6	2
6. Transport	6+	7	4	5+	7+	1	4	8+	7	7	4	7	5	4	6
7. Action	4	6	8	11	11	6+	12	4+	10	4	7	6	7	8	9
8. Referral	6+	8+	7	2+	3+	2+	8	4+	5	6	10	8+	9	7	7
9. Housing	10	12	9	1	1	11	5	1	1	9	8	12	10	9	8
10. Morale	9	10	10	7+	3+	5	1	10	3+	10	9	10	8	10	10
11. Meals	11	8+	12	4	2	2+	10	2	2	11	11	8+	11	11	11
12. Counsel	12	11	11	12	12	9+	11	11+	12	12	12	11	12	12	12

appointed in the progress of recreation as a goal, while staff rank its progress far above its importance to them.

2. *Outreach*: This goal represents a continuation of Project FIND for many SOS's. It ranks second in Composite Rank, as in Frequency of Mention, but rather low in Rank of Interest. Both staff and community persons view outreach as showing greater progress than importance in Interest.

3. *Income*: It is interesting to notice that the staff ranks income support at the top of its Composite Rank, although this goal falls to third place overall. For each group's Interest, income support shows greater importance than progress.

Clients commented on their desires to use their full abilities in a job or to receive higher pay; they did not feel their needs were being met in these areas. One client, living in a public-housing project, complained that her rent had been raised when the rental manager learned of her WORK employment. Though this causes her some hardship, she intends to continue her job; the psychological benefits to her self-esteem outweigh the financial problems. . . . Project WORK has been quite successful in placing people in jobs; very successful in making people feel worthwhile, increasing their self-esteem and position in the community; and successful in providing a supplement to the elderly people's incomes. . . . The most outstanding problem of the program is the inability of the Project to encourage community agencies to put WORK employees on the agency payrolls. . . . Since community agencies have not picked up the cost of the Project WORK employees, the employees have provided essentially free help to the agencies using them.

4. *Education*:

As the program of personal visitation and club work began to be felt in the community, several basic problems emerged with regard to the original objective of assessing employment potential and opportunities. One problem was the fact that many of these older citizens had never learned the basic skills of reading, writing, and arithmetic. To meet this need, the parish school board offered space and materials in order than an adult education program for senior citizens might be organized. . . . One of the students interviewed had never attended school at all—and she was 77 years old. The expression on her face, and the thrill she seemed to feel, as she wrote her name for the interviewer cannot be communicated on paper.

She said that learning to write her name was the greatest thing that had ever happened to her. Tears flowed from the eyes of this 77-year-old black woman as she pleaded with the interviewer to help open up the school again. . . . Almost all the persons interviewed held that this educational program was second only to the minor-repair program.

This citation shows how one program emphasis shifts to another. Education ranks fifth in mention among goals, and in its Composite Rank as far as progress toward goal achievement is concerned, is fourth from the perspectives of SOS staff and community persons. Clients rank their Interest in education much lower, ninth, but staff perceive progress toward educational goals as second only to morale.

5. *Health*: Community members give health a Composite Rank on progress of second, showing variance with every other rank for this goal, and placing their Interest in health progress near the bottom, eleventh. This may reflect some unwillingness on the part of the community to admit that all is not well with its older poor population.

6. *Transportation*: Having read the need for transportation in narrative after narrative report, one might have expected this goal to achieve a rank higher than sixth. The staff ranks transportation highest in importance, but no other ranks come close to this. The community persons interviewed, for instance, rank transportation eighth, showing some clear disagreement with SOS program staff. One wonders whether these are mere differences in individual perception, or whether the absence of transportation seriously threatens the staff with having to reallocate resources away from other programs in order to bring services to older poor clients, or bring these clients into the Centers. Certainly, the top rank given to transportation by SOS staff ought not be ignored in program planning.

Transportation is a major need, and Progress on Wheels has brought many elderly people out of isolation, at least for minimal, essential services. The program does not pretend to be comprehensive for the individuals involved; they are not thereby involved in social, recreational, educational, or vocational activities. But the transportation provided, while minimal and sharply restricted, is nevertheless a critical means of reducing isolation and providing the elderly poor with at least basic protection from such misfortunes as insufficient food, poor medical care, lack of Medicare, loss of Social Security benefits, and the like.

7. *Action*: Ranked in the lower half, as far as program emphasis is concerned, is the goal of social action. Ostensibly, CAA programs are action-oriented, beginning as they do with organizational development, and then moving into advocacy and other civil activities. Frequency of Mention for action drops from clients (fourth), to staff (sixth), to community persons (eighth), and the same pattern shows in the Composite Ranks for goal importance. Interest, however, demonstrates the reverse order of emphasis: community persons show greatest Interest and clientele least Interest in social action. All three populations share the perception that SOS progress toward the goal of social action ranks very low: eleventh, twelfth, and tenth, respectively.

> On such legislative reform as tax relief, consensus prevailed and it was possible to mount a campaign of advocacy. . . . A contingent of senior citizens went to Madison to testify for tax relief for the aged. . . . On short-term, immediate and small issues, like getting a street light or stop sign, it was more difficult but still possible for local residents to organize, get a hearing, apply pressure, and get results that could mean a victory. On larger, immediate issues that required a sustained organizational drive, as in the freeway fight or in the current investigation of nursing homes, it was still harder to sponsor social advocacy. . . . Some small benefits have resulted from advocacy, but the needs that the social advocacy program tries to meet more than justify the Project's existence.

8. *Referral*: OEO Guidelines *e* and *f* emphasize that SOS's are to make full use of existing community agencies and resources. While referral receives average rank in Frequency of Mention, it achieves a higher Composite Rank because of the Interest that clients and community persons have in this goal. Interestingly enough, both clients and the community appear more satisfied with the progress toward achieving the goal of referral than does the SOS staff, who rank progress eighth. Perhaps the staff has more real knowl-

edge of the actual referral of clients to other agencies than either the older poor or community persons possess.

9. *Housing*: Clientele and community rank housing at their primary Interest, both in importance and in progress. The staff, however, ranks this goal eleventh in importance, but fifth in progress. The Composite Rank averages seven because housing is mentioned relatively infrequently by all groups interviewed. This information poses a puzzle for program planning: should decision proceed on the basis of interest, risking the unpopularity of a housing program; or should its low Frequency of Mention be ignored, and programs be designed on the basis of the high Interest shown by some clients and community persons in housing? The low rank allocated housing by SOS staff may either reflect their inadequate skills to effect better housing, or their feeling that this goal is handled by programs other than the CAA.

> An elderly lady . . . returned home one day to find that her home and all her belongings had been burned to the ground to make way for a redevelopment area. Although notices to vacate the houses in her area had been posted prior to the fire, the lady was not able to read so was quite ignorant of the plans to burn her home. Since the lady had not been informed of the intended fire by any other source, she had made no provisions for moving. Although shocked by the loss of her home and all her worldly possessions, she managed to find another house in very poor condition six blocks away. She began paying rent on the house with the understanding that the owner of the property would repair the house to a livable condition. While awaiting the repairs, she moved into a single room in a house nearby. She continued to pay rent on the house for five months although the promised repairs were never made and she never moved into the house. The sixth month she did not pay the rent and was promptly evicted from the house she had never lived in. The ESR staff member cites this as an example of why SOS is needed— to organize people, to help them see they do not have to be victims of the system, but that they can help to shape it. He called this the advocacy role, part of its purpose being to keep the system honest.

10. *Morale*: The goal of boosting client morale ranks low in Frequency of Mention, and equally low in importance as far as community persons' Interests are concerned,

the staff's view of its importance being the highest. But in spite of these relatively low rankings on Interest importance, the staff ranks progress toward achieving morale as first. This perspective receives strong confirmation from the 3-4 rankings of SOS clients and community persons. Although infrequently mentioned, morale captures the interest of SOS groups, especially insofar as morale offers a goal toward which progress can readily be felt.

> A number of elderly persons who are in a precarious state of health, but who continue to live alone, request that the Center phone them once a day to see that they are all right. If there is no answer on the second day, the aide checks with neighbors or family to determine the reason. In some instances, the service has been requested by families who live far from the elderly person. . . . About 24 calls are made daily.

11. *Meals*: Like housing, food and meals rate high in Interest among clients and in the community. Meals also engage the Interest of the staff, who disagree that progress is as great as perceived by other groups. Again, the relative infrequency of mentioning meals as a goal contributes to its low Composite Ranks.

> While Greenville's program must receive a low-moderate rating in terms of its compliance with OEO guidelines for SOS programs, I think it only fair to point out that, considering the small amount of funds being expended, the program was almost condemned to remain limited if it was to effectively fulfill its objectives. Getting involved with broader concerns might have dissipated staff time and program funds to such an extent that instead of being able to feed 126 old persons five times a week (26 *over* quota), many fewer and less regularly served meals might have been the outcome.

12. *Counsel*: The goal of providing guidance and counsel to older poor persons ranks at the bottom of the list of twelve program emphases. It is the least frequently mentioned, and Interest in it is low even among the staff who rate its importance slightly higher than other groups involved in the SOS.

Summary of Program Goal Rankings

Reviewing this information about SOS program emphasis, recreation is by all means the first priority in program goals, followed by outreach and income support. Education, health, and transportation follow, and then the gap widens until we reach social action and referral, goals below the half-way ranking. Housing, morale-boosting, and meals rank very low, and counseling at the bottom of the list.

A glance at clients' Composite Ranks shows only one major discrepancy: progress toward referral does not match the importance that clients attach to this goal. For SOS staff members, Composite Ranks of goal importance and progress toward goal achievement show only minor discrepancies. Comparing the clientele with the staff, the only major difference between them appears with regard to health: staff rank the importance of health much higher than do clients. When attention is paid to community persons' Composite Ranks, discrepancies appear between outreach and health goals. The community ranks the importance of outreach above progress toward its achievement, and conversely ranks the importance of health below progress toward its achievement. In its optimistic ranking of health progress, the community also differs from both SOS staff and clients. The only other major difference between groups concerns social action: clients rank its importance much higher than do community persons.

All felt that realistically they had done a good job so far in "just getting things afloat" and in getting the idea of such centers over to the community. They remarked on their increasing visibility to the community, e.g., "the judge was popping in every once in a while," the police were covering the parking meters in front of their meeting place on certain specified days, local merchants—like beauty operators and bankers—were offering door prizes and soliciting business from them as well as offering "specials" to aged persons, etc. The center hostess proudly introduced her Indian foster child, a young lady of thirteen years, who was regularly stopping by after school with her friends to chat with the people at the center, and was planning a dinner to be served by her fellow junior high school students to the SOS folks. This subcenter and two others had taken an active part in local festivals by submitting floats made by them and by putting on entertainment for the citizenry at large during the celebrations, e.g., *Cheese Day* and *Homecoming Day*.

Discrepancies in Social Action Rankings

In terms of OEO Guideline *d*, calling for "a high degree of community organization activities . . . to be the vehicle for increased community influence for the elderly," the overall below average ranking of social action as a program emphasis indicates that this criterion has not been generally set or achieved by the SOS. Perhaps most significant in this regard, however, is comparison of the frequency with which this topic is mentioned by different groups, and the rank of Interest they show in this goal. Table 3-XIV displays this information.

The staff appears to mediate between clients and community persons with regard to both the frequency with which social action is mentioned (clients, 4; staff, 6; community, 8), and perceived importance of social action as an Interest (clients, 11; staff, 6+; community, 4+). All three groups rank progress toward the goal of social action as low or very low.

Further study of Table 3-XIII gives some indication of how social action is perceived by each group. Notice the discrepancy between clients' Frequency of Mention for this goal,

TABLE 3-XIV
Social Action as an SOS Program Emphasis

	Frequency of Mention	Interest	
		Importance	Progress
Clients	4	11	11
Staff	6	6+	12
Community	8	4+	10

4, and their Interest ranking of its importance, 11; and contrast this information with the community's Frequency of Mention rank, 8, and Interest rank of importance, 4+. On these two measures, the staff ranks social action about 6. And, no matter how frequently each group mentioned social action, or what importance each perceived it to have, all rank progress toward its achievement very low, between 10 and 12.

Suppose SOS staff were intuitively knowledgeable of these perceptions? How might this information affect program planning and execution? Clients talk about action, but their interests are elsewhere. Community persons lean toward action, but they don't talk much about it. The staff of an SOS might very well place its attention elsewhere among the list of program emphases. In view of client-community differences, SOS resources might well be allocated toward achieving goals other than social action. As a result, progress toward client-mentioned and community-important social action goals, might be as minimal as Table 3-XIV indicates Interest to be.

Another hypothesis, somewhat confirming this, appears from classifying program goals into two major classes: emphasis on change versus emphasis on service.

SOS EMPHASIS ON CHANGE VERSUS SERVICE

We found it profitable to classify SOS programs according to their emphasis on *change* as opposed to *service*. An emphasis on change means that a program aims to develop, reinforce, and sanction a person's capability to cope with problems of age and poverty. An emphasis on service means that a program aims to provide, supply, and support solutions to problems of age and poverty. Service, unlike change, does not require a person to learn or acquire capability, but is satisfied with delivering help to people. Change activities teach new skills, provide insights into problems, encourage self-help, and so modify the habitual behavior of persons with regard to their problems. Services include recreation, outreach, transportation, and meals, whereas changes include education, income support through employment, organization for social action, and improved self-image.

A change/service ratio was obtained by classifying evaluators' interview results into the two classes: change and service. A change/service ratio was then determined for each SOS, and programs ranked according to their emphasis on change rather than on service. Spearman rank order correlation coefficients were computed to test for the significance of program component differences between high and low change/service ratio SOS's.

1. *Client characteristics*: There is a positive, but not significant correlation between client age and the change/service ratio ($r = .275$). This indicates that SOS's with a high percentage of clients 65 and over tend to be oriented toward change. Other characteristics of clients such as income or the percentage of males showed no significant correlation with the change/service ratio.

2. *Director characteristics*: There is an inverse relationship between the director's youth and client perception of progress in change-oriented programs: younger directors tend to be associated with service rather than change programs ($r = .518$, .05 level of confidence). No relationship appears between the sex of the director, for example and the change/service ratio.

3. *Program characteristics*: Size of budget has no relationship to the change/service ratio ($r = .070$), nor does budget size show a relationship with the number of other agencies and organizations related to the SOS.

In summary, by calculating the emphasis in each SOS toward changing persons in order that they develop greater capability to cope with age and poverty, versus serving persons in order that they survive better under existing conditions, a ratio could be assigned to each program. Those programs whose change/service ratio was highest in the direction of an emphasis on change were (1) more likely to have a greater percentage of clients sixty-five years and older, and

(2) were more likely to have a program director who was also advanced in age. Therefore, the likelihood that an SOS will be change-oriented depends heavily on both its clients and its program director being older.

We hypothesize that older SOS Program Directors empathize with clients rather than sympathize with them. There is a slight indication that older program directors are less likely to have occupational histories in the helping or service professions, coming instead from administrative and secretarial jobs, and so may take a more straightforward approach to change.

That programs with older clients are also more likely to be change-oriented raises some questions. Does this mean that the over-sixty-five population feels it has less to lose and more to gain by change rather than service? Does it mean that the person over sixty-five, born in 1906 or before, in the prime of life during the Depression, questions the ethics of service programs and prefers do-it-yourself? Does it perhaps mean that the over-sixty-five clients identify more with the community's norms toward self-help? Evidence from this evaluation cannot answer these questions, but confirms the wisdom present in OEO guidelines calling for careful consideration that programs focus on older poor persons, engaging them in policy-making activities, and that program staff also be in the upper age brackets.

EPILOG

In the *Report of the Special Senate Committee on Aging,* 92nd Congress, First Session (#92-46), the results reported in this chapter were presented. After summarizing those results, which "provide clear and convincing evidence of the effectiveness of senior opportunities and services projects, the Committee strongly urges that full funding be provided for SOS programs during the next fiscal year."

Chapter 4

THE PSYCHOLOGICAL ASPECTS

ALLEN R. COHEN

Average life expectancy has been extended to the point where those who reach middle age may expect to live on the average another 25 years. As a result, a smaller part of our lives is being spent in the traditional adult roles of making a living and child rearing. However, personal recognition, social status, human companionship and usefulness are still sought and achieved largely through parental and work roles despite the fact that more of us are now living beyond the period of life in which these roles are completed. The years following the completion of these tasks are beginning to represent an extension of life marked by a shortening of hours of work, both on the job and in the home. Thus we are faced with a new turning point in life which relates to our acceptance of the goal of a long and leisurely life without having yet adjusted to the fact that we are actually achieving it.

Expectations and duties for the earlier years are fully defined by a long tradition. There are few choices to be made in childhood or in the early adult years. A person knows pretty much what is expected of him, but this is not true of the later years. There are few guidelines because no society has ever before known the mass extension of life and leisure that is upon us.

In a culture that has been heavily oriented toward work

and production, it is natural for many of us to seek opportunity for the kind of creative expression and individuality once provided on the job. Total retirement from work looks attractive in the early work years but as the time approaches, many become ambivalent about or resist it altogether because of the increased leisure time with little or no means to occupy one's self. The problem is to find community involvement that satisfies the need for recognition, social status, and individual achievement.

Removal of many tasks from the home and simplification of others has led women to seek satisfaction outside the home before their children have grown. This makes it easier to find means to spend their leisure time when parental duties are finished. But for those who are influenced by the strong vestiges of tradition, remaining at home until the children have left, the changing role becomes difficult. In either instance, the object is to find an outlet that will give a sense of purpose adequate to sustain interest.

The question that arises is how to adjust to life in a changed society growing out of unprecedented productivity, more and more leisure time, and increased life expectancy. People reaching this stage need to find fulfillment in life by utilizing their leisure time for new and different activities designed to give them unique satisfactions. It is important to avoid becoming occupied with busy work that yields little and results in boredom and dissatisfaction.

Older persons exchange economic pressures of youth and maturity for the social restrictions of age. Like adolescence, there is a change from known relative security to unknown insecurity. The very personality traits that enabled the older person to dominate successfully and to gain prestige in early and middle maturity may now stand in his way if he accepts the altered conditions of later maturity. The prime need is for self expression and for continued opportunities to make contributions to mankind.

Aging should be viewed as a natural phenomenon and a basic characteristic of all living matter. It is best understood as a continuous process of progressive change in all structures and functions of the body. As the efficiency of its physical and psychological machines decreases, one is forced to make certain adaptations and adjustments in his way of life.

The psychological problems of aging are therefore usually associated with the readjustments the person who is growing older has to make to the changes which overtake him. Since people usually repeat previously established methods of dealing with conflicts or problems, the reactions to the various changes in old age will be directly related to previous life adjustment.

Not only is it necessary to readjust in old age as the situations change but also to every change to which we are exposed through our lifetime. The stresses encountered in old age are perhaps most comparable to the stresses in our adolescence, which is another period of emotional disturbance in which our adjustments are likely to be more strenuous even than in old age. Most people get by adolescence and most are likely to keep their equilibrium within fair balance through the process of getting old.

There are wide individual differences in people in the psychological aging process. In general, however, there is a decrease in memory for recent events which represents a turning away from the painfulness of the present. In contrast, there is a sharpening of memory for the past, especially when life was successful. Also evident is a more assertive attitude possibly as a compensation for insecurity. Other characteristics include mild depression caused by isolation and a feeling of loneliness along with a tendency toward introversion. The death among people in the same age group contributes to the above and seems to add an increase in sensitivity.

On the other side of the coin, there appear to be some psychological gains in old age that may compensate in part for the losses. Although as one grows older the opportunities to improve one's social and occupational status diminish and often disappear after retirement, some people seem to adjust to this process by reconciling their goals to actual achievement. Old age, by narrowing the future, may help an individual to accept his past. The aging process provides an opportunity for a person to understand and utilize formerly unacceptable drives or character traits. To accept old age means to give up a belief that the future promises what the past has denied. Growing old can bring about greater self-understanding and self-acceptance along with some release from the stresses and disappointments of earlier years.

Later life for most people is also characterized by a reduction in physical activities as well as social interaction. With a reduction in energy, aging individuals become willing accomplices in the process of separation from active society. They are more content with this disengaged position in society than if their former, more active position had to be maintained. This will vary somewhat because of differences in temperament and experience, inner drives and needs for gratification. It will also differ for men and women, but basically a substantial reduction in physical activity can be expected.

In this regard, cerebral function has come to be regarded as the most dependable servant that can be called upon over a long span of years. The brain virtually becomes the sanctuary of the middle and later years. This remarkable organ can be the greatest source of pleasure, amusement, and satisfaction. If properly used it can improve so much with age that it provides us with one of the greatest sources for successful life adjustment.

As mentioned previously, the adjustment of the aged is a direct continuation of his adjustment from infancy on. With good mental hygiene throughout life, the problems of old age will be minimal. The better one's previous mental health, the more readily will they accept old age, the better will they be prepared for it and the more easily will they find pleasures in new things to substitute for those no longer available to them. One's earlier satisfactions became the foundation and the guarantee of emotional well-being in later years.

REFERENCES

Birren, James E.: *The Psychology of Aging.* Englewood Cliffs, N.J., Prentice Hall, Inc., 1970.

Geist, Harold: *The Psychological Aspects of the Aging Process.* St. Louis, Mo., W. H. Green Co., 1968.

Havinghurst, Robert J.: *Older People.* New York, N.Y., Longmans, Greens and Co., 1953.

Williams, Richard H.: *Process of Aging.* New York, N.Y., Atherton Press, 1963.

PERSPECTIVES ON THE OLDER AMERICAN IN A RURAL SETTING

E. GRANT YOUMANS

OBJECTIVES AND ASSUMPTIONS
THE RURAL SETTING
THE STUDY DESIGN
AUTHORITY VALUES
RELIGIOUS VALUES
ACHIEVEMENT VALUES
DEPENDENCY VALUES
PESSIMISM
DISCUSSION

Research literature on human aging has expanded enormously in recent decades. During the first half of the century (1900–1948), about 18,000 publications on aging were reported, but in the twelve years following (1949–1961) over 34,000 publications appeared (Shock, 1951 and 1963). It is a reasonable expectation that research activity will continue to expand on a topic of such vital concern as human aging.

In a research field that is growing so rapidly, there has been a notable omission—namely, the limited number of reported studies of older persons living in rural environments in the United States. Such a deficiency is not too surprising. It is characteristic of American society that innovations and new fields of inquiry emerge in urban centers and then gradually spread to the more remote rural areas. The discipline of social gerontology, a late arrival to the disciplines concerned with aging, has followed this pattern. Almost all social gerontologists are urban dwellers, and their research efforts have been directed mainly to studies of human aging in city environments.

The paucity of information on older persons living in rural areas of the United States has placed practitioners in an awkward situation. In recent years, public and private organizations have shown increased interest in the social and economic problems of older persons in rural environments. Efforts in initiating programs and services for these people have been handicapped by lack of current and reliable data.

OBJECTIVES AND ASSUMPTIONS

Several objectives and assumptions underlie the presentation of materials in this paper. The general aim is to provide some perspectives on older Americans living in a rural setting. It is assumed such information will be useful to practitioners involved in designing programs and services. A second assumption is concerned with the inadequacy of reporting only on the objective conditions and circumstances of life of older persons in rural environments. The identification of indicators of the social and economic conditions of the rural aged is vitally important. But practitioners need additional information to initiate successful ameliorative programs. They need data which probe beneath the social and economic conditions to reveal the underlying subjective values, beliefs, and attitudes of their prospective clients.

Many practitioners have painfully discovered that it is the subjective aspects of human behavior that are often resistant to innovations and changes. Medical practitioners commonly report their bafflement and dismay when health programs they advocate are rejected by the very prople who would benefit. Welfare workers often report discouragement and demoralization in their efforts to help clients who persistently spend allotments in seemingly irrational and foolish ways. Barrett (1961) points out that the beliefs and values held by any group of persons constitute the very core of their behavior. Knowledge of these subjective elements can provide clues to practitioners about the willingness of prospective clients to accept and participate in rehabilitative programs.

A third assumption relates to the lack of standards by which to assess or measure the life of aged persons in either the objective or subjective domain. In the absence of such criteria, it is assumed that data on the beliefs and values of older rural persons will be more meaningful when they are compared with those of urban older persons.

A fourth assumption and objective pertains to the continuity of programs and services. Practitioners are continually faced with the difficult task of making judgments about the suitability of their programs for future groups of aged persons. Younger aged persons, if they survive, will become older aged persons. Although younger and older age groups live in the same society, the experiences of the formative years differ as a reflection of technological and social change. In a rapidly changing society, such as the United States, younger age groups may internalize basic vaules substantially different from those of their elders, and even from those of age groups a few years older. Successive age groups, in turn, both reflect and forecast changing values and beliefs. Thus data comparing the values of older and younger age groups can offer clues about the nature of emerging society and provide bases for developing long-range programs.

In the following pages, data are presented relevant to the preceding objectives and assumptions. The next section outlines some of the more salient characteristics of rural settings. The section on the study design provides details by which data were collected on beliefs and values of older and younger age groups living in two subcultural areas—one rural and the other urban.

The substantive portion of the paper includes analyses of the selected values and beliefs and suggests some implications for practitioners. It is to be noted that the geographic areas studied are not representative of rural and urban environments in the United States. The findings may suggest hypotheses for studies in other rural and urban areas.

THE RURAL SETTING

Historically, the word *rural* has referred to the country. It comes from the Latin word *rus,* or *ruris,* meaning open land. The term suggests open space, a predominance of agricultural occupations, a low density of population, a closeness of the people to the natural environment, and less social mobility than is found in urban areas. The individual living in a rural society typically has fewer contacts with others. He tends to associate with people from a rather small geographic area, and his relationships with these people are of long duration.

In recent decades, rural areas in the United States have undergone substantial changes (Rogers and Burdge, 1972). There has been a shift from the traditional rural way of life to a more complex and technologically advanced type of society. Trends toward modernization of rural life are characterized by increased productivity, fewer farms, and more part-time farming; more specialized and increasingly efficient agricultural businesses; more complex consolidations of social organizations, such as schools, churches, and business enterprises; improved transportation and communication facilities; and greater movement of people from place to place. with an accentuated importance in secondary relationships.

Approximately one-third of the 20,000,000 men and women aged sixty-five and over in the United States live in areas designated as rural—on farms, in villages and towns, and in open country. This number is substantially increased if older persons living on open land outside of metropolitan centers are included under the category of rural.

Older rural persons, like other categories of persons, are by no means homogeneous. A typical rural senior citizen does not exist. The rural aged include a wide diversity of subcultures and social groupings, such as the Negro, Spanish Americans, American Indians, Appalachian subsistence farmers, the Wyoming cowboy, the Alabama patriarch, the coal miner in rural Pennsylvania and in rural Kentucky, the Wisconsin dairy farmer, the merchant in a small town or village, the factory worker who once commuted to his job, and a variety of persons who retire to rural areas to escape the congestion and discomforts of urban life.

It is commonly believed that the rural aged enjoy advantages, such as abundant fresh air and sunshine, out-of-doors activities, a simplicity of life moving at a slower pace, and the emotional supports of close family and friends.

This idyllic picture of rural America has been created mainly by popular writers, just as the idealized version of the American cowboy has been implanted in the consciousness of America by Eastern novelists. The glorification of rural life does not appear to stand the test of careful scrutiny, either in the distant past or in contemporary twentieth century industrialized America. Euripides, the popular dramatist of ancient Greece, appeared aware of the disadvantages of rural life when he said that the first requisite to happiness is that a man be born in a famous city. In the United States, Henry David Thoreau, who became famous when he attempted to escape the evils of industrialization by becoming a hermit in the woods near Walden Pond, is alleged to have said that it makes little difference whether one is committed to a farm or to a county jail.[1]

Contemporary studies (McKain, 1957; Youmans, 1967) provide documentation of the distressing conditions of life experienced by substantial numbers of older rural persons in the United States. On almost every indicator of well-being the rural aged are more disadvantaged than the urban aged. Characteristically, rural persons, compared with their urban

---

[1] Acknowledgement is made to Calvin Beale.

counterparts, have poorer physical and mental health, smaller incomes, more deteriorated housing, fewer opportunities for satisfactory social relationships, more inadequacies in transportation facilities, and fewer social and medical services.

THE STUDY DESIGN

In 1969, data were collected by means of structured interviews from 805 persons who comprised probability samples of men and women aged twenty to twenty-nine and sixty and over living in a rural county of the Southern Appalachian Region and in a metropolitan center located outside of the Region.[2] The metropolitan center had a population of about 150,000 and the rural county of about 6,500. City blocks in the urban center and small areas of land in the rural county constituted the sampling units and these were selected according to a table of random numbers to yield approximately 400 cases from each residential area. The urban sample included 237 younger and 165 older persons, and the rural sample included 127 younger and 276 older men and women. No institutionalized persons were included.

All homes in each city block and in each area of rural land in the sample were visited by an interviewer to obtain information from persons in the two stipulated age groups. If a prospective respondent was not at home on the first visit, an appointment was made for a subsequent interview. If more than one person in the same household were to be interviewed, special effort was made to guarantee independent responses. In most cases each respondent in a household was interviewed alone. In the few cases where this was im-

[2] The study was made jointly by the U.S. Department of Agriculture and the Kentucky Agricultural Experiment Station and partially supported by grant number MH-16722-01 from the National Institute of Mental Health to the University of Kentucky. Interpretations are those of the author and not necessarily of the U.S. Department of Agriculture or the Kentucky Experiment Station. Acknowledgment is made to J. S. Brown, A. L. Coleman, J. H. Copp, T. R. Ford, M. R. Janssen, and J. O'Donnell for advice and assistance; to W. Baldwin, J. Meddin, and N. Peterson for field work; and to C. Morgan for assistance with tabulation.

possible, the interview with one person was completed before another was started. The questions which elicited information for this report were interspersed throughout a fifteen-page interview schedule.

The respondents were almost entirely of the Protestant faith, predominantly married, and predominantly white, except for the eight percent Negro in the urban center. About one-third of the older persons were widowed. Women outnumbered men in the samples by a ratio of 6 to 4. In both residential areas, the younger age groups, compared with the older, had received more formal education, had higher incomes, and had greater representation in the professional and white-collar occupations. The median years of formal education of the younger and older aged persons in the city were 13.8 and 10.1, respectively, and in the rural area, 11.1 and 7.8 respectively. In the urban center, the median annual incomes of its younger and older persons were $6,015 and $3,885, respectively, and in the rural county, $3,999 and $1,773, respectively. The younger generations revealed greater geographic mobility in their backgrounds than did the older age groups. The oldest person interviewed was 93, and the median age of the older persons was 69. About two-fifths of the older people considered themselves retired.

The term *value* refers to a complex of knowledge, beliefs, attitudes, and ideas by which a person or group expresses ways of looking at a situation (Anderson, 1964). Values were assessed by presenting each respondent with three statements about selected values in American society, such as authoritarianism, dependency, achievement, religion, and despair and pessimism. Respondents gave an *agree, don't know,* or a *disagree* answer to each statement. These responses were scored one, two, and three, respectively, permitting a mean score range from three to nine for each set. The lower the score, the stronger the belief in or adherence to the value orientation. Intercorrelations among statements on each scale ranged from .74 to .97, indicating that the items in each set did assess a common underlying dimension.

AUTHORITY VALUES

Patterns of authority in any subgroup can provide useful clues to practitioners in developing programs. Stability and order are based, to a large extent, upon vesting authority in mature and responsible members of the society and upon the acceptance of these authorities by successive age groups. Many young persons in American society reject and challenge traditional patterns of authority. The high visibility given to movements of social protest by the news media fosters the notion that American society is undergoing rapid change in its value systems and that these changes are producing turmoil and discomfort. The important question in this paper is twofold. Are the rural persons more authoritarian in their outlook than their counterparts in the metropolitan center? Do authority patterns appear to be undergoing greater change in the rural or the urban area?

Older and younger persons in the two geographic areas responded to statements assessing four aspects of authoritarianism: (1) beliefs that schools and colleges should be more strict, should constrain the freedoms of youths, and should place more emphasis on training for vocations; (2) beliefs that young people should spend more time working and less time running around, should face up to the real problems of life, and should not get all the good things in life too easily; (3) beliefs that the husband should play the dominant role in the family, such as pay the bills, make repairs around the house, and not be required to do the dishes; and (4) beliefs that young people should have more respect for authority, that personal matters should not be pried into, and that young people basically like to have definite rules to follow.

Responses to the statements about authority suggest that this value is more firmly held in the rural area than in the metropolitan center. The older persons in the rural environment scored higher than urban older persons on three of the four measures of authoritarianism. The one item on which the older rural and urban age groups did not differ significantly was that assessing respect for authority. The younger rural persons also scored higher in authoritarianism than did the urban younger people on three of the four measures. The two younger age groups did not differ significantly in their beliefs about husband dominance in the home.

Beliefs about traditional patterns of authority appeared to be undergoing less change in the rural area than in the metropolitan center. Younger persons in the southern Appalachian region were offering a weaker challenge to institutional authorities than were younger men and women in the urban center. Differences in authoritarian scores between the younger and the older age groups in the metropolitan center were greater than those between the comparable age groups in the rural community on three of the four assessments—schools, youth, and respect for authority. On one item there was greater disparity between generations in the rural area than in the urban center—on the belief that the husband should perform the dominant role in the home.

The significantly weaker support for authoritarian values evidenced by the younger age persons in comparison with their elders suggests an emerging value system inconsistent with the structure of large-scale industrial and governmental organizations which characterize the corporate state. Every age ends to develop organizational forms appropriate to its needs, and perhaps the prevailing forms of bureaucratic structure are undergoing change (Bennis, 1970). In developing programs, practitioners in social gerontology might be cognizant of anti-authoritarian trends in society. Successive groups who enter the old age category in the future probably will be more democratically oriented and will expect a more active role in designing and carrying out programs.

RELIGIOUS VALUES

In writing about the southern Appalachian region, Thomas R. Ford (1962) states it is virtually impossible to understand fully any aspect of life in the region without taking into account religious values. These values underlie and exert complex and subtle influences on many other attitudes and beliefs. The resulting behavior may puzzle outside observers, and often is not fully understood even by people in the region themselves.

Religious values were appraised by presenting each person with three statements: (1) the belief that religion is the one thing to be relied upon, (2) the belief that there is a divine plan and purpose for every living person and thing, and (3) the belief that the Bible is God's word and all it says is true.

Responses to these statements indicated that younger and older persons living in the rural area were more fundamentalistic in religious outlook than were those living in the urban center and that in both geographic areas the younger persons were less committed to traditional religious values than were their elders. The responses also revealed a greater disparity in religious values between younger and older persons in the metropolitan area than between the two generations in the rural area.

It can be inferred from the age group differences in religious values presented that successive age groups will probably live in a society of decreasing primary and sacred values and increasing secular ones. It is generally recognized that primary values and beliefs have been instrumental to families in providing care and emotional support for older persons. With a decline in primary and sacred values, aged persons probably will receive less attention and care from their families and more from secondary public sources.

A decline in primary support values for the aged probably will influence successive aged groups to fall back on their own resources. Persons who enter the old-age category in the future in the two geographic areas probably will be motivated to form a more distinctive subculture with a stronger sense of group identity than exists at present. The growth of an aging subculture (Rose and Peterson, 1965) will provide a means of social and psychological support for the aged and will enable them to form stronger pressure groups. The increased knowledge and sophistication, the higher educational level, the improved health and economic conditions of succeeding cohorts of the aged will enable them to resist vigorously against the inequalities imposed upon them. They will have greater access to the means of uniting in action to win public support for benefits. These societal trends undoubtedly will focus private and public attention on a salient issue in American society—that is, what criteria should be used in determining the portion of goods and services to be diverted for the benefit of the aged population?

ACHIEVEMENT VALUES

According to historians, a key value in the development of American civilization has been the strong belief in achievement. Commitment to the work ethic and to the notion of success, it is alleged, has played an important role in the technological and economic growth of the Nation.

In recent decades, probing questions have been asked about the traditional value of achievement in American society. Do younger generations tend to reject the idea of hard work and achievement? Does the emergence of a *welfare state* repudiate the old-fashioned belief in dedicated effort? It is readily observable that increased length of life has placed more and more older people in a non-work status. On the other hand, substantial numbers of older persons seek *second careers*. According to Jaffe (1971), an important element in finding a second career lies in the older person's motivation for achievement. It would be important to know if older persons in a rural setting are more dedicated to achievement than older persons in a metropolitan center. It would also be important to know whether young adults in a rural and an urban environment give strong support to the value of achievement.

Achievement values in the study reported here were assessed from responses to statements about the rewards of hard work and about opportunities for success. The specific statements were: An ambitious and hard working person can always get ahead in the world. People who are at the top of the success ladder deserve to be there. With effort and ability any person has a good chance of becoming an outstanding success.

Responses to these three statements revealed significant differences between the older men and women in the two geographic areas. The older persons in the metropolitan center gave significantly stronger support to the value of achievement than did the older persons in the southern Appalachian region sample. No significant difference in achievement values was found between the younger persons living in the urban and in the rural community. In the rural area studied, older and younger age groups did not differ significantly in their achievement values. In the urban community, on the other hand, the younger aged persons registered significantly less support to the value of achievement than did their elders.

This study suggests the hypothesis that the metropolitan environment is producing younger generations who are disenchanted with opportunities for achieving success in American society. The apparent eroding of a work ethos in the metropolitan center would suggest that an increasing value is being placed on "nonwork" or "leisure" identifications. It can be inferred that successive generations in the urban environment will probably develop a "mixing" of leisure and work components.

The orientations toward work values in the urban center studied have important implications for many middle and older age persons in that area. An increased emphasis upon leisure pursuits with a decline in work values may result in a smoother and less abrupt transition from work to retirement life for increasing proportions of older aged persons. In addition, the emerging attitudes and values toward work may serve to facilitate the shortening of the work week and the earlier retirement of persons in the urban area. Some older age persons, on the other hand, may find themselves in conflict with these emerging trends. Those older aged persons who share the traditional dedication to the work ethic and who may want to work may have difficulty in finding employment. One economist (Spengler, 1969) points out that employment opportunities for the aged will probably be even less satisfactory from 1970 to 2000 than they were in 1960.

DEPENDENCY VALUES

The foregoing findings on achievement values and beliefs suggest that the traditional and frontier-like virtues of individualism and resourcefulness are not strongly sustained among older and younger persons in the sample from the southern Appalachian region. An important question may thus be asked: Does a lack of motivation for achievement imply a subscription to values associated with dependency? Answers to such a question, it is assumed, would have a bearing on the kinds of programs to be initiated for the older people.

Two measures of dependency were included in this study. One assessed dependency on one's family, such as beliefs and attitudes that a person should always give financial help to his relatives if they are in need, that a person should be able to count on financial support from his family and relatives if he needs it, and that a person should always ask the advice of his immediate family before making any decisions. A second set of statements assessed dependency on government, such as beliefs that the government should make every effort to increase welfare payments to people who need it, that the government should provide a job to everyone who wants one, and that the government should provide free food for families in need.

Responses to these statements revealed a stronger support of dependency values in the rural area than in the metropolitan center. Persons aged sixty and over in the southern Appalachian region sample were significantly more dependent on their families and relatives and on their government than were persons of the same age living in the metropolitan center outside of the Appalachian region. Comparisons between rural and urban younger persons revealed a similar pattern. The men and women aged twenty to twenty-nine in the rural environment were significantly more dependent on their families and on their government than persons of comparable age in the urban area.

In both geographic areas, the responses of the younger men and women suggest a consistency with their anti-authoritarian attitudes. The younger age groups revealed a greater degree of independence than did their elders, but the differences between young and old were greater in the metropolitan center than in the rural area. In the urban area, the younger age group was more independent of their families and of their government than was the older age group. In the rural area, younger persons were significantly more independent of their families and relatives than were their elders, but the two age groups in the southern Appalachian region sample did not differ significantly in their dependency on government.

PESSIMISM

Numerous publications have examined the *culture of poverty* in the United States (Larner and Howe, 1969; Will and Vatter, 1965). These reports have stressed the idea that this *culture* consists of a design for living shared by large numbers of persons who are shabby and defeated, permeated with failure, impervious to hope, and engulfed in misery. People in poverty areas, it is alleged, tend to retain these attitudes and characteristics despite increased productivity and attempts to modify welfare programs. As a consequence, this design for living is passed down from generation to generation.

In recent decades, the *war on poverty* has been instrumental in focusing attention on poverty in rural areas of the United States (Breathitt et al., 1957) and especially has called attention to the distressing conditions existing in the southern Appalachian region (Harrington, 1962; Weller, 1965).

It might be useful to compare feeelings of pessimism existing among older and younger persons in two geographic areas—one an area in the southern Appalachian region and the other a metropolitan center adjacent to but outside of the region. It would be especially rewarding if some clues could be detected about the nature of emerging society in the two areas.

Pessimistic feelings were identified from three statements

adapted from the anomia scale designed by Srole (1956). The three statements were: "In spite of what some people say, the life of the average man today is getting worse, not better. Nowadays, a person has to live for today and let tomorrow take care of itself. There is little use in writing public officials because they are not really interested in the problems of the average man."

Responses of agreement or disagreement with these statements revealed that older and younger persons in the southern Appalachian region sample were significantly more pessimistic in outlook than were persons of comparable age in the metropolitan center. The data also revealed that in both geographic areas the older persons were significantly more pessimistic than the younger ones, but that the difference between generations was greater in the urban center than in the rural area.

It is inferred from the findings in this study that pessimism and despair may be of declining importance in the future of the two geographic areas. This optimistic interpretation applies in greater degree to the urban center than to the rural area, since there was a greater generational difference in the metropolitan community. It is recognized that pessimistic feelings may increase as people grow older. However, only longitudinal studies of the same persons over extended periods of time can demonstrate the extent to which these occur.

DISCUSSION

The foregoing findings on values and beliefs suggest several questions. In what ways may the age groups be characterized? How may the differences be explained? What are some implications of the differences?

It appears that older and younger age groups in the samples from the southern Appalachian region, compared with their counterparts in the metropolitan center, were more authoritarian in their views, more fundamentalistic in religious outlook, slightly less motivated toward achievement, more closely identified with their families, evidenced a greater dependency on government, and revealed greater hopelessness and despair. In both geographic areas, it appears that the younger men and women, compared with the older persons, tended to be more urbane and sophisticated, more knowledgeable and better informed, more liberal and tolerant, and more secular and independent in their values and beliefs.

Two hypotheses appear relevant to explain the differences in values between older and younger persons. One is that the differences may be interpreted to represent changes to people as they age. Comparative studies of age groups are popular in social gerontology, and differences found are often implicitly or explicitly suggested to be part of the aging process. Such interpretations provide a simple explanation. With the passage of time, younger people will grow up and mature to be like their elders. Thus each generation can predict with considerable accuracy the values of succeeding generations, and a high degree of stability and security can be anticipated in society.

Unfortunately such an interpretation seems to encounter difficulties. One example germane to social gerontology serves to illustrate this problem. Proponents of disengagement theory (Cumming and Henry, 1961) compared younger and older persons and concluded that the normal process of human aging involved an inevitable and a universal severance of relationships with others. Critics of the theory (Maddox, 1964; Rose and Peterson, 1965; and Youmans, 1969) point out that alleged disengagement in later life is not necessarily inevitable nor universal, and that a major weakness in the theory is failure to give adequate attention to societal changes.

A second hypothesis is that the differences in values existing between older and younger persons is a reflection of social change. The younger men and women included in the samples were born in the decade 1940 to 1950 and undoubtedly internalized values different from those of the older-aged persons born before 1910. It is probably a safe assumption to say that an age group will maintain substantial continuity in the values it internalized and "crystallized" (Mannheim, 1952) during its formative years. Psychiatrists and clinical psychologists offer abundant evidence of the extreme difficulties encountered in their attempts to change basic beliefs of their patients. Several social scientists suggest that socialization after the formative years is concerned mainly with overt behavior and not with basic values, and that society is unwilling to incur the high cost of redirecting the basic values of adults (Brim and Wheeler, 1966; Rosow, 1967).

It is recognized that some modifications in values will occur in any age group as it moves through the life course. However, the nature of such changes is difficult to ascertain. Only longitudinal studies of the same persons over periods of time can determine the modifications that take place. Few longitudinal studies have been made in social gerontology, principally because they are extremely difficult and expensive.

One longitudinal study directly related to the issue at hand may be cited. In 1955–1957, a research team of physiologists, medical clinicians, psychiatrists, psychologists, and sociologists examined a broad range of biological, attitudinal, and behavioral characteristics of forty-seven healthy older men whose mean age was seventy-one years (Birren et al., 1963). In 1967, a follow-up of this group of men provided an opportunity to replicate some of the analyses used in the earlier study and to obtain a limited "longitudinal" view of human aging. The findings in the follow-up study showed that the elderly men gave evidence of a high degree of stability in their activities, relationships, attitudes, and general outlook on life. Some changes did occur among the men but these did not suggest a systematic shift toward the less favorable characteristics (Youmans and Yarrow, 1971).

The age differences in values and the interpretation of these differences to be a reflection of social and technological changes in American society have important implications for researchers and practitioners in social gerontology. The data presented here offer some clues about the nature of emerging society. The values and beliefs of the older age group probably exemplify the traditional or folk culture which may be passing out of existence (Lerner, 1958). In contrast, the values of the younger age group probably reflect the emerging society and may constitute what Boulding (1969) calls a newer supercultural system. It is probably a safe prediction to say that many problems of American society will revolve around the tensions and stresses generated between the traditional and the emerging values.

The values and beliefs examined in this report suggest additional questions related to changes occurring in the United States. Since values and beliefs tend to reflect and forecast technological and social change, one would expect greater differences in values between old and young in those areas of rapid change—namely, in the urban centers of the nation. The findings in this study support this expectation. Greater differences were found between the values of the older and younger persons in the metropolitan center than between the values of the older and younger generations in the rural area.

The smaller disparity in values existing between old and young in the rural area may prove to be a psychological advantage. Toffler (1971) has examined what happens to people when they are overwhelmed by the bombardment of stimuli arising from the accelerative thrust of social change. He uses the term *future shock* to describe the shattering stress and disorientation induced in individuals when they are subjected to too much change in too short a time. It is inferred from the data on values presented in this report that social change is occurring at a slower rate in the rural area than in the metropolitan center. Consequently, it can be inferred that the people in the rural area will experience less psychological stress in coping with change than will their counterparts in the urban center.

Another question pertaining to social change is concerned with the rural-urban *gap* in values and beliefs. Some sociologists contend that rural-urban differences in values and beliefs are decreasing (Rogers and Burdge, 1972:4–8).

The findings in the study reported here suggest an opposite trend in the two geographic areas. Greater differences in values and beliefs were found between the urban and rural younger age persons than between the urban and rural older generation. This finding suggests the tendency to widen the urban-rural value *gap*. It appears that values in the rural area may become more distinct from those in the urban center, an omen not salutary to the welfare of the rural aged. This tendency may be ameliorated somewhat by the migratory patterns of the young rural people as they continue to move to urban centers. On the other hand, succeeding age cohorts who remain in rural areas may be more sharply differentiated in values from those existing in urban centers.

The differences in values and beliefs reported in this paper should provide clues useful to practitioners who are designing programs and services for aging persons. Present programs in social gerontology have focused on such problems as income, housing, nutrition, health, and recreational opportunities. While these needs of older persons will continue to be important, additional needs will probably emerge that also are important. Future groups of older persons in the two areas studied probably will be more sophisticated, better educated, have more money, possess better health, and be more active than the present aged. It is probably a safe prediction that these persons will demand more sophisticated programs and services to meet their differing psychological needs, and they also will probably demand a more active voice in determining the specific nature of such programs and services.

REFERENCES

Anderson, A.: *Systems of Orientation.* Dictionary of the Social Sciences. Glencoe, Illinois, Free Press, 1964.

Barrett, Donald N.: *Values in America.* University of Notre Dame Press, 1961.

Bennis, Warren G.: Post Bureaucratic Leadership. In Michael, Donald N. (Ed.): *The Future Society.* New York, Aldine Publishing Co., 1970.

Birren, J. E.; Butler, R. N.; Greenhouse, S. W., and Yarrow, M. R.: *Human*

Aging: A Biological and Behavioral Study. Washington, Public Health Service Publication 986, 1963.

Boulding, Kenneth: The Emerging Superculture. In Baier, Kurt and Rescher, Nicholas (Eds.) : *Values and the Future.* Glencoe, The Free Press, 1969, pp. 336–352.

Breathitt, Edward T., et al.: *The People Left Behind.* President's National Advisory Commission on Rural Poverty. Washington, D.C., U.S. Government Printing Office, 1967.

Brim, Orville G., and Wheeler, Stanton: *Socialization After Childhood: Two Essays.* New York, John Wiley and Sons, 1966.

Cumming, E., and Henry, W. E.: *Growing Old.* New York, Basic Books, 1961.

Ford, Thomas R.: *The Southern Appalachian Region: A Survey.* Lexington, University of Kentucky Press, 1962.

Harrington, Michael: *The Other America.* New York, Macmillan Co., 1962.

Jaffe, A. J.: *The Middle Years.* Washington, D.C., National Council on the Aging, 1971.

Larner, Jeremy, and Howe, Irving: *Poverty: Views from the Left.* New York, William Morrow and Co., 1969.

Lerner, Daniel: *The Passing of Traditional Society.* Glencoe, Illinois, The Free Press, 1958.

Maddox, G. L.: Disengagement theory: a critical evaluation. *Gerontologist,* Pt. 1, 4: 80–82, 1964.

Mannheim, Karl. 1952. The problem of generations. *Essays on the Sociology of Knowledge,* ed. Paul Kecshmetic. New York: Oxford University Press.

McKain, Walter. 1957. Aging and rural life. *The New Frontiers of Aging,* ed. Wilma Donahue and Clark Tibbitts. Ann Arbor: University of Michigan Press.

Rogers, Everett M., and Burdge, Rabel J. 1972. *Social Change in Rural Societies.* New York: Appleton-Century-Crofts.

Rose, A. M. and Peterson, W. A. 1965. *Older People and Their Social World.* Philadelphia: F. A. Davis.

Rosow, Irving. 1967. *Social Integration of the Aged.* New York: The Free Press.

Shock, Nathan W. 1951 and 1963. *A Classified Bibliography of Gerontology and Geriatrics.* Stanford, California: Stanford University Press.

Spengler, Joseph J. 1969. The aged and public policy. In *Behavior and Adaptation in Late Life,* ed. Ewald W. Busse and Eric Pfeiffer.

Srole, Leo. 1956. Social integration and certain corollaries: an exploratory study. *American Sociological Review,* 21: 709–716.

Toffler, Alvin. 1971. *Future Shock.* New York: Random House.

Weller, Jack E. 1965. *Yesterdays People: Life in Contemporary Appalachia.* Lexington: University of Kentucky Press.

Will, Robert E., and Vatter, Harold G. 1965. *Poverty in Affluence.* New York: Harcourt, Brace & World, Inc.

Youmans, E. Grant, ed. 1967. *Older Rural Americans.* Lexington: University of Kentucky Press.

———— E. Grant. 1969. Some perspectives on disengagement theory. *Gerontologist,* Pt. 1, 9: 254–258.

————, E. Grant, and Yarrow, Marian. 1971. Aging and social adaptation: a longitudinal study of healthy older men. Patterson, R. P., and Granick, S. *Human Aging II: An 11-Year Follow-up Biomedical and Behavioral Study.* Washington, D.C.: U.S. Public Health Service Monograph.

Chapter 6

TRANSPORTATION PROBLEMS OF THE OLDER AMERICAN

IRA KAYE

As a society, we are justly proud of the increased life expectancy of our people. As social scientists we recognize that one important indicator of social growth is the life expectancy factor. We tend to denigrate societies, nations, or cultures with a life expectancy factor significantly lower than our own.

Absent from the list of indicators, however, are life enhancing factors for people as they attain greater life expectancy. In our society there is a tendency to make it more and more difficult for the elderly to have access to those basic services which make life desirable and sometimes even possible. The needs of the elderly for food, income opportunity, welfare, education, recreation, and just the general need to participate in the life of the community are made increasingly difficult of fulfillment because one of their most critical needs is ignored. That need is mobility. By mobility we mean the capacity, capability, and the opportunity to move. Transportation is only the physical means of moving and is one way of satisfying the need for mobility.

Material prepared for the 1971 White House Conference on Aging, while open to some question on detail, provides us with as good a planning tool as is required to define the dimensions of the problem. There are 20 million persons over the age of sixty-five residing in the United States. Of these, 6.6 million live in the central city; 5.8 million live in suburban areas and 7.6 million live in rural areas. While this indicates a not too dramatic spread of the places where the elderly live, it does indicate that our rural areas have a disproportionate demographic percentage of population who are elderly. Conversely, the rapidly growing suburbs too small a percentage. The numbers of elderly will continue to grow. By 1985 it is estimated there will be slightly more than 25 million and 28 million by the year 2000. By 1985 nearly 10 million persons will be over seventy-five and there will be another 7.5 million in the sixty to sixty-four age bracket.

Since our society views transportation as a commodity which must be bought, one dimension of the problem is the economic ability of the elderly to purchase transportation. Considering families whose head is over sixty-five, 22 percent have income below the poverty level of $3,400 for a farm family of four and $4,000 for a nonfarm family of four; an additional 15 percent have income defined as the near poverty level, exceeding the poverty level by 10 percent. Sixty-three percent attain an income level sufficiently high to eliminate the ability to pay for transportation as a factor of the problem. The near poverty group must be included in the number who, under our present concepts, cannot afford transportation, since experience tells us that large numbers of this group fall into the poverty group from time to time, responding to the general vicissitudes of making it in our society. When we consider persons over sixty-five living alone or with nonrelatives we find 42 percent have income below the farm poverty level of $1,700 for a single person and $2,000 for nonfarm; 28 percent live at the near poverty level and only 30 percent have income above the line where cost of transportation ceases to be a problem. An older person living alone or with a nonrelative is probably excluded from the present transportation market almost entirely. Elderly people living in institutions are excluded from these statistics.

Most public transportation, and to a large extent private transportation is geared to the home-to-work-to-home trip. Since only about 20 percent of the elderly are regularly employed, the transportation needs of the elderly flow against established patterns. In urban areas, the origin-destination pattern of their trips are diverse and do not conform to the radial pattern into and out of downtown areas. In rural areas, so many do without mobility that a pattern is hardly discernible. In all geographic settings, the older person's trips are, to a large extent, to obtain health assistance, shopping, and for social or recreational purposes. They seldom take evening trips; in many areas with good reason they fear for their safety. In the urban areas seldom do they impose on the rush hour crunch.

In typical urban areas identified as having an above national average of elderly persons, here is what we find:

Atlanta, Georgia Model Cities Area: Total population, 45,000 people. There are no physicians, dentists, large chain grocery stores or banks. All three pharmacies are located in the western section of the area. Public transportation is grossly inadequate and 50 percent of the elderly have incomes of less than $1,000 a year. The recent bus fare reduction from 40 cents to 15 cents if sustained will help out.

Seattle, Washington: 20 percent of the Model City area's population is over sixty-five years. A large number of the elderly are single men. There is no nursing home in the vicinity. It lacks basic transportation services and affords hardly any life support services.

A study of five cities in Ohio: Cleveland with 167,000 elderly; Toledo, 70,000 elderly; Springfield, 17,000 elderly; Portsmouth, 8,000 elderly; and Logan, 1,500 elderly generally representing over 20 percent of the population in each city indicated the following: 42 percent reported the need for transportation beyond any available; 58 percent had income under $2,400 per year, indicating that they had little or no money left for transportation after basic life support expenditures were provided for. The need for transportation was identified as follows: shopping 24 percent; visiting friends

23 percent; attending church 23 percent; health care 22 percent; recreational and social activities 14 percent.

In typical rural areas the situation is even more appalling.

Iowa: The percentage of elderly residing in rural Iowa is rising rapidly. Twelve counties already have 16 percent of their population in the upper-age bracket. Former Governor Blue has stated, "Transportation is a major problem for people residing in small communities and in rural areas. Passenger service by railroad is almost nonexistent, and where it does exist persons go long distances to reach terminals that accept passengers. Transportation by motor bus is also nonexistent in a large portion of the small towns . . . and in many of the smaller communities there is no taxi service." To this we must add in many of these communities there are no ambulance facilities either.

Eastern Kentucky: The isolation of the elderly is much more severe than that of the generally considered isolated total population. The President of the Senior Citizens Association of Eastern Kentucky has stated, "The need to see a physician, to purchase drugs, to purchase groceries, is a hard one to fulfill for the older person. He must depend upon the public facilities offered, and in the rural areas this is limited mostly to taxicabs which are expensive. Neighbors oftentimes offer their services in assisting the older person with his transportation needs, but too often this is not dependable enough to offer the senior citizen the security he needs."

Central Mississippi Delta: A representative of the Tufts Delta Health Center, funded by the Office of Economic Opportunity testified at hearings of the United States Senate Special Committee on Aging that almost total lack of transportation is a major obstacle to the provision of health care. Few elderly people in that area of Mississippi have access to transportation. Many of them are forced by these circumstances to give up part of their food to buy transportation to purchase food stamps.

West Virginia: At the State Forum which preceded

the White House Conference on Aging, the following was related. An old man in a rural area near Charleston spent one-third of his monthly Social Security check for a single trip to the doctor in Charleston. Living in an area with neither bus nor taxi service, he paid a neighbor $9.50 to drive him for a 9:00 a.m. appointment. The doctor did not see him until 2:00 p.m. so he had to give his waiting neighbor a dollar for lunch. The doctor charged him eleven dollars for the visit and a laboratory test. Two prescriptions cost him $9.53. His total expenditure was $31.03 none covered by Medicare. He spent 10½ hours from the time he left home in the morning until his return. His neighbor who was put out by the delay told him the next such trip would cost him $12.00. Although the doctor told him to return for a follow-up examination and treatment, it would be a very long time before he would visit a doctor again.

One physician at sixty years of age told the Forum that he had to keep very long office hours virtually seven days a week because he and one other physician aged eighty-five served their entire county of 17,000 persons. He stated, "We see people who have been sick or acutely ill for several days and we sometime ask why have you waited so long? They say, 'Well, I live in such and such a place, it is only Saturday or Sunday that I can get anyone to bring me to the doctor's office.' The people are working during the week and there are only one or two cars in the community and therefore we have got to depend when they are not working or on Sunday."

To the elderly this lack of access to transportation adds to his isolation, his ill-health, his poor nutrition, and makes the so-called "Golden Years" sound with a brass ring. To the society which allows this condition to exist or continue, a warning should be sounded to reexamine values and priorities.

What of the large number of older persons whose income level makes mobility affordable? We are living through an era which has witnessed a sharp decline in public transportation. For a variety of interrelated reasons an industry-wide deficit of $11 million in 1965 has risen to $130 million in 1968 and is still rising. Attempts by the industry to recoup its earnings by increases in fares shows that in spite of a 300 percent rise in fares between 1945 and 1968, the number of passengers using public transportation has decreased by two-thirds. In the latest fifteen-year period 120 companies have disappeared; of these seventy were in cities of less than 25,000 people. Because of this trend, mobility and transportation has meant the private automobile in a growing number of localities. The elderly as a group have severe handicaps which affect their ability to drive automobiles under current conditions. This is so in spite of the estimate that 81 percent of the elderly could travel without assistance. Ten percent of the elderly have impaired peripheral vision. Fifteen percent have hearing losses. Generally they have difficulty with multifaceted tasks and 20 percent suffer from neurological depression. Many, from time to time, are under medication that slows reactions. Although the University of Denver Law School study in March, 1970, indicated that drivers over sixty-five averaged 37 percent fewer accidents than would exist if their proportion of accidents were in exact ratio to their driving population; represented 7.4 percent of the total driving population in the thirty states and the District of Columbia area surveyed but were involved in 4.8 percent of all accidents; averaged lowest of all age groups in the frequency of injury producing accidents; and average 7 percent fewer fatal accidents, the older driver faces tougher and rougher licensing requirements and largely discriminatory insurance rates. Many companies arbitrarily cancel-out elderly drivers as bad risks even though they have a favorable accident record. Assigned risk plans to which those who desire to continue to drive must turn means not only higher costs, but these must be paid in one lump sum. One is therefore not surprised to find the elderly in the Transportation Workshop at the White House Conference pressing for a strong recommendation of No-Fault Insurance.

Highway construction, including the interstate systems,

require speedier traffic flow, shorter reaction times to get on and off the system and adjusting to rapidly changing traffic conditions. Since the elderly usually drive older cars, this too adds to the handicaps. The private automobile is at best a dwindling resource to afford mobility to the elderly. The modern highway system has had one additional negative effect on the ability of older Americans to travel. The decline of public transportation which has been discussed above is directly related to the death of public transportation in small towns and rural areas. The ability of the great national bus lines to speed along the interstates and other major highways means the bypassing of larger segments of rural areas, small communities and their beleagured people. This factor combined with the increased and more efficient transport of goods by truck has encouraged the railroads to shut down or curtail service in these same areas. As more and more families leave the central city to reside in suburbs linked by beltways and radial highways, the elderly have less access to public transportation. Since the general society's life style requires the use of the private automobile, transportation planning too often becomes highway construction. Until recently it was nothing else. It is almost axiomatic that the needs of the elderly rarely is considered in such planning. Nor have there been mechanisms through which the elderly themselves could participate in such planning. What public transportation remains is based on the home-to-work trip. As we have seen, this virtually eliminates the older person as a user. It has been observed by most urbanologists that most new activity centers tend to be located more and more on the fringe of jurisdictions. This trend assumes the availability of a private automobile or even two to provide adequate mobility for the residents. Those who cannot afford the luxury of this mode become immobile and isolated. Those older persons who can afford to own and operate a car feel constrained to limit themselves to drive only at certain times of the day in which they feel it is safe to drive. Many are issued licenses which specify daylight driving. Dr. Gelwick of the Gerontology Center, University of California at Los Angeles has found that the improvement and expression of our highways and the development of expressways and freeways have produced compartmentalized cities. Instead of neighborhoods, we now have the medical center, the business center, the shopping center, each of which may spread over many acres of land. Once an older person reaches one of these centers and parks his car he may find it extremely difficult to reach his ultimate destination. With the decline of the neighborhood, the center becomes the only resource for the fulfillment of shopping, medical, and other needs of the elderly. He then asks, "Of what use is it to take an elderly person to the corner of the shopping center if there is no internal transportation system to assist him in traversing the several acres of parked cars or moving from area to area within the center?"

A problem so severe has challenged some communities to seek solutions. Those working on the general problem of transportation for the elderly have sought to determine whether the elderly are better served by transporting services to the elderly or by transporting the elderly to the services. From another perspective they have sought to determine whether the elderly are better served by a transportation system designed exclusively for them or by a comprehensive system for the community at large which plans for the special conditions and needs of the elderly.

Since as a nation we have made only sticking our toe in the water efforts so far, these questions remain largely unanswered. At best we can describe without evaluating the options and alternatives thus far tried. For starts let us examine what federal legislation exists which could provide us a basis for programs to overcome the mobility handicap of the elderly. Under the Highway Safety Act of 1966 (P. L. 89-564) the Secretary of Transportation is authorized to establish performance standards for state highway safety programs to implement these standards. Two such standards, driver licensing and pedestrian safety, are of particular interest to the elderly. It is to be noted that only one of these really affects the older person as a user of transportation. To date, the only recommendations on highway design affects the elderly persons as a pedestrian. Measures have been taken to eliminate steps, steep grades and traffic lights which require fast and aggressive walking to make a crossing safely. As we have already noted, the Driver Licensing Program correctly seeks uniform, national standards to remove potentially unsafe drivers from our highways. This program cannot increase the number of elderly drivers.

Under its legislative authority to conduct research and planning, the Department of Transportation has conducted a very few studies and/or evaluations of programs. One was the evaluation of the Raleigh County, West Virginia, project funded by the Office of Economic Opportunity as a demonstration project for a limited, definite period. A substantial percent of the people served by the projects were elderly, poor persons residing in isolated rural areas around Beckley, West Virginia. Special nonwork trips were provided which improved (any trips had to be an improvement) service to the elderly. The study recommended the use of school buses, mail trucks, and improved service from the local Community Action Agency bus. It suggested an experiment with transportation stamps or vouchers. It did not result in the Department of Transportation providing the funds for a continuation of the project to enable it to test out the suggested modifications.

The Department funded a study of the transportation problems of the urban disadvantaged which includes elderly as well as physically handicapped younger persons. This attempted to get at the equipment and hardware problems of the elderly and physically handicapped as they face all types of air and surface transportation. A report entitled *Travel Barriers* was issued. It is available from the Clearinghouse for Federal Scientific and Technical Information, Springfield, Virginia, 22151 (PB# 187,327). The study team consisted of social scientists, systems analysts, and designers. Subways, buses and trolleys, train, and airplane barriers were studied in relationship to an index which measures the percent of disadvantaged individuals who are prevented from traveling or are discouraged by the prospect of travel because of the particular barrier. These matrices then gave the designers a crack at suggesting design changes in vehicles, cars, and airplanes as well as terminals and baggage handling arrangements. The suggestions and recommendations are still under study. As we shall see, a beginning has been made in their implementation in a few of Urban Mass Transit Authority's Research program.

Section 16 of the Urban Mass Transportation Act of 1964 states that 1½ percent of the total funding of UMTA Programs *may* be set aside to assist state and local public bodies and agencies to provide mass transportation facilities and services for elderly and handicapped persons. Data to date indicates that this section of the act has not been properly utilized. This is the only specific approach mentioned by the President in his message to Congress on the Aging, dated March 23, 1972. There have been, however, several research, development, and demonstration projects funded by UMTA which indicates that at last the Federal Government may be moving to find answers. These consist of an advanced people mover system in Morgantown, West Virginia. One hundred vehicles are to be especially designed to facilitate use by the elderly and the handicapped. These vehicles and all stations on the system provide wide aisles, extra wide doors, open floor space, and elevators to accommodate disabled or aged riders.

Haddonfield, New Jersey, has a Dial-A-Ride demonstration project. One vehicle of its contemplated twelve will be specially equipped with a lift device to handle wheel chairs. Currently under development are new bus specifications for special features which will ease travel for the elderly and handicapped. The innovations include bus floor level with curb heights, wider aisles and tracks or canes. In the lower Naugatuck Valley in Connecticut, a suburban area of which 10 percent of the population is elderly there is a project based on transportation services to health and medical facilities. The demonstration seeks a test of demand-responsive, fixed route services and a combination of both.

There is a project in Helena, Montana, which has no public transportation except expensive taxicabs. A multimodal, demand-responsive bus system designed to meet the mobility needs of the elderly is the basis of the project. The local taxi company will operate the system. If the experiment is successful, the city will continue to operate the system at the cessation of federal funds.

Summing up the Department of Transportation effort for the White House Conference on Aging, its own task forces stated, "In all fairness, it must be said that to date the impact has been minimal."

Just as the efforts of the Department of Transportation includes approaches which serve only the elderly, as well as a few that see the elderly traveller as only one component in a comprehensive system, the Office of Economic Opportunity has funded a few urban and about 50 rural transportation projects testing both approaches. Unlike the Department of Transportation which cannot see itself authorized to provide rural transportation, or use highway trust funds for public transportation, or any funds for operation subsidies, the Office of Economic Opportunity has found the flexibility, if only limited appropriations, to move into the breach. Since it is charged with aiding people to break out of poverty cycle, it could start with the demonstrated needs of the people. We have seen how the elderly poor are more severely handicapped by the lack of transportation than the elderly taken as a group. Thus any transportation system geared toward the needs of the poor, benefit the elderly as well. And in those rural areas totally deprived of public transportation, the institution of almost any system places an additional resource and alternative to the elderly as a group.

Early studies such as Project FIND identified the need for transportation. It seems superfluous to continue to research this point. However there is still a lingering debate about the feasibility of bringing the service to the people rather than the people to the service. Under the national emphasis program provided for in Section 222a (7) of the

Economic Opportunity Act of 1964 as Amended (42 USC 2809) (Senior Opportunities and Services), many centers provided Meals on Wheels or other food delivery services, mobile vans for food stamp registration or delivery, social security information and services, and other categorical services. There have been efforts in some of the health programs to provide mobile medical and dental vans. While some have proved successful and meet specific needs especially of the relatively small percent of the elderly who are house-bound, they are costly. The elderly do not see them as the preferred solution. While a visit is pleasant and breaks the monotony, it does not bring the elderly into the community. He still has many economic, social, and psychological needs untended that he wants and needs to do for himself. The examples of the Office of Economic Opportunity effort, usually operated by a local Community Action Agency reported below rely on transportation in the accepted meaning of the term to meet the older persons needs.

In Maine there are two prototype programs. In Kennebec and Somerset, two twelve-passenger vans and two nine-passenger station-wagons are operated by the CAA staff. They are used mainly to transport the elderly for required medical services. In York County, however, the county acquired a bus with funds from its surplus commodity program. It was utilized as the CAA's local share to bring in an Emergency Food and Medical Services program. The driver is paid under the Emergency Employment Act. The bus carries 17 poor persons a day from the rural areas to Portland. While its program was not set up for the elderly, as a group they have benefited most.

In New Hampshire, Rockingham County uses five twelve-passenger vans to transport Head Start pupils. In the period between the time classes start and the homeward journey begins, the vehicles are used to transport the elderly for all types of trips. The CAA uses part of its local initiative money and part of its Emergency Food and Medical Services grant to keep the program in operation.

In Vermont, The Champlain Valley Transportation

Corporation (CVTC) was started as a nonprofit corporation in 1969 to serve the rural counties around Burlington, Vermont. It has nine ten-passenger buses and three sixty-passenger buses which run daily routes to pick up general passengers, many of whom are elderly. It has contract or charter services for a variety of older persons' activities. It also delivers parcels. Two counties have initiated a demand activated dispatch system instead of fixed routes to determine the effectiveness of this approach in promoting mobility for otherwise isolated persons. The Corporation is governed by a board of low-income people elected by the low-income residents from the four counties served. It determines the routes, the mode of operation, contracts with state agencies and assists in staff selection. The board includes a large number of older persons. They attend local CAA meetings, as well as senior citizen groups and hold public hearings to remain responsive to their local communities. CVTC also has a garage component utilizing manpower trainees to do repair work on low-income peoples' cars at low prices. This service aids the elderly car owner.

In New Jersey, Progress on Wheels serves the elderly in rural counties in northwest New Jersey. The CAA obtained a government surplus bus. A trading stamp drive was organized, and the stamps redeemed for sufficient cash to maintain the vehicle. Volunteer drivers were recruited and the service transported older persons to meet their overall needs. Eventually a cash grant was obtained from the Office of Economic Opportunity which enabled the program to purchase two nine-passenger vehicles. These are supplemented by eight sedans and three stationwagons some of which are owned by the drivers. The project employs thirty-two people; only the director and his administrative assistant are not elderly. Regular routing schedules would have placed the service under State transportation regulations so it operates on a modified demand responsive basis. The elderly telephone requests for services to schedulers at the POW office. The schedulers obtain drivers and arrange all trips. Referrals from social service agencies, physicians, and other such sources are also honored. The part-time drivers are paid up to the Social Security-authorized maximum. Other drivers are paid depending on ownership of the vehicle for mileage and time. As successful as this program is it has difficulty in maintaining its funding status.

In North Carolina's Appalachian area, The Green Eagle Transportation Cooperative serves Watauga, Avery, Mitchell, and Yancy Counties. WAMY Community Action Agency sponsors the program, but the operation has been delegated to Green Eagle. There are 530 members who purchased stock at $5.00 a share. Only Cooperative members may ride the bus, but this has been interpreted to mean that any club or group with a member who owns a share of stock can charter vehicles for the whole group. Thus senior citizen organizations can charter buses from the cooperative.

In addition to the Raleigh County Experiment, previously discussed, West Virginia's Pride in Logan County Community Action Agency is about to launch a system which meets community needs but thereby takes care of the needs of the elderly. It will be under contract with the Department of Labor's WIN (work incentive) program, Head Start, Social Security and other service agencies to provide transportation for medical assistance, the welfare office, Social Security office, etc. The drivers will be WIN enrollees. They will have thirteen weeks of work experience training. After training they will be employed by the Transportation System. Training will be provided by the Department of Public Safety, County School System and vehicle manufacturer.

In Maryland, the Community Action Agency in Anne Arundel County organized a transportation cooperative with funds from an OEO Research and Demonstration grant. They were able to acquire, through the Economic Opportunity Loan Program administered by the Farmers Home Administration, a cooperative loan to buy buses. This is the only example of a transportation cooperative aided by the credit facilities of the Farmers Home Administration. The fixed routes service areas where a substantial part of the riders are elderly.

In Pennsylvania, three CAA's serving the rural counties of Erie, Crawford, Warren and Forrest run a comprehensive system tailored to the needs of the elderly. Volunteer drivers with accident-free records and adequate insurance are utilized. They are reimbursed only for the costs of operating the vehicle. Persons desiring to ride contact the CAA which establishes a pick-up route. The driver picks up the rider at his residence.

The rider makes a cash donation to the program for the service. Since the system is operated by a nonprofit corporation it is enabled to accept such donations, yet run a regular route free from the jurisdiction of the Public Utilities Commission. It has achieved an effective degree of coordination with the agencies, some of which alter schedules to meet the transportation schedules to better serve the client riders.

In Oregon, the CAA in Jackson County developed a system called Operation Transport and received OEO funds in June of 1971 to provide low-cost transportation for the poor, especially the elderly poor. This system combines a carpool, rural taxi service, central city interagency shuttle and intercity bus service. A local existing transit company and colleges are involved in managerial and research aspects of the system. The project aims to help create a local transit authority and to influence private transportation industry to meet rural poor people's needs, especially those of the older person.

There are small, initial efforts like these in several other states. Those students interested in more details are directed to the Appendix which lists specific agencies to contact for information on their particular systems. The termination of federal support of the Community Action Program after Fiscal Year 1973 will have an extremely negative impact of these germinal programs. It will be interesting to see how many receive continued support through revenue sharing.

In addition there are a few programs directly funded by the Office on Aging. In February, 1972, Maine became the first state to receive funds under the Older Americans Act to implement a program specifically for older persons. Project Independence serves three western counties in Maine— Androscoggin, Franklin, and Oxford. Free transportation is a key feature of this project which includes a variety of other activities including information-referral service, health screening, homemaker and home health nursing service, and leisure time activities. An elderly person needing transportation calls a toll-free number to make arrangements with a dispatcher. Usually twenty-four hours notice is needed, but emergency arrangements can be made on shorter notice. To begin with, the six mini-buses operate nine to five week days, but it is expected that hours and days will be expanded once the program gets underway.

In addition to these OEO efforts, at least fifty cities and communities in the United States have reduced transit fare programs for the elderly. In some communities participation in such programs is limited to the low-income elderly. Almost all of them require presentation of Medicare or other identification cards. The December 1970 report by the United States Senate Special Committee on Aging indicates that the impact of reduced fare programs for the elderly show that such programs help the elderly and that ridership does increase. However, there is still some question about the effects the programs have on transit system revenues and operations. Reduced to basics—does the system bear the expense, or does the general community, through tax dollars?

The New York City experiment provided for 15 cent fares (half the regular fare) for all persons 65 and over, not fully employed, to ride buses and subways during the hours of 10:00 a.m. to 4:00 p.m. and 7:00 p.m. to midnight five days a week; all day on Saturday and Sunday and Holidays. The city, at the outset of the program, agreed to pay the transit authority 5 million dollars for six months plus administrative costs. During the ensuing two years, the City agreed to pay 30 million dollars for the program. To overcome the taint of welfarism, approximately 1,000 commerical and savings banks served as registration points for the elderly wishing to participate in the program. Senior Citizens Centers, labor unions and neighborhood centers also participated. About 600,000 older persons registered for the reduced fares. As of May, 1970, 73 percent of those eligible had registered. It is of major interest, however, to learn that the middle-class elderly appear to be most responsive. Registration in poverty areas of the city are lower than the rest of the city. It may well be that some low income older persons cannot afford even reduced fares. It may also be noted that poverty areas usually have fewer participating banks and reduced information sources.

Both the buses and the subways have shown a substantial increase in ridership during the hours on which reduced fare participants are eligible to ride.

The Chicago experience has not yet been properly evaluated so that there is only a limited basis for judgment. Its format is similar to that of New York City and the elderly are charged a half-fare rate of twenty cents. Since the Chicago Transit Authority is required by law to pay its operation costs entirely out of revenue from the fare box, a city subsidy was not possible. Since there has been revenue loss for the period in which the program operated, the transit authority is reluctant to continue it. However, a fair analysis of the loss indicates that it is not possible to definitely tag the program with the blame for the loss. While it was true that the ridership increased during the hours that reduced fare participants were eligible to ride, there was no correlation shown between that fact and the overall decline in revenues.

It is difficult to generalize from the small sampling of experience that exists. Most programs have initial difficulties with Public Transit or Utility Commissions over franchises, schedules and rates. Sometimes an existing company that has virtually abandoned its franchise suddenly protests that its rights are being invaded. Local taxicab companies also complain of unfair competition. Cooperatives have been denied tax exempt status by Internal Revenue Service local offices. Many programs suffer from the effects of failing to run adequate feasibility studies or origin destination studies. Rarely has operating expenses for the early lean years been anticipated. Government agencies may extend credit or even grants for the acquisition of vehicles but rarely do they provide the operating subsidies to launch a healthy program. Government surplus vehicles are convenient to acquire but too often they are in need of immediate costly repairs or need excessive maintenance to keep them going, and too little has been set aside for such contingencies. Moreover the Office of Management and Budget required the General Services Administration to severely limit the ability of community groups to acquire surplus vehicles for such uses. If we have learned anything from our experience to date it has been the complicated nature of setting up a transportation system. It should not be undertaken lightly and only with the most expert help available.

As we have seen, most of these programs are in the nature of experimental or demonstration programs and will terminate when the demonstration period runs its course. The Senate Committee comments: "The frustration, disappointment and bitterness engendered by the termination of the services—desperately needed by the elderly recipients—may not dissipate early. There is a need to consider the social implications of demonstration programs that are terminated after changing the lives of the participants." This, unfortunately, is true for all sections of the population affected by demonstration grants. Yet, since Congress and the Office of Management and Budget rarely respond except to data retrieved through the experimental, and research and demonstration approach, they alone have the ability to mitigate or eliminate the social evil complained of.

The immediate future is a bit more promising than the recent past. The 1971 White House Conference on Aging saw transportation as one of the top three problems facing the elderly and made the following recommendations:

1. The Federal Government shall immediately adopt a policy of increasing transportation services for the rural and urban elderly. The policy should be flexible encompassing various alternatives. Both system subsidies

and payments to elderly individuals may be needed, the choice depending upon the availability and usability of public and private transportation.

Subsidies should be made available not only for existing systems, but also for the development of flexible and innovative systems, especially where there are no existing facilities.

Financial support should be directed toward accomplishing program purposes such as:

1. Reduced or no fare transit for elderly people.
2. Operating and capital subsidies.

2. The Federal Government shall act immediately to increase support for the development of transportation for all users, with special consideration given to the needs of the elderly, the handicapped, rural people, the poor and youth.

3. Publicly funded programs for the elderly shall be designed so that transportation will be required as an integral part of these programs, whether transportation is provided directly by the program or through other community resources. Public policy shall require coordination of existing transportation and/or new planned transportation with publicly-funded programs for the elderly.

4. The Federal Government should move immediately to adopt a policy which will both increase the level of funding available to the development and improvement of transportation services and also foster the coordination of all forms of transportation, public and private, at federal, state, regional, and local levels of responsibility.

The Congress of the United States is urged to immediately adopt legislation to convert the Highway Trust Fund into a General Transportation Fund to be utilized for all modes of transportation.

A portion of the General Transportation Fund shall be

made available for the development of new transportation services and the improvement of existing transportation services for the elderly.

5. A broad program to develop people-delivery systems in rural areas should be undertaken such as those by the Federal and State Governments, based on demonstration projects by the Office of Economic Opportunity, the Appalachian Regional Commission, Green Light, and others.

Legislation should be passed enabling and requiring public, social, health and employment services in rural areas to help provide transportation and outreach; removing legal barriers such as taxi rates and car, taxi, and school bus insurance restrictions to such transportation services; and financing such services for older people in rural areas.

This last recommendation came from the Rural Older People Task Force. Many other recommendations worthy of consideration by the serious student and decision maker can be found in the Report to the delegates of the Transportation Section.

These recommendations reflect the concerns of many people, from almost all walks of life, and from all sections of the country. It is important to note that the elderly, as well as the technicians, felt that a comprehensive system would better answer the needs of the elderly for mobility, than one fashioned exclusively for the elderly. Once again our older persons have opted to remain part of a viable community instead of a service-privileged group.

There are at least twelve legislative proposals in both Houses of Congress currently being considered which deal with the transportation problem of the elderly. Some provide priority in the allocation of UMTA funds to cities which will institute reduced fare programs for the elderly; some (please note) authorize special emphasis on transportation, research and demonstration projects; there are none that address themselves to the request for a comprehensive system sought by the conference.

What of the future: The urban elderly can look forward to a continuation of the reduced fare trend. They may even be able to experience routing and scheduling more to their needs with less emphasis on the home-to-work trip. They certainly stand to benefit from experiments in the redesign of all elements in transportation. Vehicles will be designed which will eliminate the climbing of steps for entrance and exit. Special seats for the elderly and other handicapped, even the possibility of travelling with one's own wheelchair is achieveable. Acceleration and deceleration will be geared to the safety of the elderly passenger.

The San Francisco Bay Area Rapid Transit System will provide:

Elevators to help nonambulatory or feeble persons move vertically from street to train platform, equipped with telephone and controls within easy reach of wheelchair occupants.

Restrooms with special design features for elderly and handicapped, including doors wide enough for wheelchairs.

Stairways in stations with handrails on both sides extending 18 inches behond top and bottom steps. Special parking facilities for handicapped will have especially wide stalls that are located close to stations.

A wheelchair occupant will be able to ride easily over the gap between train platform and the BART car floor, pass through the door and move from one end of the car to another. This extra width will undoubtedly be helpful to older ambulatory persons during crowded rush hours.

A loudspeaker system, as well as highly visible signs, will assist those with impaired sight or hearing.

Special services gates and fare collection machines will be installed in stations.

Closed circuit television communication systems, special directional signs, and low placements of public telephones and elevator buttons will also provide special assistance to the elderly and handicapped passenger.

The Metro contemplated for Washington will incorporate many of these features. It is important to note that all of the features discussed represent existing technology. If the elderly had an institutional mechanism through which they could bring their special needs before the transportation and community planners, all systems could be made responsive to the needs of the elderly.

A recent study entitled, "Communications Technology for Urban Improvement," indicates that with existing technology we can organize and operate a personalized dial-a-vehicle system to serve the elderly; create a system which would enable a person to telephone any bus stop and obtain precise information on when various buses will arrive at the stop. This would make it possible for the elderly to avoid safety and weather problems. We have little or no information on the cost to society to utilize the technology on hand. But we do know the cost in human suffering of the elderly if we do not make the effort.

In rural areas, the future is much less certain. Until we achieve a national growth policy which seeks the type of rural development capable of reducing outmigration of young people, it is doubtful whether any decision maker will authorize the investment in total resources necessary to provide adequate public transportation for our rural people including the elderly. Recent advances in communication technology including the communication satellite system could lessen the need for transportation, although we should not be deceived into thinking that these advances will eliminate it. What is required is a realistic appraisal of the transportation/communication mix necessary to properly serve our rural areas, its people, and especially its elderly. An urban level of services in a rural residence could thus be achieved and the "Golden Years" become a reality.

One approach which has not yet been explored, might be to combine all of the existing transportation and communication resources in given multicounty rural areas and with a systems approach fashion a people-serving comprehensive system. The resources spent by the Postal System to pick up and deliver mail; by the school system in picking up and delivering children; by the social service agencies to serve their individual clients; by the military with their underutilized maintenance and training facilities all represent a sizeable investment. If this investment could be restructured into a single system, it could provide a basis for a people transport system at fares all could afford.

As an example, Switzerland has a highly developed Postal Passenger Service which appears to be a model we should examine closely as it is relevant to the transportation needs in this country. The Swiss PTT and private licensed companies under contract with PTT provide public bus transportation and mail conveyance in areas where no railway service is available. The Postal Passenger Service is legally bound to keep its rates as low as possible and uses idle and reserve vehicles for extra trips, particularly for tourists, to generate additional income. The postal bus network extends over 4,700 miles, providing service to 1,600 villages; the average length of a route is about 7.5 miles. Vehicles are made to specifications of the PTT and are flexible enough in design to be used for a variety of assignments. The PTT owns garages for maintenance and repair work. In the last few years there has been more than a 5 percent increase annually in the number of passenger service. The PTT states, "It has always been one of the foremost duties of a government to promote good transportation facilities at reasonable charge." That philosophy seems to be the foundation which makes possible such a progress transportation system.

Institutional and functional trade off's would be required. But weighed against the human tragedy imposed by lack of mobility, none of these trade off's seem insurmountable. The elderly would benefit most from this approach. In most cases the duration of the ride is not that important to them if it is certain, safe, and comfortable. The ingenuity that brought a human to the moon ought to be able to figure out how to get an older person from rural West Virginia to Charleston to see his doctor in less than a day and for less than a third of his Social Security check.

REFERENCES

U. S. Department of Transportation: Federal Highway Administration; Bureau of Public Roads. *The Transportation Needs of the Rural Poor.* (RMC Report # UR-072) December, 1969.

Office of Economic Opportunity; Office of Program Development. *A Study of the Transportation Problems of the Rural Poor.* (RMC Report # UR-171) January 7, 1972.

United States Senate Special Committee on Aging. *Older Americans and Transportation: A Crisis in Mobility.* 91st Congress, 2nd Session Senate Report # 91-1520. December, 1970.

Straszheim, Mahlon R.: *The Federal Mass-Transit Capital Grant Program* Program on Regional and Urban Economics Discussion Paper # 53. Harvard University, Cambridge, Massachusetts, August, 1969.

Straszheim, Mahlon R.: *Transportation Policy as an Instrument for Altering Regional Development Patterns—Misdirected Emphasis?* Program on Regional and Urban Economics Discussion Paper # 52. Harvard University, Cambridge, Massachusetts, August, 1969.

1971 White House Conference on Aging. *A Report to the Delegates from the Conference Sections and Special Concerns Sessions.* November 28,– December 2, 1971.

Office of Economic Opportunity. *Summary of Conference on Rural Transportation.* November 25–26, 1968. Kimley-Horn and Associates, Inc., Raleigh, North Carolina, February, 1969.

Conference on Poverty and Transportation, June 7, 1968. American Academy of Arts and Sciences, Brookline, Massachusetts. Clearinghouse for Federal Scientific and Technical Information. PB 180 955/PB 180 956.

Department of Housing and Urban Development. Committee on Telecommunications National Academy of Engineering. *Communications Technology for Urban Improvement.* June, 1971.

Office of Economic Opportunity. National Council on the Aging Senior Opportunities and Services Technical Assistance Monograph # 4. *Developing Transportation Services for the Older Poor.* May, 1970.

Office of Economic Opportunity. Abt Associates. *The Causes of Rural to Urban Migration Among the Poor.* March 31, 1970.

Office of Economic Opportunity. National Council on Aging. *The Golden Years—A Tarnished Myth.* January, 1970.

Tarsi, Charles A.: *An Outline and Suggested Methodology for New Transportation Programs.* Progress on Wheels, Belvidere, New Jersey.

Department of Housing and Urban Development. National Council on Aging. *Special Handling Required.* June, 1971.

Department of Transportation. Abt Associates, Cambridge, Masshusetts. *Travel Barriers.* Clearinghouse for Federal Scientific and Technical Information, Springfield, Virginia PB 187 327.

Chapter 7

RELIGIOUS NEEDS OF OLDER AMERICANS

John McDowell

THE NEED FOR COMPANIONSHIP
PASTORAL COUNSELING
CHAPLAINCIES

The human person is a whole being, not a composition of different natures. Therefore, religious needs are inter-related and interdependent with economic, physical, psychological, social, cultural, and other types of human needs.

Religion may be described as "the response to all of life," as "the search for meaning in the range of life experiences."

The choice of behavioral patterns that express one's "response" or "search" for the ultimate meaning is largely culturally determined. Whether one worships in a church or synagogue, or in neither; how one expresses his sense of relationship with God and his fellow human beings, ritualistically or with studied informality; in company with many people or few is likely to be determined by the family and community in which one grows up. Likewise what particular group of people one associates with for religious activities is determined more often by personal and social history than by objective rational choice.

A current trend to ecumenism in religious associations within Christian communions and the ordinary person's lack of concern for esoterica of theology is removing for many people the guilt feelings and damaging familial alienation that once characterized a person's break with his own traditional religious group. Religion is becoming more truly than ever "a personal matter."

However, it is likely to be one factor in determining whom a person seeks to associate with, even a person who is not currently an active member of a church or synagogue. Therefore, in dealing with the Older American sense of loneliness which characterizes the latter years of many, the religious congregation (of whatever faith) is a resource to be sought out by practitioners with older people.

THE NEED FOR COMPANIONSHIP

The need for someone to talk to, to play games with, or just to "sit with" is one that does not require a professional competence, but rather a congenial human being with some time. It can be met by an organized program of volunteer visitors, many of whom may be older Americans themselves and subject to similar feelings of loneliness.

It is reasonable to look to a church or synagogue suggested by the person being counseled for this kind of service. If no such service is found to be available at the time of first contact, the rehabilitation counselor need not be inhibited from pursuing it further. Steps which would be appropriate include an appeal to the pastor to take initiative in starting a program with the client of the moment as the first recipient. If the pastor is unwilling to act, he may be willing to suggest one or two members of the congregation who might be approached. If the pastor and congregation seem preoccupied with other concerns, a council of churches or some other interchurch or interreligious agency may be able to start a "friendly visiting" program or to direct the counsellor to some other religious group that may be more willing to undertake to organize this kind of volunteer service.

The risk involved in "by-passing" a pastor who cannot be

moved into taking some responsibility for helping to get a needed program launched should be carefully weighed. Some clergy will bitterly oppose any attempt to secure action on the part of a group of their parishioners which is not under their own auspices. Others will be most willing to give anyone, inside the parish or outside, a "hunting license" to enlist whatever support he can for a needed community program. More often the pastor will be cooperative, although the time and energy he himself can give to it will be limited. He may well introduce the counsellor to the chairman of the group within the congregation who is most likely to be responsive to a request for a friendly visitor service.

Many pastors, often in a cooperative effort with others, are already moving toward organization of a program of service to older Americans in their own homes which will include not only "friendly visiting" to lonely persons, but also specific types of personal or household service on a volunteer basis. For example, transportation to a weekly senior citizens club meeting, to church on Sunday, to the clinic or drugstore, or to the supermarket for a weekly shopping trip are all services that are being undertaken by a church-related volunteer organization in many communities. People with "handy-man" skills around the house can be enlisted on a volunteer or modest fee basis, to do the chores in a home or apartment that the older person is no longer able to do herself (or himself). Churches and synagogues across the country are being encouraged by their national organizations to initiate such programs within their parishes and communities. The "ecumenical spirit" which currently prevails makes it unlikely that such programs in a locality will be limited to those narrowly considered "members" of the sponsoring religious organization. An inventory of such programs among the religious organizations of a community would be desirable as part of the "orientation program" for a new rehabilitation counselor.

PASTORAL COUNSELING

There is a recognized competence in pastoral counseling which is developed through organized programs of professional training in theological schools of all major faith groups in America. There are problems which people have which pertain particularly either to their current or previous religious affiliation or to their sense of relationship (or lack of it) to a supreme being. These problems may complicate the resolution of economic, social, familial, physical, or psychological situations. For help with such problems the pastoral counselor is needed as part of the "service team" for older Americans.

The rehabilitation counselor rightly objects to the idea that "common sense" is all the qualification that a good counselor needs. So also the competent pastoral counselor objects to the idea that anyone who considers himself a "religious person" is competent to provide help with spiritual or religious needs.

Let us look at some of the needs of older persons which have a religious component calling for the special knowledge and skill of a pastoral counselor.

Guilt feelings. One cause of mental ill health in a person of any age is a sense of guilt, a feeling that one has transgressed some higher law, or, to put it in the religious vernacular, that one has "sinned." Any attempt to determine whether one actually has transgressed any law, "higher" or otherwise, is irrelevant. It is the individual's feeling that he has violated some standard or rule that he believes imperative which can be dehabilitating.

If the guilt relates to alienation from an earlier religious belief or association, it is clearly a matter requiring a pastoral counselor's help. If it relates to behavior which the client perceives to be in violation of his own expectations of himself; Judeo-Christian religious teaching of a God who "forgives sins" brings a message of release and new hope. It is the mission of the minister, priest or rabbi to communicate this message to all who are tormented by their inner sense of wrongdoing.

Guilt feelings are not restricted to older people, but older persons are not immune to them. When they constitute a particular problem of an older client, the services of a pastoral counselor should be sought by other practitioners involved.

Facing death. As the years pass, even the physically healthy older person realizes that death is an event certain to occur in the relatively near future. The older person who has developed the ability to cope with the vicissitudes of life in a resourceful and responsible way prepares for death in the same way. He puts his affairs in order, makes sure that his last will and testament expresses his current wishes, and arranges for a cemetery lot or other arrangements for the care of his physical remains.

The older person who exhibits this healthy approach to the end of his life, nevertheless encounters some complications, often arising out of the American sociocultural pattern of avoiding consideration of death and dying except for promotion of elaborate and expensive funerals. The responsible older person who knows himself to be "on his deathbed" and fears mainly that his stay there shall be unduly prolonged, often finds his doctor unwilling to talk frankly with him about his physical prospects. His family and friends play out a charade to the effect that "you will be up and about in a few days" (or weeks). Too often he faces this unknown and essentially "unknowable" life experience deprived of the opporturnity to "talk it out" with those close to him with whom he is accustomed to talk over major events. The pastoral counselor may be the understanding listener with the dying patient. Hopefully in these last days he can help to bring reality and trust into the relationship of the patient with surviving spouse, with son or daughter, or with a close friend. To do this the pastor's work is more with the family or friend than with the patient.

Beliefs about the meaning of death and what is after physical death will differ from one religious group to another and sometimes among various clergymen within the same religious group. Nonetheless the pastor can reasonably be expected to have training and experience in counseling people who are facing the end of life. If the older person expresses a preference for a religious faith or denomination, the chances are that a pastor from that group will be most likely to be helpful.

The task of making available to the older person pastoral counseling will differ depending on the situation, for example:

(a) If the older person is a regular member of a parish, his or her own pastor will arrange to be available, if he knows of a patient's illness or if the older parishioner seeks his counsel before illness strikes. The rehabilitation counselor or other practitioners working with such an older client have only to determine who the pastor is, to what extent he has been working with the client, and to establish some orderly means of communication with the pastor in relation to this client.

If the older person is living away from his home parish (for whatever reason) a call to his pastor from the rehabilitation counselor should bring about a visit, or the name of a substitute pastor in the community where the client now lives, or some other arrangement for service.

(b) If the older client has not had any recent active affiliation with a congregation or parish, a pastor of his faith or denominational preference can be consulted to discover whether he is able and willing to serve or whether there is an ecumenical agency in the community which has pastoral counseling as one of its purposes. In some communities there are pastoral counseling centers set up for the purpose of providing such service to people who have no pastors of their own or who choose not to use him, for some reason. Councils of churches, urban ministries, Protestant chaplaincies supported by a number of churches are types of Protestant agencies that can be turned to in some communities for pastoral care of religiously unaffiliated persons. There is a staff member in Roman Catholic dioceses who can arrange for pastoral care on request for persons not currently related to a parish but who prefer the ministry of that Church.

CHAPLAINCIES

The 1971 White House Conference on Aging recommended "that all licensing agencies in the State require that institutions caring for the aged must provide adequate chaplaincy services. In certain instances in which cooperating church organizations cannot obtain financial support for such service, government should be empowered to supply it upon recommendations of the State Commission on Aging or other appropriate agencies." (From Working Draft of Conference Recommendations.)

For a number of liberal Protestant communions the establishment of a chaplaincy service to agencies serving older people does not present major theological or jurisdictional difficulties. In fact, church leaders are willing to recognize that such agencies, particularly those under proprietary or nonsectarian auspices, have a right to expect that churches will provide chaplaincy services to their aged residents. However, these ventures tend to be low on the priority list in the budgets of most congregations in the community where the services are needed. In some denominations it is only recently that clergymen serving as chaplains (to hospitals, prisons, courts, institutions for the aging) were given the ordinary "fringe benefits" (e.g. retirement fund, health insurance, car allowance, housing allowance, etc.) accorded the parish minister. Some chaplains still may not have these benefits and protections.

The suggestion that governmental funds be allocated to provide for chaplains in such institutions raises many questions. There is the obvious constitutional question of "the establishment of religion" by use of public funds. There is also the prophetic—moral issue now being raised with respect to military chaplains, i.e., does the religious community by acceptance of salaries for its chaplains in the armed forces forfeit its right to condemn "an unjust war." With respect to agencies serving older people the issue would be that one function of a representative of the churches (and synagogues) should be to express a judgment about any practices of the agency which dehumanize or degrade the elderly people whom it serves. This can be and is carried by some institutional chaplains to the point where community support is mobilized to bring about needed changes in the institutions. Question: Can this function be performed by a chaplain whose salary is paid by the institution or by the government which licenses it?

The concept of a chaplaincy could be broadened to include a "ministry to Older Americans" in the community as well as in institutions, so that older persons in need of pastoral care would have it available whether or not they are actively related currently to a congregation or parish. The fact of the matter is that the counselor of older Americans in many communities may be forced to engage in a community organization—social action enterprise in order to assure pastoral counseling for the people in his or her clientele. This should be considered no less appropriate than community action to secure adequate housing, health services, and nutrition for older Americans in the community.

MEETING THE REHABILITATION NEEDS OF THE OLDER AMERICAN

JOHN G. CULL AND RICHARD E. HARDY

DEFINITION OF THE OLDER AMERICAN
EMOTIONAL ASPECTS OF AGING
PSYCHOLOGICAL ASPECTS OF AGING
EMPLOYMENT NEEDS OF THE AGING
SOCIAL NEEDS OF THE AGING
SUMMARY

DEFINITION OF THE OLDER AMERICAN

The purpose of this chapter is to outline some of the rehabilitation needs of older Americans. It will cover some of the emotional, psychological, employment, and social needs of these individuals. Before looking at these specific areas, it would be appropriate to identify this segment of our population. In rehabilitation we tend to be quite exact in our functional descriptions or definitions of a disability group. For example, in mental illness there are numerous specific diagnostic categories which describe the psychological function of the individual; in cardiac involvement there is the functional heart classification; almost all state rehabilitation agencies use a rather specific range of IQ to define mental retardation, and IQ is a quantified approach to describing intellectual function; however, the term "older Americans" is filled with ambiguity. We use many other terms which are just as inadequate—the aged, the aging, senior citizens, geriatrics, golden-agers and many others. Not only are the names for this segment of our population indefinite and inadequate, the definitions are just as confusing. Almost all the definitions use age rather than function as the criterion. As many will recognize this is foreign to professionals involved in vocational rehabilitation since we pride ourselves on taking the humanistic or functional approach with individuals.

As professionals in rehabilitation, we prefer the term industrial gerontology or the industrial geriatic. According to Norman Sprague (1970), industrial gerontology is the study of the employment and retirement problems of middle-aged and older workers. It is the science of aging and work.

Industrial gerontology begins where age *per se* becomes a handicap to employment. Age discrimination in employment may start as early as age thirty-five or forty in some industries and occupations, and it begins to take on major dimensions at age forty-five. Federal and state legislation impose age discrimination in employment policies generally around the ages of forty to sixty-five. However, as in other disability areas of vocational rehabilitation, this condition (age) becomes a factor of concern only when it constitutes a handicap to employment.

Industrial gerontology is concerned with aptitude testing, job counseling, vocational training, and placement. It is concerned with job adjustment, job assignment and reassignment, retention on the job, redesign of the work requirements, vocational motivation, and mobility.

We believe the similarity between the concerns of industrial gerontology and vocational rehabilitation and the degree of overlapping in these two areas are both impressive and remarkable. So programs in industrial gerontology are highly significant to the individuals charged with responsibilities for program planning and program development in vocational rehabilitation as well as the practitioner in the field. Historically, vocational rehabilitation has been a medically-oriented program. We have worked exclusively with medical disabilities which impose vocational handicaps. There are many in vocational rehabilitation who have been advocating a change in the philosophy of our profession. This change would result in our working with individuals who have a vocational handicap regardless of his physical or medical status. Recently (through P.L.89-333, 1965) there has been a major step forward in this direction—the expansion of the definition of eligibility to include behavior disorders. This is the first nonmedical, social disorder with which we have worked. We are firmly convinced one of the next nonmedical disability groups we will expand our definition of eligibility to accept and serve will be the industrial geriatric. This is why we feel we should start gaining program experience through our workshop programs now.

Before discussing the specific needs of this segment of our population as outlined above, we would like to state a basic position which we feel we all accept but often forget. The similarities between any section of our population and the population as a whole are much greater than the dissimilarities. The industrial geriatric or "older American" is more like than unlike the clients on our existing case loads. Programatic changes which are needed to adapt our services to this population will be minor and tend to be changes in emphasis rather than changes in direction. Programs for the aging in workshops are completely compatible with existing service programs.

EMOTIONAL ASPECTS OF THE AGING

A very interesting trend has occurred in our culture which has resulted in creating emotional needs for the "older American"; age is no longer related to conformity behavior (Cull, 1970). Traditionally we have revered our elders. In our culture we can see this reverence in the admonishments of the Old Testament. In the Indo Iranian and Hindu cultures we can turn to the Rig Vedas, the Upanashads, and the Bhagavad-Gita for the same admonishments. Since the beginning of time, cultures and societies have turned to their elders for judgments, decisions, values, and mores. The elders have determined the future of the tribe, culture, or society. This has been true universally until the past generation. The current generation of elders have been socially, economically, and vocationally emasculated. They have become a lost generation. They grew up expecting, and with every reason to expect, to mature into a role of influence in our culture. This is a very enviable role and one generally anticipated with a degree of eagerness. To become an elder had meaning, purpose, rewards, and status.

However, after the revolution in technology we now turn to younger, more aggressive, more highly trained individuals to make decisions. The demands for speed and innovation are the two factors which have robbed older people of what they viewed as a birthright. Everything which smacks of seniority is under fire—even the committee hierarchy in Congress.

The result is this lost generation of elders has become confused, disoriented, relegated to an inferior role with a great amount of condescending expressions of concern. Rather than arriving at a state which would bring status and reverence and one filled with meaning and purpose, they have been pushed to early retirement, then isolated and forgotten. No wonder many are concerned, bitter, and resentful.

The most important need this group of individuals has is to feel useful. While much can be said for our new sophisticated decision-making theories, there is a great manpower pool of years of experience going to waste. This pool of manpower should be mobilized by our workshops for the benefit of both parties. While production and income supplementation will solve some of the problems of the aging, the workshop can solve many others. In workshop operations, it has been found (Johndrow, 1970) that if older workers are placed with younger retardates, the production of both groups increases and the discipline problems with the retarded youngsters are reduced. This arrangement also seems to be an effective motivating factor for the older worker. Life is becoming more meaningful for them—they are more useful. From the workshop's point of view, this arrangement is beneficial since it reduces the need for intensive professional supervision and simultaneously increases production.

PSYCHOLOGICAL ASPECTS OF AGING

When we think of the psychological aspects of aging, we almost automatically think of reduced intellectual ability. Almost all research studies between Galton's in 1883 up to Lorges in 1947 have indicated there is a decline in intelligence with age. The decline was supposed to be progressive beginning after a peak at age eighteen to twenty-five. However, more recent studies indicate this is not the case. It appears as if there is a plateau established at approximately age twenty-four to twenty-five. This plateau is stable until about age seventy. The objections to decline in intellectual abilities center around (a) the speeded nature of the tests and the decline of the individual's reaction time as opposed to intelligence, (b) the scores being dependent upon acquired and stored knowledge and older subjects being more remote from the time of schooling and having less schooling, and (c) the tests being constructed so they are more appropriate to younger subjects than older subjects. There is little if any reliable evidence that the older individual undergoes significant intellectual decline.

Testing deficits may be explained by lack of motivation, lowered reaction time, lack of familiarity with the testing orientation, as well as the considerations above.

A second factor to consider under psychological aspects of aging is the pathological mental conditions among the aged. This factor is probably the largest precluding factor in vocational rehabilitation's accepting and serving the aging population. There are statistics which support the position that age invariably brings on mental aberrations. During the last third of a century the admission rate of geriatrics in our state hospitals has zoomed.

There are many articles now appearing in the literature which indicate the state hospital geriatric wards are serving more as human warehouses and foster homes than bona fide treatment facilities. The high rate of admissions is partially explained by social and cultural factors rather than emotional factors. Due to the removal of much of the stigma attached to mental illness, many adults have older relatives committed on the slightest pretexts since this is a convenient solution to a social problem.

We are not trying to explain away the problems of the aging. Some are very serious and need the attention and concern of all of us; however, the problem is not of the magnitude we in vocational rehabilitation suppose. In the past we have felt the problems were insurmountable so we ignored them. The life expectancy for this attitude is indeed very short. It is incumbent on us as professionals to understand the problems of these people and mobilize our efforts to solve them.

In the psychological aspects of aging, one explanation of the increased incidence of a type of mental illness lies in the role they are required to accept. The current life style in our culture leads toward older citizens feeling much less secure, unhappy, nonproductive; they generally live in a home situation in which they have at best an ill-defined role; there is a feeling of dependence rather than independence which leads to self-respect. Their future is narrowing, constricting, and bleak with a diminishing health status (physical and emotional).

The last factor we will discuss in the psychological aspects of aging which is related to vocational rehabilitation is the psychological set of the older individual. All of us view ourselves as workers. If we become unemployed, we still tend to view ourselves as workers and as such are capable of work. The longer we are unemployed the more narrowed and rigid our view of our capabilities of working become. While employed, our psychological set relative to our capabilities for work is highly flexible. We feel we can do our job and many variations of our job in many different locations. The longer we are out of work the more rigid our psychological set of ourselves as workers becomes, until finally we become convinced we are no longer workers. This is very obvious among the coal miners of Appalachia. They can function only as coal miners in their local area. Since there are no jobs, they are unemployable. They no longer view themselves as workers.

This phenomenon is particularly appropriate with the aging. The longer they have been unemployed and the more they felt pushed out of their last job, the less they will characterize themselves as "a worker" or productive individual. Since the older individual has a rather strong need to be considered a useful person, but is unable to do so, his psychological adjustment to aging will be quite difficult.

The older worker can be a highly productive worker; therefore, a workshop administrator should be keenly interested in adapting and extending existing service programs.

Now, what can the workshop do? First, the workshop should modify its work adjustment program for the older client. As with other clients this should be a sequentially or graduated program providing positive, concrete feedback relative to progress and production and should require not only repetitive tasks but should include a program of graduated decision-making responsibility. Most of us in vocational rehabilitation fail to recognize the need for work adjustment training for the older worker of average intelligence with a work history. We feel he can just go back to work. In our approach to the practice of rehabilitation work, adjustment training is for the client with just the opposite qualities—young, mentally retarded and no work history—but the purpose of the work adjustment training is the same in both instances—the establishment of an appropriate psychological set. With the young retardate, we are trying to establish the self-concept of a worker; with the other worker, we are attempting to reestablish this concept.

Next, we feel workshops should extend their service programs to develop satellites in the geriatric wards of state hospitals. There are many indications that the majority of the patients on these wards are not in need of psychotherapy as much as they need redefinition of their role in society. A satellite program of a workshop can be developed which would incorporate a work adjustment training program and a remotivation program and would provide many avenues to facilitate the psychological adjustment to aging. The establishment of a program such as this will broaden the client experience background and add depth to the client-ability factor of the workshop which obviously will broaden the spectrum of subcontract work the workshop can attract. It is a basic principle of workshop administration that the more heterogeneous the clientele of a workshop the more flexible and diversified will be its negotiations for subcontract and prime contract work.

In the satellite program, which we are proposing, there should be a provision for a full array of services within the satellite system for those whose maximum capabilities are at the state hospital terminal placement level. There should also be a built-in opportunity to progress through interim placement in the workshop and when appropriate on to industrial placement.

EMPLOYMENT NEEDS OF THE AGING

Employment fulfills many functions and needs for all of us. As individuals we are what we do. In our culture we are identified by what we do for a living. Our economic status, self-concept, social status, friends, and community activities are to a great extent determined by our jobs. All of these factors which have direct bearing upon personality integration deteriorate in unemployment.

In the face of economic inflation, more and more concern is being expressed relative to retirement programs which provide fixed incomes. The inflationary spiral which we have had in this country for the last decade has seriously jeopardized or destroyed the stability of fixed-income retirement plans.

Therefore, the employment needs of the aging are two faceted—first, employment supplies many social and psychological needs which are essential to the individual and secondly, and more mundanely, employment needs of the aging include the provision for basic subsistence.

As we have outlined above, the older worker can be a highly positive asset to a workshop since the workshop can uniquely meet many of his needs while he is contributing to the economic stability of the workshop. The productive older worker is interested, in many cases, in supplementing his fixed retirement income; therefore, his employment needs are uniquely adapted to workshop production. His interests and vocational and production capabilities can be developed to the point of permitting the workshop to attract a diversity of subcontract work; and if properly planned programs are instituted, the workshop will be able to attract national industrial contract work on a long-term basis.

The workshop also can institute a program which will meet the social and psychological aspects of employment needs of older workers who have solved the problems of basic subsistence. For most bright, alert, aggressive retired persons, retirement, unless impeccably planned, soon begins to pall. The avocational pursuits which held so much attraction on the "pre" side of retirement soon become stultifying and deadly on the "past" side of retirement. Fishing, bridge, hiking and so forth soon fail to fill the void left by the demands and rewards of employment. Consequently, many retirees are looking for an opportunity to utilize the talents, abilities and proficiencies they have developed and perfected over many years of employment.

We are amazed that workshops have failed to adapt the SCORE concept (Service Corps of Retired Executives) on the local level. We feel these people represent a vast untapped reservoir of manpower in our communities. In some limited situations workshops have solicited volunteers composed of retired teachers to teach remedial subjects, but we have in our communities retired workers who were supervisors, foremen, managers and executives concerned with purchasing, marketing, production, accounting, plant layout and efficiency, and contract procurement—the same concerns we in workshop administration have. We believe a workshop administration can be highly self-serving and still meet some of the employment needs of retired workers by developing a program to utilize these people's talents in the operation, development, and administration of the workshop.

They can be used on a continuing volunteer basis in areas such as remedial education, production supervision, quality control, or on a consultative basis for marketing, contract procurement, et cetera. We feel this approach will gain the workshop not only improved efficiency in operations and administration but a wider base and greater degree of community support for its programs.

SOCIAL NEEDS OF THE AGING

It is difficult to separate the social needs of the aging from the other needs discussed above. Almost all of the needs outlined above have direct social implications.

The social needs of the aging, as well as other needs, are the same as for all populations. They need satisfying relationships with their peer groups, security in interpersonal relations (they need to know who they are and have a sense of identity), recognition for achievement and acceptance.

Generally the aging process is also an isolating process. As people grow old and retire from work, their environment shrinks drastically until, in many instances, the individual withdraws into isolation. In this situation he becomes highly ego-oriented, selfish, and preoccupied with himself and his bodily functions to the point of becoming hypochondriacal. If the social needs of the individual continually fail to be fulfilled, this psychological and physiological deterioration will continue. Once established, this pattern of isolationism is extremely difficult to break since chronic behavior in the aged is relatively easy to establish and the drive for change and new experiences is subdued in them. Individuals in this social isolation system are so obvious or noticeable, regretfully they form the stereotype we have of the older persons. This is an unfair stereotype; but as all stereotypes, it is a highly persistent image highly impervious to change.

Most of the suggestions made above regarding the extension of service programs in the workshop to meet the various needs of the aging will also meet the social needs of the aging. Perhaps a specific action the workshop could take would be the development of a service center for the aging. This action would be directed objectively at the social needs.

SUMMARY

In summary, we feel it is particularly good community planning to plan for a workshop to become the focal point of services to the aging population within a community. We feel:

1. The workshop should create and develop an administrative policy and an operation climate which will attract older citizens to contribute to the goals of the workshops.

2. Workshops should extend the orientation of their existing service programs to include the aging—this includes all programs from work adjustment training through terminal placement.

3. The workshop should establish satellite programs in areas with a high concentration of older nonworkers—state hospitals, senior centers, and homes for the aged, et cetera.

4. The workshop should be flexible in its approach to workers. It should permit and encourage part-time workers—workers who produce according to their own needs and schedules rather than adhering exclusively to the workshop's schedule.

5. The workshop should moblize the retired people in the community to contribute their talents to the objectives of the workshop. In this we are advocating a local adaptation of the SCORE (Service Corps of Retired Executives).

There are several other areas in which a workshop can become involved in the needs of the aging, but we feel these are perhaps the prime areas.

REFERENCES

Cull, J. G.: Age as a factor in achieving conformity behavior. *Industrial Gerontology,* Spring, 1970.

Galton, F.: *Hereditary Genius.* New York, 1891.

Johndrow, R. F.: Personal communication, 1970.

Lorge, I.: Intellectual changes during maturity and old age. *Rev Educ Res, 17,* 1947.

Sprague, N.: Industrial gerontology: A definition and a statement of purpose. *Industrial Gerontology,* Spring, 1970.

Chapter 9

THE ROLE OF WORK IN MEETING NEEDS OF THE OLDER AMERICAN

J. D. HODGSON

O ne of the tests of any society is how well it treats those who have grown old in its service. On this test our own society does not always get the highest marks.

Let me say at the outset I know it is not uncommon for public officials to paint in glowing terms all the measures they are undertaking. It would be easy for me to do this. I could dwell at length upon my own department's efforts to abolish job discrimination against older workers. I could point to the more than 30,000 compliance contracts we made last year, with age discrimination barriers removed from 100,000 jobs. I could talk about our manpower training programs and the $300 million we are spending this year on job training for those who are forty-five and over. I could note we require that at least half of the participants in our Operation Mainstream shall be forty-five or older. I could remind you we insist people over forty-five be given special consideration in filling public jobs under the recent one billion dollar Emergency Employment Act.

But this kind of self-congratulatory listing contributes little. Whatever the program, whatever the group being helped, we know the need always seems to outrun available resources. So I would like to strike out in another direction, one that I think might be more helpful. I would like to confine my chapter to the role of work in filling some of the needs of the older person. And, I would like to hazard an observation or two on strategy to realize these needs.

130

What are the work needs of the older person? Well, of course, these needs vary with the individual, with the situation, and with age. It is difficult to lump them all in one big pot. Still, I think we can make a few general observations.

First, we should appreciate that work may often mean something different to the older person—both something more and something less—than to the younger one.

Some common worker needs are not always present among older workers—for example, the need to develop a skill, to build a career, to feed a growing family, and so on. Income, of course, is important to *any* worker. But income for the older worker may often be needed as much to sustain dignity as to maintain living standards. So psychological needs must be coupled with recognition of economic need. The need to be active, to be part of something, to contribute something worthwhile, to stay in the main stream—these psychological needs are often part of the driving force that keeps the older person in the workforce. They should not be ignored.

A second need relates to unemployment problems of the older worker. While they may not be broad, they are, in instances where they exist, very deep. We know geographic pockets of severe unemployment exist among older workers. We know whole industries pass from the scene, leaving a residue of stranded older workers. We know job skills of some specific older occupational groups have become outmoded. And we know that when older workers *do* experience a job loss they often have an acutely serious problem in finding another job. Last year, for instance, even though the rate of unemployment for the older worker was quite low, the duration of unemployment for those who did lose their jobs was more than twice the national average. Every plant closing we have studied reveals the same pattern—older workers are the ones who experience serious problems in becoming re-employed. The pattern is evident. The young move with job opportunity; the older worker often does not. Community and family ties lessen geographic mobility. Reduced incentive to acquire new skills limits occupational mobility.

This should be understood as fact rather than merely deplored.

So here we have two major work needs—the psychological needs that jobs supply and the specialized employability problems of those older workers who find themselves out of jobs. These are needs that differentiate the older from the younger or even middle-aged worker.

Now, how do we go about seeing that these needs are recognized and filled? Here I believe a shift in strategy might help.

I have spent a lifetime in what I call the "people business"—that is, dealing with problems of people. A compassionate person who deals with people problems cannot but be touched and even overwhelmed by the needs of the aging in our society. So one who observes and works with these problems wants to make sure they are understood and presented in a way and at a place where they are apt to receive both the amount and kind of attention they deserve. It is my impression this is not now being done as effectively as it could be because the *special* needs of older workers are not being pointed up. Instead, the plight of the older worker *in general* has been the focus of the attention. This plight, I believe, has been well dramatized and well presented. But a more sharply tailored approach may now be more effective.

Let us start with an examination of what groups representing the older worker are up against when they attempt to get recognition for his unemployment problem in Federal legislation. They are up against two major things. First, limited resources—unhappily resources are always limited. Second, they face strong competition for the resources that do exist. So when one attempts to dramatize the unemployment problem of the older worker in the *traditional* sense—that is, in terms of the number or proportion of his group that are unemployed—there are some facts that make the effort an uphill struggle.

Remember, I noted that many groups are competing for whatever resources are available. Let's look at the claims that can be made for some of these groups. Though there are several, I will touch on only three—the young, Blacks and other minorities, and veterans. First, let's look at the young. Here are some recent unemployment figures—those supplied by the Bureau of Labor Statistics for October, 1971:

> For the age group 16–19 unemployment is 16.4 percent.
> For those age 20–29, unemployment is 7.2 percent
> For those age 30–55, it is 3.6 percent
> For those 55 and over, it is 2.9 percent

Not a strong argument for giving extra attention to the older group, is it? And yet to the older group that knows full well many of its members often have serious unemployment problems, these *overall* figures provide little comfort.

Now look at figures for the two other groups that compete for attention. The current unemployment rate for Blacks and other minorities is 9.5 percent. And during the past year the unemployment rate for our Vietnam veterans has averaged 9 percent.

So here we observe what can be called the competitive dimensions of the problem. In terms of proportions—the traditional measure of the unemployment problem in this nation—other groups have an awesome competitive edge. Unemployment rates for these groups are from three to five times as great as for the older age group. In fact, the older age group figure is only half the national average.

So if the aging attempt to compete for attention in Congress on a traditional basis—that is, on the amount of unemployment—they find themselves swimming upstream against a strong current. But here it is important to understand that quantitive figures tell a limited story. They conceal a lot of discouragement, wasted talent, and acute human misery.

What then can be done? It seems to me two approaches should be emphasized. One of these approaches is to emphasize the *specialized* needs that I have spoken of earlier. I suggest that those who champion the cause of the older worker shift their sights somewhat from a generalized concern for levels of unemployment to a different focus—a focus concentrating on the special need of the older worker who is without a job and the companion psychological needs of the older worker. This may mean specialized help for unemployment problems. And it may mean specialized kinds of manpower programs to meet special job needs.

And, while we are talking about strategy, it may mean something else. It may mean more concentration on the local government level than in the past.

In a big country, federal legislators are apt to concentrate on the big picture. Special needs of special groups, particularly needs that often vary widely by situation and community, have difficulty competing for attention.

This circumstance prompts me to wonder about the wisdom of prompting categorical programs for the older worker at the Federal level. Such programs face the most demanding competition from other groups who contend they have a superior claim. We must recognize that work needs for the aging differ by age and circumstance. Those who are familiar with categorical funding know how difficult it is to recognize properly such differences in federal program administration.

There are clearly areas in this nation where needs of older workers are preeminent—rural areas, retirement communities, many suburbs, areas of declining industrial employment, etc. If more funds were available with localized control in these communities the needs of the older worker would no doubt get a better break than they do now. For all its shortcomings, city hall is still more accessible and more attuned to local needs than a distant federal bureaucracy. Until now, however, at city hall and other local levels a shortage of funds has limited the extent of help for needy citizens.

This condition is, of course, what President Nixon sought to remedy with his revenue sharing concept—a concept that permits local governments to respond to the needs of their own citizens without being constrained by the ill-fitting regulations of a remote federal agency. Certainly the Manpower Revenue Sharing Bill proposed by the administration would be a big step forward in achieving this objective. Thus, as a matter of strategy, perhaps local government levels should be the subject of increased attention among older workers.

Well, I have offered these suggestions as a friend of the older worker and a student of his needs. But I do not want to leave you with the idea that you discontinue your efforts on the federal level. Nor do I want to suggest that we in the Labor Department are not developing some of our own recipes to give the older worker a better break in the future.

One of these is our Senior Community Service Project involving a $1.6 million grant to the National Council on the Aging. We and the Council have joined in providing special work experience and training help to hundreds of a special group—chronically unemployed older workers. Though the program still has nearly a year to run, we are about ready to pronounce it a success. It will no doubt be continued and it is a good candidate for expansion.

In the city of Louisville we have another fascinating experimental project under way. Here the Employment Service and the Senior House of Louisville provide a unique type of service to help retirees get either full or part-time jobs through use of older worker volunteers. These volunteers are used to uncover suitable job openings. Even at this early stage of the effort we find a high percentage of those seeking this service are being placed in jobs. Accordingly, I am directing expansion of the program by bringing in representative older worker service organizations in order to make use of their resources and know-how as well as those of the Employment Service.

Then in Minneapolis we have something under way that really has exciting promise. Here the Department, working with the State and the Minneapolis Rehabilitation Center, has developed a comprehensive package covering training for all phases of service needed by older workers who are seeking jobs. This approach has worked so favorably in Minnesota that I have directed it be extended to eight other States within sixty days. If the program continues its present promise, it will be extended nationwide.

There is a bundle of related subjects that consume our interest at the Labor Department. New pension protection and liberalization measures, the popular Green Thumb

Program we run with farm organizations, fascinating findings and developments with regard to second careers for older workers, the additional funds we are devoting each year to manpower programs and how the amount of money available would take a quantum leap forward under the Administration's Manpower Revenue Sharing Bill—these are part of a veritable laundry list of items that might be of interest.

In closing let me say this. From a study of advance conference reports I notice things like income, health, housing and transportation may rate higher priority among the interest of the aging than do problems of employment. We in the Department of Labor, however, believe the employment needs of the older workers are often acute, that they deserve specialized attention, and that we should play a role in providing that attention. We will continue to do so.

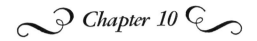

Chapter 10

PRERETIREMENT COUNSELING

H. Charles Pyron and U. Vincent Manion

In our society the institution of retirement is creating a new life-cycle role for an ever increasing number of people whose labor is not considered essential for the supply of goods and services. For this reason, retirement represents a transition from a productive to a nonproductive economic role in society. For the individual this transition often poses significant social and psychological problems resulting from the termination of a life-fulfilling work role.

The research indicates that older workers are being subjected to increasing pressures to retire earlier. Recent research indicates that nearly all (93%) of 201 companies surveyed have an early retirement provision. Moreover, the survey found that in 1968 about one-half of all retirements from the companies were "early" retirements.

The research revealed that the majority of employers offer "inducements" to older workers to elect early voluntary retirement and 54 percent of the companies surveyed offered some type of financial incentive to retire early. Moreover, about one-half of the companies impose some type of re-employment restriction upon the retiring employee which generally guarantees against his re-employment with the company.

Although the number and proportion of the retired population is increasing, little empirical research has been focused upon the possible social and psychological disorganization resulting from the termination of a life-fulfilling work role and the transition to retirement. There are, however, a number of indications that people do not always adjust well in retirement. The suicide rate is much higher for white males over sixty-five years of age (Birren, 1964). Many retirees, who have not adequately prepared financially for their retirement, end up experiencing financial deprivations because of reduced income. There is also a commonly observed, but apparently unverified, phenomenon that many people have strokes, heart attacks, and psychological breakdowns immediately following retirement. The interesting thing seems to be that this has very little to do with age, but appears to be related to the fact that they are no longer working.

Most of these indicators of poor retirement adjustment have not been documented by research. However, they do seem, in total, to indicate that people who do not prepare both psychologically and economically for the impact of not working, of not having the close association of being on the job, of no more responsibility, loss of routine, etc., may have serious adjustment problems. Further, it may be argued that employees will make a better adjustment to retirement if they plan for retirement—psychologically, financially, and in health areas.

Some companies, after considering the indicators described, have felt that it is the company's responsibility to prepare the employee for retirement through a series of intensive counseling sessions. The logic for this kind of thinking goes something like this: The person has spent his entire working life, or at least the last ten to twenty years before retirement, with the company. Thus, the company feels that they must not only provide for the financial adequacy after retirement, but also they have a responsibility to "re-program" the man so that he will be able to adjust psychologically in retirement.

On the other hand, some companies have viewed preparation for retirement as an individual responsibility. This is in keeping with the American tradition of saving for later security and the individualism which characterizes American industry. Thus, any company "counseling" program is seen as an interference in the employee's private life. Still other companies feel that the problems of retirement and aging are for the community, state, and federal governments to solve.

MODELS OF PRERETIREMENT COUNSELING

In general, presently offered preretirement programs represent variations of three basic models. A brief review of the models is presented as follows:

a. Traditional programs consisting of lectures by subject matter specialists in a typical classroom setting. The general objective of this model is: to provide helpful information and stimulate planning for retirement.

b. The group discussion program. This type of program utilizes a test consisting of short case materials oriented toward problems in retirement and audiovisual aids to stimulate discussion.

c. The structured T-Group method oriented toward retirement and life planning. The program is structured to the extent that the trainer (teacher or group leader) introduces exercises and topical matter relevant to the participants which is then processed in the group setting.

HISTORY OF PRERETIREMENT PREPARATION PROGRAMS

While the views of personnel managers differ widely as to the need for preretirement counseling and the propriety of the company providing it, many companies report that they have some form of preretirement counseling.

Although the origin of the first program of this type is presently obscure, companies which have embarked upon preretirement preparation programs have followed either the individual counseling approach or the group approach. In commenting upon these approaches, Hunter (1968) observes that while little is known about the origins of the individual approach, group-type preretirement planning programs can be traced to the pioneering work of two American universities: the University of Chicago and the University of Michigan. Both of these institutions have developed educational programs for use by industry in helping them prepare their older employees for adjustment to maturity, retirement, and old age.

The growth of preretirement counseling programs is indicated by the National Industrial Conference Board (1964). In tracing this growth, the Conference Board cited research which reported that "a survey of seventy of the largest companies in the U.S. in 1951 indicates that 37 percent had some type of counseling; in 1952, 54 percent of 657 companies had it; and in a 1955 Conference Board Survey, 65 percent of 327 companies had preretirement counseling." A 1964 survey by the National Industrial Conference Board reported that of the 974 companies surveyed, 65 percent had some type of preretirement counseling.

The foregoing reports would seem to indicate that following a rapid growth in the adoption of preretirement counseling programs in the early 1950's, the installation of new plans has leveled off and remained at about 65 percent of the companies surveyed. This assumption, however, is rather tenuous because of the difficulty in evaluating the data reported by companies as to what actually constitutes a preretirement counseling program.

Only a limited number of surveys have been aimed at determining the extensiveness or comprehensiveness of the counseling programs offered by companies. Wermel and Beideman conducted a nationwide study in 1961. Its purpose was to determine what companies were doing to prepare their older workers for retirement. In their work, they attempted to differentiate between programs designed primarily for explaining the company's retirement benefits and those programs whose *principle aim* is to help employees *prepare* for retirement.

By analyzing the responses, Wermel and Beideman discovered that company programs could be grouped into *two* categories: The limited programs and the comprehensive preparation-type programs. A "limited" program was defined as being concerned primarily with the financial aspects of retirement, with emphasis upon giving the employee information about his retirement benefits, options, pension, and encouraging him to make financial plans. Individual counseling might have been provided if requested by the employee, printed matter might have been distributed providing information on retirement planning, etc., but this was very much incidental and not an explicit goal of the counseling program.

The "comprehensive" program, on the other hand, was defined by Wermel and Beideman as going beyond financial planning and dealing with planning for retirement adjustment, such as physical and mental health, use of leisure time, etc.

Using this method of classification, Wermel and Beideman determined that 161 or 40 percent of the 415 responding firms qualified as having a "limited" counseling program, and that 136 (33 percent) were in the "comprehensive" category. A more recent study attempted to determine the extent and comprehensiveness of preretirement counseling programs in Western companies (Pyron, 1969). A detailed analysis of the content of twenty company programs was made and revealed that only twelve responding companies, or 20 percent of those having programs, had instituted programs which satisfied the criteria of an "intensive-comprehensive" counseling program. The characteristics of the twelve programs are described as follows:

1. The programs had been established for at least five years.
2. The company had adopted a mandatory retirement policy.
3. Counseling was conducted on company time.
4. Employees were exposed to more than six hours of counseling.
5. Counseling commenced at age sixty or earlier.
6. Personnel counseling records were maintained by the company.
7. Counseling program coverage included all or a majority of the following subjects:
   a. Pension and Social Security benefits
   b. Personal financial planning
   c. Health after retirement
   d. Housing and living accommodations
   e. Leisure time activities
   f. Retired work activities
   g. Legal aspects.

While the prevalence of preretirement counseling programs in industry has been the subject of several surveys as previously discussed, few studies, however, have attempted to establish the reasons such programs were established, their objectives or their value to the firm or to the individuals.

In the Wermel and Beideman study the main reasons given by companies for not establishing a program were lack of employee interest and shortage of personnel to administer the program. Of the 105 firms who indicated an interest in the programs, the main reasons given for deferring a decision were the need for further study on cost and organizational responsibility and the desire to wait until other companies had obtained enough experience with such programs that the results could be evaluated. The major reasons for establishing a preretirement counseling program were the following:

—It carries out the basic purpose of a pension program and helps the retiree plan and live a successful retirement.

—It increases public relations and helps attract and retain better employees.

—It increases the efficiency of the prospective retiree and provides an incentive for the employee to retire before he becomes physically unable to work.

—It is an important contribution to good management—employee relations.

Wermel and Beideman concluded that the various motives offered by management in supporting preretirement counseling indicated an awareness of a growing responsibility toward the welfare of employees as a result of social and economic circumstances. According to Wermel and Beideman, the following management comment was typical of responses received: "Just as we accept the necessity of providing group life insurance, hospital-surgical-medical benefits, and retirement income, because we have advanced in our attitudes of what obligations a corporation has toward its employees (and because it is *good business*), we must now face up to the establishment of a preretirement counseling program."

While varying motives underlie the extablishment of preretirement counseling programs, the program coverage and counseling techniques have also been varied to meet specific needs within resources allocated.

The National Industrial Conference Board (1964), as a result of a survey of 974 companies, labeled programs as either "Benefit Plan" counseling or "General Counseling." "Benefit Plan" counseling was described as limited to three topics only: the amount of company pension; other benefits and services provided by the company after retirement; and Social Security benefits and procedures.

Overall, the NICB Study found that 30 percent of the 974

companies offered "General Counseling" and of these, only about 10 percent scheduled group sessions. The majority of programs using the individual approach provide for interviews with the employee. These interviews usually are arranged at strategic times prior to retirement, some companies schedule the first interview five years before retirement, while others delay the interview until it is necessary for the employee to execute the necessary legal documents incidental to retirement.

"Preretirement counseling," as the term is now being used, is often an inaccurate description of how the counseling process is presently conceived and conducted. To be most effective, the relationship between the counselor and the older employees should be characterized by an atmosphere of trust, understanding, genuineness, warmth, and empathy. Employees should not be merely recipients of a lecture or a handout of reading material.

Wermel and Beideman (1961), after examining the type and content of counseling programs reported in their survey, developed a model retirement preparation program. This program was described as having three main objectives:

1. To stimulate and encourage employees to plan for retirement.

2. To time the programs so that employees could develop and test their plans before retirement.

3. To provide the necessary aids for employees to use in carrying out their planning.

The salient features of the model plan included the following:

1. An initial "reminder" is given to employees at age fifty (50) and an invitation is extended to take part in the program.

2. During the next eight years, participants are provided with planning materials, books, literature, etc.; recognition is afforded older workers in the form of long-

service clubs, extended vacations and more frequent medical examinations.

3. At age fifty-eight (58) employees and their spouses are invited to attend a series of ten group discussions. These weekly discussion sessions cover the subjects of financial planning and budgeting, physical and mental health, leisure-time activities, matters of housing, including change in location, and community resources available.

4. In the years following the group discussions, the indirect method of counseling is resumed and consists of providing materials and the opportunities for recognition and socialization. A year prior to normal retirement, a personal interview is scheduled with the personnel department to discuss pension benefits, retirement data, etc.

5. For employees who elect not to retire at the normal age of sixty-five (65) and desire to continue to the mandatory age of sixty-eight (68), the model program provides for a one-month leave of absence at age sixty-six (66) and a three-month leave of absence at age sixty-seven (67). During the three-year period the older workers train their replacements and undertake special tasks which utilize the experience, yet do not require long-term continuity.

6. After retirement, the model program provides for "keeping in touch" with the retirees and including them in special company functions and programs.

EFFECTIVENESS OF PRERETIREMENT COUNSELING

A few companies which have initiated preretirement counseling have attempted to conduct an evaluation of their program's success. Wermel and Beideman (1961) note that when company evaluation was attempted the evaluations were based, for the most part, on three main factors: (1) employee participation in preretirement activities; (2) employee reactions to the various services offered; and (3) observed change in the attitudes that employees held toward retirement.

Hunter (1962) notes that little, if any, effort has been made by companies to control the quality of programs or to evaluate results. Franks (1962) suggests that this is probably due to the fact that most companies do not view a preparation for retirement program as a major requirement in the management of the company.

In reviewing objective-type research which has been done to determine the effects of participation in programs, Hunter (1962) cited three studies (Mack, 1954; Hunter, 1957; and Burgess, 1960).

In the Mack Study, 281 subjects who participated in sixteen (16) different programs in the Chicago area filled out a "Retirement Planning Inventory" at the beginning and end of the program. On the basis of statistical tests, Mack concluded that the program reduced fear and increased positive attitudes toward retirement, increased constructive planning for retirement, and effected desirable behavior change in retirement preparation.

In Hunter's Study of 73 hourly workers age 50 to 65 in Niagara Falls, New York, before and after program data were obtained in order to study change in retirement attitudes, retirement planning information, plans for retirement, and plans put into action. It was concluded that significant changes took place in each area investigated except that of retirement attitudes.

Burgess's study reported results of a two-year research project which compared changes in attitudes toward retirement among two hundred subjects who participated in a preretirement discussion program as opposed to changes in attitudes of a matched group of subjects who had not been exposed to a program. The highest gains were found in retirement planning, financial planning, retirement anticipation, and retirement living. Only moderate gains were found in such categories as retirement attitudes, social adjustment, and mental outlook.

In more recent research, the University of Michigan

(Hunter, 1968), conducted a longitudinal study of preretirement education. This study, which is believed to be the most complete and objective evaluation conducted to date, was concerned with assessing the effects of an educational program on both the temporal and qualitative aspects of adjustment following separation from work. The study population included an experimental group of workers and wives who had been exposed to the discussion meetings and a control group of workers and wives who were not exposed to preretirement sessions.

The three major null hypotheses investigated were: (1) that workers who participated in the program would not score higher on adjustment measures than workers who had not been exposed; (2) that there would be no difference in mean change scores over a two-year period; and, (3) that there would be no difference in mean scores or mean change scores because of race, education, income, and marital status.

The major findings of the study reported that "from the analysis of mean scores, experimental subjects had higher mean scores on half of the indices, but that none of these differences were statistically significant." However, the test of differences between mean change scores made it possible to reject the null hypothesis and to credit the preretirement education programs with having had the important effects of:

1. Reducing dissatisfaction with retirement;

2. Reducing worry over health; and

3. Encouraging participants to engage in all kinds of activity including social activity with friends and members of the family.

Most of the statistically significant gains by experimental subjects occurred during the first year of retirement, and they tended to persist into the second year, but at a somewhat diminished level of significance.

The analysis of the effects of the program on the adjustment in retirement of subgroups based on race, education, income, and so forth, suggested the possibility that the program was more effective with white subjects, with subjects who completed eight or nine grades in school, and with subjects who were born in an English-speaking country.

In another recent project (The Drake University Preretirement Planning Center), an attempt is now underway to provide preretirement education to prospective retirees and to assess the program's effectiveness. In the first annual report of operation (Drake University, 1968), the center reported that over five hundred participants had attended a seven-week series of programs covering the topics of company fringe benefits, employment after retirement, estate planning, investments, leisure-time activities, psychological aspects of retirement, and Social Security—Medicare.

The program's effectiveness was assessed through a continued monitoring of changes in adjustment and of attitudes, through evaluation of program satisfactions and dissatisfactions, and through actual behavior changes. A psychological scale designed specifically for the project demonstrated both statistically significant and positive changes in adjustment and attitudes toward retirement.

In the most comprehensive study yet done on the effectiveness of preretirement counseling, Greene, Pyron, Manion, and Winklevoss (1969) conducted depth interviews with 648 retirees and older workers in eight companies. Four of these companies had conducted an "intensive" preretirement counseling program for several years, and four other "matched" companies were selected who did not have programs. (Companies were matched on product produced, size, and geographic location.) The major findings of the study were the following:

Adjustment to Retirement: A major effort was made in the study to isolate the factors related to adjustment in retirement. Major findings are:

1. Adjustment scores were significantly greater for the retiree who had the greatest retirement income, who perceived this higher income to be "adequate," and

who experienced the least decline in living standards after retirement. Finances do appear to be very closely related to retirement adjustment. These findings are consistent with previous studies of retirement adjustment.

2. Health is importantly related to adjustment in retirement, i.e. the better the retirees' health (as well as attitudes toward the state of health), the better will be adjustment in retirement.

3. In reviewing all of the various measurements of retirement activities and their relationship to successful adjustment in retirement, clear evidence exists that well-adjusted retirees are those who are more active than less-adjusted retirees. In addition, better-adjusted retirees appear to have increased both the number and extent of their participation in activities since retirement. This would indicate that well-adjusted retirees increase their activities after retirement, and are not just more active people before retirement. However, the evidence shows that retirees who participate in preretirement counseling increase their activities *before* retirement.

4. On each of the specific factors, such as attitudes toward work, the job, supervision, and the company, there were significant differences between well adjusted and poorly adjusted retirees. In any case, high job satisfaction is positively related to adjustment in retirement. If a retiree was satisfied with his job, his supervisor, and the company before retirement, he was much more likely to fall into a high adjustment in retirement category than was true if he had negative attitudes in these three areas.

Resistance to Retirement: For the group of 232 older employees, resistance to retirement was variously related to certain factors as follows:

1. The higher the monthly income and the less the ex-

pected change in the standard of living after retirement, the less the resistance to retirement that may be expected. Employees with a negative attitude toward their present financial status tend to resist retirement more than those with a more optimsitic present attitude.

2. In comparing the relationship between resistance to retirement and present level of participation, intensity, and enjoyment of activities, as well as expected level of participation, intensity and enjoyment of activities after retirement, we found only one significant relationship. This relationship was between resistance and expected change in enjoyment of retirement activities. Those older employees with less resistance to retirement were quite likely to expect activities in retirement to become more enjoyable.

3. Resistance in retirement varied according to the degree to which retirees believed common "stereotypes" about retirement (these stereotypes were inaccurate and negative beliefs).

4. Employees with poorer present health resisted retirement more than those with better health. Thus, those employees who are least able to work are resisting retirement the most. Again, the most plausible explanation is either that employees *resent* (and therefore resist) *being forced* to have to quit because of poor health, or, since resistance is inversely related to planning, those who are now being forced to retire because of health are even more resistant because they know they are not prepared to retire.

5. It was noticed earlier that there appeared to be no evidence to support the theory that employees who have more off-the-job activities, or enjoy them more, will be less resistant to retirement. Conversely, we did not find that employees who get more of their satisfaction on the job are more resistant to retirement. Likewise, resistance did not appear to be re-

lated to job morale, attitudes toward company, supervisor, or skilled level. Thus, there was little support for the theory that the highly motivated, highly job- and company-oriented employee will resist retirement the most.

Preretirement Planning: The effects of preretirement planning for the entire population of retirees and older employees were examined with the following results:

1. A highly positive, significant relationship was discovered between financial planning and level of retirement income. Retirees who planned in advance apparently not only have a larger income but are also more *satisfied* with their level of retirement income. The lack of financial planning is very closely related to high resistance to retirement among older employees. Employees who are making many plans tend to believe their retirement income will be more than adequate, whereas those who made no plans tend to believe their retirement income will be less than adequate.

2. Planning also seems to pay off in more activities after retirement.

3. People who are well-adjusted in retirement have done more planning for their health needs than those who are less well-adjusted. However, there was no relationship found between amount of planning for health needs and better health after retirement. There was no relationship between planning for health needs and resistance to retirement, nor between the amount of planning and actual health. One of the reasons we may not see a stronger relationship here might be because there was such a small amount of planning for health needs reported by employees and retirees, and what planning there was might have been relatively ineffective.

4. Of the eight companies, four had preretirement

counseling programs. The "graduates" rate the program as "helpful," but the objective data is generally lacking which shows that it either made an impact on their awareness or on their planning. However, the results indicate that attendance in the program *does* result in more effective *adjustment* in retirement. Consequently, the results of this study raise questions about the exact nature of the relationship between program content, planning, and adjustment; and further research is needed to clarify these questions.

There was considerable evidence that resistance to retirement is characterized by a high degree of "wishful thinking." In fact, this may be the variable which allows the high resistor to be that way, which allows him to rationalize away the need for planning and even the need to admit that he someday soon must retire. If this explanation is plausible, then we must seriously question the validity of the present form of some preretirement counseling because of its apparent inability to confront the resistor with a more realistic view of his present and future needs. Indeed, there was much evidence reported in this study to support the conclusion that, whereas the counseling programs were praised by a high percentage of those who attended, they did not appear to have produced much planning. Again, this seems to indicate that the preretirement counseling programs were being evaluated on the basis of their personal interest of entertainment value, not their effectiveness in producing a great deal of specific planning; *however, the counseling did produce overall less resistance and more adjustment.*

The major emphasis of the Greene et al. research was to determine an answer to the question: "Does preretirement counseling contribute to effective adjustment after retirement?" Four different analyses, comparing preretirement counseling with various measurements of retirement adjustment were made: (a) The responses of retirees who had taken preretirement counseling from the four companies with programs were compared against the responses of those who had not from all eight companies. (b) The same comparisons were made, but only within the four companies with programs, so that retirees who had chosen to participate in preretirement counseling were compared against those who had chosen not to participate. (c) The responses of all retirees from the four companies without programs were compared against the responses of all retirees (both with and without counseling) from companies with programs.[1] (d) Finally, the response of retirees and employees who had participated in preretirement counseling and thought it was very helpful were compared against the responses of those who had participated in counseling but did not think it was that helpful.

Findings were as follows:

A. When comparisons were made between responses of retirees who had and had not taken part in preretirement counseling, significant differences were found on many of the adjustment indicators, suggesting that retirees with counseling were experiencing more effective adjustment in retirement than those who had not. Specific areas where significant differences were found between the two groups included overall adjustment, rated adjustment (perceived by the interviewer), amount of planning done for retirement, belief in stereotypes of retirement, adequacy of income, subjective rating of health, and number of retirement activities. In addition, on six (6) more of the dependent variables the data appeared to be in the direction of expectation, that is, more favorable adjustment for retirees who had participated in preretirement counseling programs; but the data did not reach a level of significance which would allow for rejection of the

---

[1] There were a number of retirees in the sample from companies with preretirement counseling programs who had not been exposed to the counseling program, but it was reasoned that their might be an "osmosis" effect (i.e. an employee might, through his contact and association with other employees who had been through this counseling program, pick up a significant amount of the essential effect of the counseling). Also, since the four companies without programs acted as a control group, this analysis was a check to see how much difference there was between retirees' and employees' responses from the two types of organizations.

null hypothesis with any degree of confidence on these six variables.

B. The questionnaire responses of retirees who had taken preretirement counseling were compared with responses from retirees who had not, *within the same company*. It was by this method of comparison that the greatest differences in adjustment were found between retirees who had taken the counseling program and those who had not.

C. In the third series of tests of the nineteen (19) hypotheses, responses of all of the retirees in the sample from companies with a preretirement counseling program were compared against responses of all retirees from companies without preretirement counseling programs. In general, few significant differences were found in retirement adjustment of retirees from companies with and without preretirement counseling programs. Only in the area of number of retirement activities and the area of retirement income does there seem to be anything approaching a significant level of difference between the retirees from the two sets of companies. Although there were several other measurements which predicted more effective adjustment for retirees from companies with preretirement counseling programs, none were significant and it would be impossible to justify the existence of the preretirement counseling based on these very meager results. Consequently, it can be concluded that the effect of the rather large percentage of retirees in companies with counseling programs who had not taken the counseling tended to cancel out significant differences. Consequently, there appears to be no justification for the "osmosis" theory of preretirement counseling. An employer who supports such counseling might thus be advised to require or strongly urge attendance at preretirement counseling sessions because voluntary attendance does not produce measurable results for all employees.

D. A fourth test of the nineteen (19) hypotheses was made comparing responses of retirees who had taken the preretirement counseling program and *thought it was very help-*

ful with responses of retirees who had taken the preretirement counseling program but did *not* think it was particularly helpful or who thought it was not helpful. Only one of the nineteen indices differentiated significantly between the responses of the two groups of retirees, and this was in the wrong direction. Thus, it was concluded that there is no significant difference between the adjustment of persons who report they found the program very helpful as compared with those who report they did not find the counseling program particularly helpful. In other words, the real differences which were discovered in this study were between those retirees who have taken the program and those who have not. This would indicate that *even an exposure to preretirement counseling which was seen as not particularly helpful by the participants still produces better results than no participation in a program at all.*

The Effect of Preretirement Counseling on Older Employees' Resistance to Retirement: Approximately one-third of the persons in the Greene et al. sample were employees who had not yet retired, but many in this group had already participated in preretirement counseling. Thus it was possible to test the hypothesis that present employees who are nearing retirement and have had preretirement counseling will be less resistant to retirement, will have completed more planning, etc. than will be those employees who have not been exposed to counseling. Comparisons were made on the same basis as before, between responses of: (a) employees who had and had not taken counseling, (b) employees who had and had not taken counseling within companies where counseling was available, (c) employees from companies with and without programs, and (d) employees who had taken counseling and thought it "very helpful" vs. employees who had taken counseling and did not find it so helpful.

Findings were as follows:

A. An examination of the data relevant to the comparison of attitudes of employees who had taken preretirement counseling vs. those who had not showed significant differences on only four of sixteen indices of resistance to retirement. The most significant item which was found to differentiate those who had and had not had preretirement counseling concerned belief in retirement stereotypes, indicating that employees who had attended preretirement counseling had a much more favorable and realistic attitude toward their future retirement than employees who had not. The data also indicated that employees who had participated in preretirement counseling were presently involved in a much greater number of activities than employees who had not participated in preretirement counseling.

B. Comparing the responses of employees who had taken the program with other employees *in the same companies* who had not taken advantage of the preretirement counseling showed that approximately the same kind of results were to be found here as were found in the earlier analysis (a) comparing employees who had taken preretirement counseling vs. those employees who had not. The levels of significance for these differences, however, were considerably lower than in the previous analysis, indicating not as much difference.

C. In looking at the comparison of responses between these employees in companies with preretirement counseling programs vs. those employees in companies without preretirement counseling programs, on none of the general indices of resistance to retirement were there significant differences found at a high enough level to allow for rejection of the null hypothesis with any degree of confidence. The only thing of practical significance that might be reported is that there appears to be quite a bit more observed resistance to retirement than reported resistance to retirement. In other words, the interviewer perceived resistance during the hour interview for many employees who were not openly willing to admit it.

D. The responses of employees who had taken preretirement counseling and found it very helpful vs. employees who had taken preretirement counseling and found it not so helpful indicates no significant difference between the two groups except on three indices. Both on resistance and rating of resistance there appeared to be significant or near significant differences between the two groups of employees; and in terms of enjoyment of present activities, there also was a significant degree of difference between responses of the two groups. None of the other measurements indicated any difference between the two groups except "plans," in which there was an observed but statistically insignificant difference between the two groups.

Overall, there are some indications in (A), (B), (C), and (D) that preretirement counseling may, to some extent, reduce employees' resistance to retirement, but conclusive proof of this is lacking.

The possible effects of a preretirement counseling program on the attitudes and performance of the employees before they retired was also examined in the Greene et al. study. The seven dependent variables were attitude toward work, attitude toward specific job, attitude toward his supervisor, the company, the company's pension plan, and his attitude toward the company's mandatory retirement policy. These tests were made for the purpose of answering the question: "Does a preretirement counseling program produce work attitudes which help the older employee who has participated in preretirement counseling to be a more effective employee before retirement?" The answer appears to be "yes."

It would appear that preretirement counseling does have a positive and significant effect upon improving the morale, and presumably the work performance of the older employees. As would be expected, the greatest difference between the two groups was within companies where employees had the choice of either participating in preretirement counseling or not participating. This finding would cast even more doubt on the commonly held assumption that an employee who resists retirement is the employee who is highly motivated and very much job-oriented. Quite to the contrary, our research results indicate that employees who had participated in preretirement counseling (and who were thus more favorable toward retirement) also reported a much more positive attitude toward their job, their supervisor, and their company than did those employees who had not participated in preretirement counseling.

These results seem to support the point of view that preretirement counseling programs not only help prepare the employee for a better life after retirement, but they also may pay back dividends to the company in terms of a better work adjustment and more effective performance during the last working years before retirement.

A COMPARISON OF PRERETIREMENT COUNSELING AND POSTRETIREMENT COUNSELING AS THEY AFFECT ADJUSTMENT TO RETIREMENT

One of the companies who participated in the Greene *et al.* study encompassed two divisions; one division had for some years an ongoing preretirement counseling program, while the other division of the company had at approximately the same time installed a postretirement counseling program. This allowed the unique opportunity to compare the adjustment of retirees who had participated in preretirement counseling with retirees who had *not* participated in preretirement counseling but who had been participants in postretirement counseling sponsored by their company.

The purpose and content of the postretirement program was somewhat different in the sense that instead of focusing upon the need for preplanning, the purpose of the postretirement counseling program was to keep in touch with the employees and to see to it that they did not have significant psychological, economic, or health deprivation after retirement. The program involved meeting "emergency needs" as well as an attempt to contact every retiree at least once a year for a short conversation concerning his adjustment. From a theoretical point of view, it was our hypothesis that retirees who had participated in preretirement counseling would actually be better adjusted than retirees who had not been confronted with the necessity for planning for their retirement, even though the latter had the continued assistance of a counselor.

Essentially, the results tend to confirm that retirees who

had participated in the preretirement counseling program reflected an equal or better level of adjustment than those retirees who were involved in the postretirement program. The results indicated either a slight edge in effectiveness for preretirement counseling or no significant difference between the two treatment effects with the exception of the area of income and satisfaction with it.

For some reason, although the pension income of the two groups is as well matched as is possible to achieve in any field study, the retirees receiving postretirement counseling appear to be less dissatisfied with their income than those persons who had been involved in a preretirement counseling program. Although none of the other data on income showed a significant difference between the two groups, those persons involved in the postretirement counseling program indicated their retirement income was higher as well as indicating more satisfaction with that income than did their preretirement counterparts. The only possible explanation for this phenomenon is that in the preretirement counseling program the counselors did not spend enough time dealing with financial planning, whereas the postretirement counselors were actually counseling the retirees in a "here and now" kind of way on budget matters (and even in some cases were providing supplemental income), so that even though the actual amount of income of these two groups might have originally been the same, the persons involved in the postretirement counseling were actually utilizing their resources more effectively than persons who were only involved in the preretirement counseling. However, this is only a tentative explanation, and the data in at least one of the analyses might tend to refute it.

The test of significance which showed the most difference between the two groups, as might be expected, concerned the amount of planning they did for retirement, with the persons involved in preretirement counseling having done a significantly greater amount of planning for their retirement than those who were involved only in the postretirement program. This finding, combined with the other data, leads us to believe that there was a very positive effect from the preretirement counseling in stimulating the employee to do planning; however, apparently the effectiveness of the postretirement program has to a large extent compensated for the differential observed between retirees in other companies who had and had not participated in preretirement counseling. In other words, whereas preretirement counseling does stimulate planning and does appear to be related to more effective retirement adjustment, the fact that in this company those without preretirement counseling seemed to be as well adjusted would tend to indicate that postretirement counseling to a large extent compensates for the lack of preretirement counseling and planning.

In addition to planning, the two areas where there was a trend toward better retirement adjustment for persons involved in preretirement counseling were in the areas of number of activities and enjoyment of these activities.

Thus, in summary, it would appear that there is very little difference in the adjustment of retirees who participate in preretirement counseling and those retirees who participate in postretirement counseling. This would argue strongly for the validity of the company's postretirement counseling program in terms of producing the same results as the preretirement counseling program. The next question, of course, that must be asked concerns the relative cost of the two programs. It should also be recorded that in the interviews we found none of the (possibly assumed) negative side effects of a "paternalistic" program implied in postretirement counseling.

TOWARDS A MORE EFFECTIVE MODEL OF PRERETIREMENT COUNSELING

The research on the composition, content, and method of presentation of company-sponsored preretirement preparation programs indicates that the term "preretirement counseling" as it is commonly used is inaccurate in terms of how the counseling process is presently conceived by most professionals. Rogers (1957), Patterson (1964), Arbuckle (1963), and Tyler (1961) all would agree that counseling *must* describe an interpersonal relationship. To be most effective, the relationship between the counselor and the employees soon to be eligible for retirement should be characterized by an atmosphere of *trust, understanding, genuineness, warmth,* and *empathy.* The employees involved in preretirement counseling should be in psychological contact with the counselor and with each other, but as indicated earlier in the discussion, many of the present preretirement "counseling programs" do not conform to the above criteria for a counseling relationship. Rather, present programs are more closely aligned with an educational model and consist of lectures, handouts, and classroom type questions and discussions. In general, study materials are prescriptive in nature and advise prospective retirees on such matters as hobbies, wills, etc.

Present programs tend to fall short in dealing with the social and psychological implications of retirement, and it can be argued that the subjects covered and the materials utilized might even reinforce the individual's fears about retirement. For example, hobbies are viewed by many older people as "busy" work and an inferior substitution for useful, meaningful activity. Also, over-emphasis upon wills and dying reinforces commonly held negative stereotypes about health failure and early death after retirement.

Clearly, traditional preretirement programs utilizing information-giving in a one-way communication model do not foster the development of stimulating counseling relationships, nor do they focus on attitude change and feelings.

The purpose of this discussion, therefore, is to describe a counseling model designed to deal with the social and psychological implications of retirement for mature men and women.

One of the basic assumptions in the development of a counseling model is that the traditional *learning model* is inappropriate to the problem of planning for retirement. This is because attitudes (usually fear) toward retirement interfere with the communication process used in the typical program. The "retirement resister," for example might avoid doing any meaningful planning in the future since he never really confronts his feelings or concerns. On the other hand, some employees look forward to retirement with such eagerness that they often let *inaccurate expectations* color their thinking and distort reality, and therefore they "tune out" the preretirement lectures to avoid disturbing their preconceived idea.

The preretirement counseling model which we have found to be most effective is based on a group interaction model (Lifton, 1966). This procedure actively involves the employees in a discussion of a great many aspects of the retirement process. In addition to being presented with basic factual materials concerning retirement, subjects are able to consider their future in an atmosphere and environment that encourages and supports examination of their individual needs, attitudes, values, feelings and fears that impinge upon the forthcoming major change in their lives.

Some of the specific objectives or goals of a preretirement counseling model using the interaction approach are as follows:

1. Developing self-diagnostic skills—helping the older employee become aware of his fears and his strong motivational needs and to be able to relate them to his preretirement planning.

2. Developing communication and interpersonal relations skills. One of the most serious barriers to effective retirement adjustment seems to be the physical separation from long-established friendships both on the job and in the community (not only are job related acquaintances servered, but also many retirees move into "retirement housing" or "retirement communities," therefore severing friendships within the neighborhood where they lived for many years), and consequently new friendships must be established. Often the employee who resists retirement (and consequently planning) may do so because he unconsciously fears that he does not possess the communication and interpersonal relations skills necessary to establish new personal relationships after retire-

ment. This area might also be called "developing social relationship skills."

3. Developing attitudes of independence, rather than dependence.

4. Developing an awareness of present life-style as a basis for planning a realistic retirement life style.

5. Developing skills in life planning.

6. Developing skills and attitudes for effective problem-solving (which are considered necessary tools for adequate retirement adjustment).

7. Developing attitudes of "decision-making" and "action-taking," so that plans for retirement will be carried out after they are made.

8. Learning about retirement planning decision options.

Although this is the "heart" of the model in terms of content, it is important that the areas of skills and attitude change outlined above must be presented simultaneously with factual information. Only when all eight instructional (or learning) goals are achieved do we have an optimum expectation that realistic preretirement planning will be both completed and actualized.

The preceding goals are consistent with the objectives of the laboratory learning approach, the general learning model. This orientation, discussed by Bradford, Gibb, and Benne (1967), and others can be characterized as follows:

1. The approach represents a spirit of scientific inquiry guided by a sense of democratic values. The individual is encouraged to experiment with his behavior and his environment in order to develop a more effective and fulfilling position in society.

2. The approach attempts to increase an individual's awareness of himself and others.

3. The approach encourages the individual to become more authentic in his relationships. This assures that his

behavior more closely corresponds with his feelings, attitudes, and values.

4. The approach encourages individuals to enter relationships in the environment from a collaborative perspective. The status brought by individuals to such a relationship therefore does not prescribe the dimensions of their roles in the new relationship.

5. The approach encourages individuals to resolve conflict situations through problem-solving rather than compromise or avoidance.

One of the best vehicles through which these goals are achieved is the "training group." In this setting an atmosphere is created which satisfies the conditions discussed above. In these groups, individuals gradually become involved as they realize that it is their responsibility to participate in the group. They develop trust in the group and begin to risk self-revelation by exploring feelings, attitudes, values, fears, and aspirations with the other members. By stating their positions and working through their plans verbally and behaviorally they become committed to the plans and consequently are much more likely to act on them outside of the group (Crosby and Schmuck, 1968). Exercises and techniques are used throughout the group sessions to help an individual and/or the group work through a situation that is interfering with effective adjustment. These interventions also serve to give the members opportunities to try-out new ideas or behaviors. This experimental aspect of the learning situation is central to its success. The development of communication skills is especially important, for an effective communication process enables the retiree to function better in everything he does.

Research using the basic principles of the laboratory approach to learning have been shown to be successful in many situations. Bavelas and Strauss (1967) demonstrated that involvement of employees in decision-making processes increased their production. They gained a commitment to what they were doing. Bennett (1955) made the same point in comparing the group interaction model with the traditional lecture method. He found that the advantage of the former lies in the fact that it can affect a higher degree of *commitment to act* in the individuals involved. It is hypothesized that this process will give a group of preretirement employees the same commitment to pre-planning for their future.

Published reports of reaearch in the *Journal of Applied Behavioral Science*; in Bradford, Gibb and Benne, *T-Group Theory and Laboratory Method* (1967) ; as well as articles in the *Journal of Counseling Psychology* and the *Journal of Clinical and Consulting Psychology,* among others, document the effectiveness of the interaction model. As a brief summary of these findings, it suffices to say that as an individual is actively involved in the learning process he becomes interested in and committed to it. This situation then results in the objectives of the education or training being acted upon by the participants.

In summarizing the research in the field, several advantages of the group interaction model are noted. Group interaction provides a social situation for modifying the attitudes and judgment of group members, is more efficient in terms of time and money, provides situations for more adequate problem-solving activities, and aids members in accepting ideas and suggestions proposed by their fellow group members.

In the light of research findings, relationships can be drawn between the proposed model for preretirement counseling and the major issues involved in the process of retirement. The interaction model, therefore, is considered the most appropriate setting for individuals to confront these issues and thereby stimulate more realistic planning for retirement.

The Oregon Center for Gerontology, University of Oregon, has presented annually, for the past four years, a summer workshop *Education for the Retirement Years*. A part of this workshop consists of demonstrating for student observation, an interaction model of preretirement counseling. Typically, the interaction group members are University of Oregon classified employees nearing retirement, and their spouses. The interaction group normally consists of ten to twelve participants plus a leader and co-leader. The group meets approximately one-and-one-half to two hours each day for ten days. Each day a separate topic or retirement issue is dealt with by the group. The topics, objectives of each session, and examples of exercises used in the ten structured T-group sessions are summarized as follows:

Session 1

Topic: Orientation to Preretirement

Objectives: Create Climate for Group Discussion
            Establish Conceptual Framework for Planning

Methods: Human Relations "Warm-Up" Exercises
            Trainer Models and Instructs in Group Discussion Techniques
            Life Planning Exercises

Session 2

Topic: Attitudes Toward Retirement

Objectives: Self-Awareness of Attitudes and Feelings About Retirement

Methods: Discussion Centered on Feelings Toward Work and Retirement

Session 3

Topic: The "Facts" About Retirement

Objectives: Group Develops Discussion Agenda About Perceived Retirement Problems
            Clear-Up Misinformation About Negative Stereotypes

Methods: Individuals Express Their Hopes and Fears About Retirement
            Provide Factual Information from Research

Session 4

Topic: Income and Finances

Objectives: Develop Objective View of Financial Needs/
             Alternatives
             Provide Frame of Reference for Financial
             Planning

Methods: Financial Planning Questionnaire/Worksheet
             Provide Research Findings on Income/Estate
             Profiles

Session 5

Topic: Personal Assets and Liabilities

Objectives: Self-Awareness of Personal Resources, Interests
             and Capabilities

Methods: Self-Inventory of Interests, Under-developed
             Resources, Hopes, Wishes, and Aspirations

Session 6

Topic: Activities in Retirement

Objectives: Focus on Present Activities
             Discussion of Future Activities

Methods: Activities Inventory
             Description of a Day in Retirement

Session 7

Topic: Living Arrangements, Family and Friends

Objectives: Realistically Consider Needs for Future Living
             Arrangements
             Consider Alternatives to Present Arrangement
             Awareness of Importance of Family and Friends

Methods: Group Discussion Focused on Hopes, Plans and
             Alternatives

Session 8

Topic: Physical and Mental Health

Objectives: Understanding Relationship Between Emotional
            Well-Being and Physical Health

Methods: Health Index, Life-Review, Future Fantasy

Session 9

Topic: Social and Inter-Personal Relationships

Objectives: Awareness of the Importance of Satisfying Re-
            lationships
            Maintaining and Enlarging Social Relationships

Methods: Inventory of Social Assets
            Role Play

Session 10

Topic: Plans and Policies for Retirement

Objectives: Focus Upon the Importance of:
            Making Plans for Retirement
            Developing Policies for Retirement Living
            Establishing Personal Goals for the Future

Methods: Retirement Readiness Checklist
            Financial Plans Worksheet

The University of Oregon experience in presenting the
structured T-group counseling model to four groups of classified employee preretirees and their spouses indicate the
appropriateness of the model for preretirement counseling.
Experience indicates that an atmosphere of trust, openness,
understanding, genuineness, warmth, and empathy is readily
established within the group and the preretirees welcome
the opportunity to discuss viewpoints and concerns about
retirement with their peers in a "safe" and supportive environment. As group members explore their feelings, attitudes,
values, fears, and aspirations about retirement, there is an
observable movement toward individual problem identifica-

tion and a commitment to retirement planning and problem-solving behavior.

Whether or not preretirees who have participated in the structured T-group counseling experience follow-through on their commitments prior to and after retirement is a matter deserving further research. Although resources have not permitted such a follow-up study on all participants in the T-group sessions, there is considerable evidence indicating the probable long-term success of the counseling. For example, the group leaders have been invited to attend several group "reunions." These reunions indicate that the social relationships established in the group are continuing in nature and provide an opportunity for individuals to report on plans and experiences. Since several members of the various groups have since retired, they are eager to share their transitional experiences with those yet to retire and pass on much valuable information.

Individuals who have participated in the T-group pre-retirement counseling sessions have consistently rated the experience as being of value and some have considered the experience a turning point in their lives. One female employee had this to say, "Until I took the course I never told anyone my age. Now I know that age isn't important and I don't care who knows how old I am."

SOME IMPLICATIONS FOR FUTURE RESEARCH

1. Although preretirement counseling programs have been shown to be effective, an area for future research is to discover how they may become even better. There are a multitude of indications from the data of previous studies which lead us to believe that the results would have been even more dramatic and more positive had there been a more intensive counseling program. For example, only the University of Oregon program uses an intensive confrontation-type counseling model, and it is our feeling that, given the anatomy of resistance to retirement, successful adjustment in retirement to some extent depends upon the ability of the company to confront directly the resisting employee.

If we can as a society begin to prevent as many of the problems of adjustment to retirement which exist among our older retired citizens, through the medium of relatively inexpensive preretirement counseling programs, then we essentially through the investment of a few dollars *before* retirement can save our society tremendous costs, both economically and psychologically, in terms of the more effective life style of the retiree. Further research should develop and test new methods and models for preretirement counseling.

2. Although there were indications that preretirement counseling, to some extent, does reduce employees' resistance to retirement, we were somewhat disappointed in the lack of consistency of findings in this area. One of the kinds of followup research needed is to conduct a "longitudinal" study to check the actual adjustment to retirement of employees after they retire. In this way, a more accurate measurement of their before-and-after attitudes will be possible, and we will be able to determine more accurately the impact of pre-retirement counseling upon adjustment.

3. Research is needed to determine why some retirees adjust to retirement much more rapidly than others. The length of time required to adjust has not been found to be related significantly to preretirement counseling. More study is needed to isolate the factors which do account for the differences reported.

4. We also need additional research to explain the relationship between counseling and planning. For example, we found no significant difference in the degree of planning between employees who had been involved in preretirement counseling and those employees not involved in counseling, while at the same time we did find retirees who had preretirement counseling reporting a significant higher level of planning. Since the major goal of preretirement counseling may be to promote planning, it is somewhat disturbing to view such a result. One hypothesis is that an employee who resists retirement may be doing so with "plans" (i.e. he says "I am going to do all those things after I retire, but now I'm too busy," or "I can't retire yet because I can't afford it"), but

these statements, although they reflect an attitude of planning ahead, also reflect a superficial or inaccurate approach which thus allows him to rationalize the fact that he really does not want to retire. On the other hand, employees who have participated in preretirement counseling realize that true planning is hard work, and they may therefore tend to underestimate the amount of planning which they have actually done.

SUMMARY

There is no doubt but that the field of preretirement/postretirement counseling is emerging. As we look around us we see increasing numbers of retirees, but as the numbers grow, so do their problems of adjustment. Employment trends clearly show that more people will be retiring early, and social and psychological research studies show that the transition from work to leisure is not an easy task for most people. Finally, there is evidence that preretirement and postretirement counseling can help the retiree make a more successful transition.

Although the focus of this paper has been on an analysis of preretirement counseling programs within the employment context, possibly an even larger number of older people are participating in retirement counseling programs sponsored by private and public agenices—churches, unions, adult education programs, city recreation programs, and nonprofit organizations, such as The American Association of Retired Persons.

Therefore, it is important that in this area of counseling more people be trained, newer more effective methods of counseling be developed, and more research be conducted as a way of serving the needs of our senior citizens.

REFERENCES

Arbuckle, D. S.: The learning of counseling process, not product. *Job Counseling Psychology, 10:* 163–168, 1963.

Bavelas, A. and G. Strauss: Group dynamics and intergroup relations. In Bell, G. D.: *Organizations and Human Behavior.*

Bennett, E. G.: Discussion, decision, commitment, and consensus in "group decision." *Human Relations, 3:* 251–273, 1955.

Birren, James E.: *The Psychology of Aging.* Englewood Cliffs: Prentice-Hall, 1964.

Bradford, L., J. Gibb, K. Benne: *T-Group Theory and Laboratory Method.* New York: Wiley and Sons, 1967.

Crosby, R. and R. Schmuck: Transfer of Laboratory Training, Unpub. paper. CASEA, University of Oregon, 1968.

Drake University Preretirement Planning Center. *First Annual Report,* June 1, 1967 to August 31, 1968, Des Moines.

Greene, M. C., H. C. Pyron, U. V. Manion and H. Winklevoss: *Early Retirement: A Survey of Company Policies and Retirees' Experiences.* University of Oregon, October, 1969.

Greene, M. C., H. C. Pyron, U. V. Manion, and H. Winklevoss: *Preretirement Counseling, Retirement Adjustment and the Older Employee.* Eugene, University of Oregon, 1969.

Hunter, W. W.: *A Longitudinal Study of Pre-retirement Education.* Division of Gerontology, University of Michigan, 1968.

Lifton, W. M.: *Working with Groups: Group Processes and Individual Growth,* 2nd Ed. Wylie, 1966.

National Industrial Conference Board: *Studies in Personnel Policy.* National Industrial Conference Board, New York, NICB, 1964.

Patterson, C. H.: Supervising students in the counseling practicum. *Journal of Counseling Psychology,* 47–53, 1964.

Pyron, H. C.: Preparing employees for retirement. *Personnel Journal,* September, 1969.

Rogers, C.: The necessary and sufficient conditions for personality change. *Journal of Consulting Psychology, 21:* 95–103, 1957.

Tyler, L. E.: *The Psychology of Human Differences,* 3rd Ed. New York: Appleton-Century-Crofts, 1965.

Wermel, Michael T., and Beideman, Geraldine M.: *Retirement Preparation Programs: A Study of Company Responsibilities.* Pasadena: Institute of Technology, 1961.

Chapter 11

VOLUNTARY ACTIVITIES
FOR THE
OLDER AMERICAN

JANET S. SAINER

INTRODUCTION

As the number of older persons in our society has increased, so have the problems that often accompany retirement. Basically during the retirement years, the older adult is faced with a loss of roles and of the satisfactions previously derived therefrom. As children grow up, marry or leave home, as spouses, relatives and friends die, family ties and friendships are weakened or severed. With job responsibilities at an end, the older person loses his role as a breadwinner and as a contributor through his work to society. It becomes difficult for him to maintain his former self-image or his previous status in the community.

The result is that many retired persons suffer from increased isolation, diminishing social contacts and decreased self-esteem. Many suffer a sense of futility as they seek to fill the long hours of enforced leisure.

The real tragedy inherent in this situation is that these millions of older persons represent a tremendous untapped reservoir of talent, available time, and accumulated experience which could be of inestimable value to their communities.

SERVE (Serve and Enrich Retirement by Volunteer Experience), the largest single older volunteer program in the nation, has demonstrated that volunteer service is a way of tapping this tremendous manpower resource, to the benefit of both the retired and of the many community agencies and organizations in need of volunteer assistance.

What is SERVE? How did it start and what were its objectives? How does it function? How well did it succeed? What can we conclude from the SERVE experience? What practical guidelines does it offer in the recruitment, placement, training, and retention of older volunteers? Consideration will be given to each of these questions in the hope that a description of the SERVE experience, its principles, and findings will be of value to others interested in developing a volunteer program for the older American.

WHAT SERVE IS

The first SERVE program was started as a research and demonstration project on Staten Island in 1967. It was sponsored by the Community Service Society of New York (CSS), with partial support from the United States Department of Health, Education and Welfare Administration on Aging, private foundations, and individuals. The purpose of the three-year project was to ascertain whether persons sixty and older would find satisfaction in volunteer service. Could older persons be recruited? Would they continue to serve over a long period of time? Would their services be of real value? The demonstration project showed that the answer to all these questions was *yes,* and SERVE on Staten Island is still active under CSS sponsorship.

From an original nucleus of twenty-three volunteers who served weekly at the Willowbrook State School for the retarded, Staten Island, the program now includes more than six hundred older volunteers who give weekly service to thirty agencies and programs on the Island. Willowbrook is the setting for the largest number of SERVE volunteers; about two hundred. They assist the occupational therapist; give loving care to and feed retarded children; teach folk dancing to retarded adolescents; sew; repair strollers and toys, sort donated clothing among other tasks.

Other SERVE volunteers on Staten Island assist teachers and tutor school children in reading; restore donated books for distribution to needy children; serve as friendly visitors to hospital patients and the institutionalized aged; are office volunteers for national organizations such as the American Cancer Society and prepare bloodmobile kits for the American Red Cross.

In initiating and developing the SERVE on Staten Island program, a group approach was basic. Older persons were recruited in groups, to serve as a group, with individual assignments, on the same day each week at a given agency. This made it possible in most cases to provide group transportation from one or two central pick-up points to the agency and back. The provision of transportation is especially important for older volunteers because of the lack of public transportation to many agencies, and the diminishing strength of older persons. If they had to provide their own transportation, the effort involved and the cost would discourage many older persons from volunteering.

With large groups, SERVE on Staten Island found it practical and economical to charter school buses during school hours when the buses were available at lower cost. Taxis were sometimes used to transport small groups, again from a central pick-up point. In other SERVE programs which developed later throughout New York State, the agency sometimes provided a bus to transport volunteers to and from a central location. The group approach was used also in holding weekly group discussion meetings which were the heart of continuous in-service training for the older volunteers.

It is important to note that the group approach gives the older volunteers the opportunity for social contacts and to make new friends; one of the major satisfactions gained from volunteering, thus helping to diminish isolation and loneliness often characteristic of this age group.

This group approach also was efficient and time-saving for the agencies, allowing them to concentrate supervision on one day of the week.

WHAT SERVE ACHIEVED

There are three ways in which we can evaluate the SERVE program: in terms of its effect on the older persons who become SERVE volunteers; its effect on the agencies and organizations that were served by the volunteers; and its long-term effect in encouraging other communities throughout New York State and the nation to establish similar older volunteer programs.

At the end of the research and demonstration phase of the program, Community Service Society undertook an in-depth research evaluation of the program. Among the conclusions of particular interest were the characteristics of the SERVE volunteers and the satisfactions that they gained from their service.

The average SERVE volunteer was seventy-one years old. The majority (83%) were women. On the whole, they were older, less healthy, less well educated, less prosperous, and had much less previous volunteer experience than the traditional volunteer. Nearly half of the women volunteers and one-fourth of the men lived alone. Almost two-thirds of the women were divorced, widowed, or separated. The majority (76.4%) were retired, and had been so on the average for fifteen years.

Socioeconomic status was generally low. The majority of the volunteers and their husbands had been workers in skilled, semiskilled or unskilled jobs. Few had had professional or semiprofessional occupations. About one-third of the volunteers had not completed the eighth grade; approximately three-fourths had not finished high school and only a few had gone to college. Health problems were mentioned by approximately one-half of the volunteers. Few had ever done any volunteer work previously.

Yet despite the fact that they were older, less healthy, less well educated, and of lower socioeconomic status than the traditional volunteer, they established an excellent record for dependable service over a long period of time.

Another significant conclusion that emerged from the research study concerned the satisfactions that these retired persons gained from volunteer service. Information about individual volunteers drawn from SERVE records and staff interview with them, as well as comments made by the volunteers at group meetings, told essentially the same story. The consensus was that SERVE had given the older volunteers a goal and added new meaning to lives which too often had been empty and purposeless. It had developed new dignity and self-esteem among them; given them a sense of involvement with and for others, and provided companionship and the opportunity to make new friends. In working with the ill and the handicapped, SERVE helped the volunteers to gain a new perspective on their own problems and to adjust more easily to their own physical disabilities and health limitations. Above all, it had given these older persons a new role and the gratification of being useful and needed.

The effect of the program on the agencies served was studied also in the CSS research evaluation. At the end of the demonstration period, research staff interviewed staff members in twenty-five agencies, each of which was or had been engaged in a SERVE program. The interviews revealed a clear conviction among the respondents that SERVE had benefited their agencies.

Many thought that the agency's program had been strengthened by the regular and reliable attendance of the older volunteer over a long period of time, and by their interest, warmth, and ability. Some agency staff members had been hesitant to use older volunteers, but now they were enthusiastic about their worth. "I have learned something," said one. "I did not know old people could be such useful workers."

Some agency staff members noted with satisfaction that the numbers of volunteers had increased, their job assignments were carried out with greater competence, and they were able to relate more easily to the patients. Several noted an improvement in community understanding of their own agencies' activities and attributed this to the SERVE volunteers' interpretation and support of their agency in the community.

In evaluating what SERVE achieved, it is important to consider the applicability of the SERVE concepts in other types of communities and in other settings. To determine whether this type of program could be replicated successfully elsewhere, the Community Service Society initiated SERVE-in-New York State in 1969, under a Title III grant from the New York State Office for the Aging. The goal was to stimulate interest in communities throughout the state and to provide technical assistance to help them develop older volunteer programs, emphasizing the group approach which had worked so well on Staten Island. CSS staff was to provide consultation and guidance, but the local older volunteer programs were to be operated by a local community group or sponsor.

Through SERVE-in-New York State, many other SERVE-type programs have been started in many types of communities; rural, semirural, and urban, with many different types of sponsors; a volunteer bureau, a senior citizens center, a community council, and a school of social work to name a few. As of January, 1972, forty-two pilot SERVE programs, involving approximately 850 older volunteers, were in operation in twenty-one counties throughout New York State.

Of even more far-reaching significance is the role that SERVE has played in serving as a model for federal legislation which established the Retired Senior Volunteer Program (RSVP). The newly-created federal agency ACTION, which is responsible for RSVP and other programs, initiated eleven older volunteer programs in that many states during the summer of 1971. With a budget of $15,000,000 for the fiscal year 1972, it plans to have a great many more RSVP programs in operation by June, 1972.

We can conclude therefore that the concept of volunteer service as a new role for the retired is gaining growing acceptance throughout the nation. It is a role which promises great satisfaction, dignity and self-esteem for the aging and which opens up a tremendous new manpower resource for agencies and programs which can benefit from volunteer service.

SPECIFIC GUIDELINES

The SERVE experience had done more than demonstrate the broad philosophic concepts outlined above. It has developed specific guidelines which have proved valuable in the recruitment, placement, training, and retention of the older volunteer. These guidelines, excerpted from the Community Service Society report (Sainer and Zander, 1971) on the SERVE on Staten Island project, are as follows:

Recruitment Guidelines

1. Direct recruitment should be preceded by an assurance of community receptivity, the selection of a placement agency, and the development of a variety of specific assignment opportunities within that agency, as well as the establishment of a relationship with the network of individuals and groups that has access to and influence upon the older person.

2. Recruitment must be based upon reaching-out techniques and a willingness to go out to the neighborhoods where older persons live and meet. Older persons are not likely to take the initiative and come to a central office to apply for the opportunity to serve.

3. Recruitment is most effective when conducted by direct person-to-person contact with the potential volunteer. The use of mass media and community-wide publicity campaigns, though conducive to creating and sustaining community understanding of the SERVE program, seldom bring about immediate direct recruitment of an individual older volunteer.

4. Recruitment of older persons is more productive when it is related to one selected agency and to the choice of visible assignments within that agency, rather than to volunteerism in general.

5. Recruitment efforts should be focused on attempts to form a group of SERVE volunteers rather than to recruit and place single individuals. The opportunity to participate as a volunteer with others is encouraging to the older person who becomes more confident and interested when he sees that a group large or small will serve at one time and that he will be a welcome part of it.

6. Opportunity should be afforded to the potential volunteer to see an agency and its needs *before* he is asked to make a commitment to volunteer. The most effective approach to the establishment of new SERVE groups has been the use of a series of recruitment techniques, culminating in the *Tour-and-See* visit of the agency or institution.

7. The entire process of direct recruitment should move quickly so that the interest and enthusiasm of the prospective volunteers are captured at their height and not given an opportunity to dissipate.

8. Recruitment activities must be ongoing and continuous in order to establish new groups, to expand already existing groups, and to maintain a high level of participation.

9. The enthusiasm, interest, and experience of the volunteers, once strong SERVE groups have been formed, can be utilized effectively as recruiting agents.

Placement Guidelines

In selecting a placement agency appropriate for a SERVE-type program, the following are important criteria.

1. There must be some appreciation of the value and potential of a volunteer program *by* older persons before the placement agency undertakes a SERVE program. Support from three levels of staff is necessary: the administration, the volunteer director or staff assigned this responsibility, and line staff with whom the volunteers will be working.

2. An agency staff member should assigned to carry responsibility for the coordination and overall supervision of the program, and to work cooperatively with SERVE staff. Such staff should be available with some regularity for orientation and in-service training of the volunteers in the work setting and at the weekly group meetings.

3. There should be the readiness and ability to use the services of a *number* of regularly assigned persons on one selected day of the week.

4. Volunteers should never displace staff members. This policy may require interpretation to agency prior to the arrival of the volunteers and, if necessary, reinforcement by interpretation to volunteers.

5. Two factors; the potential volunteer's needs and the agency's needs, must be kept in constant balance. Individual opportunities should be developed which while representing real tasks and reflecting agency needs also fit the interest and skills of available volunteers.

6. In agencies where the major need is for one-to-one relationships between volunteers and patients or residents, there should be a willingness to offer assignments initially which will facilitate exposure to the agency and permit volunteers to come into contact with patients informally rather than confined to a direct one-to-one assignment.

7. An assessment should be made of the availability of a meeting room in which the volunteers can hold group sessions and have lunch, if they are at work at that time.

8. An agency should encourage expansion of its SERVE program either by absorbing more volunteers on the specific day originally selected or by adding another group on a second day of each week.

Training Guidelines

1. One and the same training programs cannot and should not be applied to all SERVE programs. Although a number of essential factors should always be included, each training program should be adapted to the needs of the placement agency, the kind of assignments available, the size of the vol-

unteer group, the interests and characteristics of its members, and the time commitment of the director of volunteers.

2. Volunteers should start on their jobs as soon as possible with training to follow rather than precede placement. General orientation should be provided to all volunteers prior to placement, but formal pre-service training should be given only in those situations in which detailed information about the assignment is necessary in order to get started on the job.

3. Training should be on the job and continuous, and related initially to a specific job assignment within a specific agency. As each SERVE program progresses, training should be broadened beyond the specific job assignment to include information about the total agency and discussion of issues of significance to older persons, the agency, and the community.

4. On-the-job supervision and guidance by the unit supervisor (line staff) are essential in order to foster the interests and skills of the volunteer, to provide him with the necessary information about his job assignment, and to motivate his continued participation.

5. The group approach to training is particularly well suited to the older person, and is also of benefit to the placement agency because it is an efficient use of supervisory time.

6. Training should be the joint responsibility of the volunteer director of the placement agency and SERVE staff.

7. The provision of lunch is an added feature which is important to the volunteer if he works beyond the lunch hour. It is of social as well as nutritional value to older persons and provides a sense of fellowship.

8. An intensive training institute for the SERVE volunteers in several agencies not only strengthens in-service training within the single agency setting but also broadens the knowledge and understanding of the volunteers. The institute, which in many ways substitutes for the pretraining required by many volunteer programs, should take place at a time when the older person has already been active and is, therefore, more interested in and responsive to absorbing additional information.

Retention Guidelines

1. Retention activities are essential and should be seen as an ongoing process permeating the entire program.

2. An important retention factor is the group approach which provides individual volunteers with an opportunity for the social interchange and mutual support that most older persons want and need; particularly the more isolated and those of lower socio-economic status.

3. Assignments which are obviously needed and useful and the expectation of regular attendance are of key importance in stimulating the continued interest and enthusiasm of the volunteers.

4. Group transportation on a regular ongoing basis is essential. It is the actual *provision* of transportation rather than reimbursement for carfare which makes it possible for older persons to go to their respective agencies week in and week out.

5. The attitude of SERVE and agency staff in making the volunteer feel welcome and wanted and in viewing him as a person as well as a giver of service is an important aspect of retention.

6. Recognition by staff and community officials of the individual volunteer and the total SERVE program serves to raise the volunteer in his own self-esteem and in the eyes of his family, friends, and neighbors. This, in turn, helps to develop the sense of satisfaction and pride which forms the basis of successful retention.

7. Identification of the older volunteer with the total SERVE program as well as with his specific placement agency should be encouraged. The SERVE training institute fosters this identification in a most effective fashion. The opportunity that SERVE offers for broad and multiple identifications, represents another stimulus toward continued participation in the program.

These then were the specific guidelines for recruiting, placing, training, and retaining older volunteers which were developed by the SERVE program on Staten Island, and tested in subsequent SERVE programs throughout New York State. As other programs utilizing older persons as volunteers develop throughout the nation, they will no doubt modify and adopt some of the guidelines to suit their particular needs and circumstances. But some principles, we believe, will remain basic to the success of all older volunteer programs.

First and foremost is an appreciation of the older adult's worth, the realization that almost every older person has something valuable to contribute if the right assignment in the right agency can be found for him.

Second is the understanding that older volunteer programs do not just happen. Staff is needed to reach out to the aging, to develop suitable placements, to provide on-going interest and supervision.

And third is the utilization of the group approach because of its practical advantages, e.g. economical transportation, efficient supervision, and because of its social benefits, e.g. opportunity to make friends.

It is our hope that in time every older person will have the opportunity and the option to serve his community as a volunteer and therby to remain a contributing, vital part of our society.

REFERENCE

Sainer, Janet S., and Zander, Mary L., SERVE: *Older Volunteers in Community Service*. Community Service Society, 1971.

Chapter 12

SENIOR CENTERS FOR THE OLDER CITIZENS

Abbe Hacker

INTRODUCTION

The first senior center in the United States was opened by the New York City Department of Social Services in 1943. This center, the William Hodson Senior Center, was founded by Harry A. Levine, welfare center administrator who learned of the terrible loneliness of the aged poor from his social investigators and was determined to do something to brighten their lives. He developed the concept of a center where old people would meet with their peers during the daytime hours when the rest of the world was at work or in school. The concept of senior centers, originally called day centers, became steadily more popular. They are now numbered in the thousands, but because of their rapid expansion an exact count is difficult. Another complicating factor is that definitions vary as to what constitutes a senior center. Most definitions call for a minimum requirement of either two or three full days of operation per week under the direction of a professional staff in a designated facility. A five-day-a-week center, however, is the minimum requirement stipulated by some funding agencies.

Senior centers have built upon their primary mission of providing opportunities for socialization. Many of today's centers offer broad cultural and educational programs, hot lunches, medical services, individual and group counseling, outreach to the isolated, volunteer services to the community, a committee system of client decision-makers, and more recently a greater emphasis on social action.

Basically, senior centers provide a preventive health service designed to help older people retain and improve their physical, psychological, and social well-being. At the centers older people learn that their individual problems are not unique, and that together with their fellow members they can attack these problems and through their combined strength effect change. In addition to being able to choose from a variety of activities, and to initiate new ones, the center members are involved in the world outside their centers. Senior centers have developed a growing importance in their communities. The importance of community involvement has been noted by John B. Martin, Commissioner of the Administration on Aging. What is needed, he wrote, are "Senior Centers which reach out with real services, as well as recreation, to bring people into the action center of a community's life" (Martin, 1971).

New staff consistently have voiced their surprise and admiration for the vitality and zest for living which they encounter at senior centers. For those who have never visited a senior center, and whose image of any institution for the aged conjures up frightening visions of decay and death, a visit to a senior center should provide a pleasant surprise. One visitor wrote the following about his first contact with center members: "What really surprised me was their endless want to welcome new people. This I can say first hand. They all seemed to be very interested in new people and welcomed them as old timers who dropped in for a visit" (Spier, 1968). In an effective center both members and staff appreciate the importance of a warm welcome for the stranger, be he client, staff, or guest.

SPONSORS AND FUNDING

The primary sponsoring agencies for senior centers are social service, recreation, and adult education agencies. Some centers are sponsored by more than one agency. For example, in New York City the Department of Social Services operates sixty-three senior centers in cooperation with a wide variety of other agencies, including public housing, education, health, and voluntary agencies, homes for the aged, veterans organizations, and center boards. Nationally, unions, faced with increased numbers of retired workers, have sponsored centers, as have Model Cities and other antipoverty agencies. In Philadelphia the dual aspects of health and recreation services are merged in the Adult Health and Recreation Center, operated by the Department of Public Health in cooperation with the Department of Recreation. An example of securing support from a number of public and private sources are the senior centers of Dade County, Florida. Their physical facilities are provided by public housing, while their program funding comes from the United Fund, plus contract agreements with government agencies.

The growth of the senior center movement has been accelerated by federal legislation, such as the Older Americans Act. This legislation has provided funds for developing center programs, although it does not fund construction costs. Federal housing legislation has made it possible for the United States Department of Housing and Urban Development (HUD) to stimulate the construction of public housing for the elderly, including space for center programs for both elderly public housing tenants and oldsters living in the surrounding community. Federal legislation had funding for senior centers, including the funding of food programs. The United States Department of Health, Education, and Welfare issued guidelines to the states in November, 1970 for carrying out the provisions of Title XVI of the Social Security Act. (Dept. of HEW, 1970). Title XVI provides for reimbursing up to 75 percent of the costs of services to the aged, blind, and disabled, including senior center services. Reimbursement is limited to services to the poor, previously poor, or potentially poor. Services may be provided directly by Departments of Social Services (Welfare) or through purchase contracts. Later in this chapter we will discuss the social action campaign undertaken by New York's seniors to eliminate a person by person means test for determining federal reimbursement for New York State's senior centers funded under Title XVI.

In addition to their primary sources of funding, centers also welcome donations of cash, goods, and services from business firms. Most centers conduct some type of local fund raising. These include white elephant sales, bazaars, and the like. Many centers also charge membership fees. A serious negative consequence of fee requirements and some fund raising projects is that they place additional barriers to the poor and hard-to-reach seniors from obtaining needed center services. A center membership culture of even token financial giving by the members can be seen as a "Not Wanted" sign to those most in need of what the centers have to offer.

Information on funding sources can be obtained from state offices for the Aging, or the Administration on Aging, United States Department of Health, Education, and Welfare, Washington, D.C. 20201. The National Council on the Aging has prepared a useful booklet on the subject, entitled, "How to Obtain Grants for Programs for the Aging Poor" (Rachlis, 1968). Your local library can be of assistance in providing names of community civic groups and agencies which are potential sources of help. The possibility of applying to small philanthropic foundations, whose modest but unpublicized resources may be more readily available than those of their mammoth counterparts, should not be overlooked.

CENTER FACILITIES

Until fairly recently those associated with senior centers used to boost of how they "made do" with run-down facilities. Only ten years ago the author had to walk down the cellar steps of a tenement and edge past garbage cans in a narrow alley to reach a center entrance. Today more recognition is being given to the need for dignified, well designed, and attractively furnished centers. Public housing architects have pioneered in this area. Recently, the New York City Department of Social Services has leased Senior Centers constructed specifically to serve the elderly. They include ramps for wheel chairs, air conditioning, a serving counter between the kitchen and dining room, and adequate toilet facilities. An important ingredient is an inviting reception area where people can be greeted. We have learned also of the necessity for sophisticated burglar alarm systems. These new centers which are highly visible and accessible, are located in the heart of poverty areas, where large numbers of the elderly live.

Ingenuity and initiative in securing space where conditions are less than ideal are valuable assets. In Long Island, New York, a recreation department coordinated many smaller units spread over a large geographic area. The facilities of libraries, Y's, youth centers, and an art league were utilized. The programs coordinator noted that there was a positive factor in the use of existing space in community buildings at hours when they were not used. It helped to develop an awareness of the needs of senior citizens by the community (Pattie, 1968).

SENIORS WHO USE CENTERS

The available evidence suggests that the vast majority of seniors currently served by centers have been fairly successful in coping with life. While not well-to-do financially, they are generally not the poorest or the most deprived in regard to social relationships. The stronger and better adjusted seniors will seek out a center, if they feel they need it. The seniors who use centers today are better educated and more sophisticated than those of twenty years ago. These people certainly should have center services available to them to help maintain their effective functioning in the community. There is a need, however, for our present centers and for new centers to reach out to the more isolated and handicapped oldsters—those most in need of the supportive bulwarks which a center can provide. This is not to say that every isolate could benefit from center involvement. For some loners, even a peripheral relationship would be too threatening. Others, however, can be helped if they can be reached. The following are examples of such efforts.

In one New York City hospital a senior center was the heart of a treatment plan for geriatric patients with emotional problems (The Geriatric Rehabilitation Center of the Kings County Hospital Center, Brooklyn, New York, 1955 to 1962). Many of these were severely depressed patients who would have faced state hospitalization. The author recalls one such patient. He had been a husky strongly built man, but now be barely shuffled along. "Isn't he too weak for rehabilitation?" asked the hospital's executive director of the center's psychiatrist. The psychiatrist replied that the man's depression was effecting his physical functioning. For several months the elderly gentleman sat in one particular chair against the wall of the center's activity room. He said almost nothing, but his eyes followed the action. One morning he found his seat occupied by another male patient. With a roar of anger he lifted the chair with its startled occupant still in it, and the transgressor barely escaped without injury. The newly active patient never developed into a socializer, but he began to dress up for special center occasions, took a keen interest in gardening, and was later discharged to a home for the aged.

Another example of a senior center which is geared to serve a special group is the Model Cities Multi-Purpose Senior Citizens Center in Baltimore, Maryland. It "provides older persons care for part of a day or week, either because they live alone and cannot manage completely for themselves, or live with their families, who need some relief." Its program includes hot, well-balanced lunches, opportunities to socialize, crafts, and therapeutic exercises (Tiven, 1971).

OUTREACH

In order to help those who could benefit from center services to actually get such services a concentrated outreach program is needed. One such program was project FIND, which sought out the "Friendless, Isolated, Needy and Disabled" aged. Twelve FIND projects were established by the National Council on the Aging and funded by the Office of Economic Opportunity in areas throughout the United States where there was a high concentration of the aged. It was discovered that there were substantial numbers of hidden aged who need and could use services, but would not by themselves come to agencies for help. Without an intensive program to seek out such people, they would not be served (National Council on the Aging, 1966).

One out-reach project director asked these crucial questions: "What are the most effective methods to find the invisible needy older person? Once found, how do we help the hard-to-reach attend our programs regularly enough to really benefit from what we have to offer?"

One program, funded under the older Americans Act, which sought answers to these questions was the Downtown Senior Center in San Francisco. The center, a refurbished storefront, was designed from the beginning to involve and serve the hardest-to-reach oldsters. Home visits were made with the residents of small hotels in the area where the aged poor lived before the center opened. The hotel managers were prevailed upon to provide space for weekly club programs. Possible programs for the forthcoming center were discussed and voted upon by the hotel residents.

During the first week that the center actually started operating, open houses were held honoring residents of each hotel. The guests appeared enthusiastic. But despite all these careful efforts most never were seen at the center again! The hard-to-reach are indeed hard-to-reach! Apparently quite a few would attend a large special function where there was little danger of personal involvement, but would go no further. Center staff fought off their discouragement and undertook a wide variety of approaches to attract their target group. A monthly bulletin was sent to 135 small hotels and left at local shops. Two neighborhood papers featured special center activities. Regular meetings were held with local social agencies to stimulate referrals. A special group was formed for new center members. Unlike the average center, where member referral is a big factor, most of the new people had to be brought in by staff. Home visiting staff were not always given the warmest of welcomes. A not uncommon greeting was: "What! Are you here again? Can't you get enough people to your Center without coming here?"

The project showed that the hard-to-reach fell into two groups: the frail with severe physical difficulties who were depressed (angry and without hope), and the relatively healthy who wanted a greater challenge than they believed most centers offered. To attract people with different needs, a well-balanced program was developed under the broad categories of fun and friendship, adult education, community resources, opportunities to serve the community, and last but not least, a hot lunch at a low price. It was found that service projects for needy children had a strong appeal for many of the hard-to-reach aged, who often could not be reached in any other way. Despite the many problems which the project faced, the center was able to develop a core of interested and interacting seniors (Booth, 1969).

Most senior centers do not have the resources to undertake this kind of comprehensive out-reach program. Nevertheless, more time and creativity invested in such efforts are needed. The following is an example of an attempt to stimulate nonattending members to renew their contact with their center:

Each active member chose an inactive member to contact during the Thanksgiving week or Christmas holidays. The contact would be made by telephone call, letters, but preferably a personal contact. For the ill or shut-in members, baskets of fruits, candies, and nuts were taken. The baskets were colorfully decorated. The active members were encouraged to invite the person he visited to come to the center on a particular day to participate in a program with him. The response was overwhelming and gratifying. Thirty inactive members visited the center and nine telephoned and two sent letters.

The active members were so pleased with their efforts and the response, that they have decided to keep in contact with the person they visited for at least two months. Hopefully the personal contact will arouse their interest in coming to the center on a regular basis (South Jamaica Senior Center, 1960).

One effective form of outreach is *visits by telephone* to the isolated, handicapped aged. A radio broadcast by a Telephone Reasurrance Service coordinator described the service as follows:

It is a program whereby elderly and handicapped persons who live alone and have limited social contacts receive regular telephone calls from a corps of volunteers. Telephone Reassurance is exactly what the name implies—a way of reassuring a homebound, isolated person that someone will regularly check on his well-being and take action if the need is indicated. In fact, during the past year, we experienced a number of emergency situations where prompt action may well have forestalled very serious consequences. But it is something else as well— and perhaps even more important—it is a service which provides continuing, warm, human, personal contacts in situations where the greatest disability is loneliness and the greatest hardship is a feeling of abandonment (Russell, 1961).

Some centers have been able to provide transportation to bring the handicapped to reunion parties with their callers. A number of centers have made special efforts to include the blind aged in their programs. Other aspects of out-reach will be included in our later discussion of community service programs.

CENTER GOALS
Individualizing the Senior Citizen

Older people, because of their diverse and lengthy life experiences, have different needs and tastes. Age differences alone between members can be up to thirty years. There was a case of an eighty-year-old mother and her sixty-year-old daughter attending the same center. One person may need an ongoing relationship with a center; another may need only one particular service; a third may come primarily to meet a mate; and a fourth to learn a new art skill or to revive a former one. The initial step in getting to know the individual and his unique wants is the intake process. It is vital to be able to know each person as a distinct human being and not just another addition to the group. A full interview may be too threatening to some seniors on their first day at the center. Nevertheless, an organized method of greeting newcomers by both staff and members is definitely called for. Many centers have developed membership reception committees in which fellow seniors escort the newcomer on a tour of the center. They explain the workings of the center and discuss possible programs of interest to the newcomer.

Early in his contact with the center, the new member should be interviewed by a staff person to determine how the center might be of service to him as an individual. A knowledge of the person's interests, family, health, education and special problems can be elicited. A personal data form is helpful in recording pertinent information. The interviewer should also be alert to an interest in special areas which the center does not have, but which might be established as part of the program. Most centers issue membership cards, and keep attendance records, which help alert them to the absences of regularly attending members.

Another important tool in individualizing the members is through individual counseling. Much of the counseling involves helping the older person to link up with community resources to get needed financial, medical, and housing assistance. It is difficult enough for a professional to negotiate the bureaucratic maze; it is no wonder that an older person with a problem can use all the help he can get. The author recalls one dramatic case, where an alert director noticed that one of his members looked paler every day. The director utilized a variety of pressures to see that the member was immediately hospitalized, where it was leaned that he was suffering from serious internal bleeding. Proper medical care was given, and the member returned to the center, extolling the director who had helped save his life.

Fighting Withdrawal Through Socialization

The benefits of opportunities for older people to socialize with their peers is dramatically illustrated by the following case history:

Mrs. Bradstone was brought to the Center by a neighbor, who explained that she had been trying to persuade her to join the Center for over a year. Mrs. Bradstone had been a widow for the past ten years, and had retreated into a shell upon the death of her only son two years ago. She was encouraged by both staff and members to take part in Center activities. This was a slow process as she never smiled or made any overtures to the others present. Gradually she began to assume some clerical duties, then agreed to act as a saleslady at the bazaar. Later she joined the sewing group and branched out into other forms of arts and crafts. Slowly she began to socialize and make friends. When election time came she was nominated for second Vice-President and was elected in spite of the fact she ran against a well-known Center member (Hacker, 1971).

The first member president of a newly formed center beautifully described the meaning of the center to older people in his installation address. He said:

Most single and unattached people have the special task of getting used to being alone and living alone. You arise in the morning and wonder, after breakfast, "Where should I go? What shall I do? Where am I needed? Who cares, anyway?" One feels the closeness of the four walls, and very often, you feel choked. You cannot stay indoors any longer, and so you go outside, still not having a sense of purpose or direction.

This marvelous center solves my problem five days a week when I realize I have the Surf Center to look forward to. It is such a wonderful feeling of sharing a common experience with people my own age. I cannot help wondering how important it could be to have centers like this one in every section of the city.

During our younger days we are busy working, building, raising our families, educating them. We are involved with the problems of sharing rich family experiences. But now, when the children are grown and they, themselves, are married and have their own personal family problems, how important, how gratifying, how meaningful it is to share our long days with good and valuable friends. Now that Senior Citizens have the time to enjoy life, to relax, to be wiser, to enjoy the wisdom of advanced age, to enjoy changed and wiser values, it is places like this Surf Center for Senior Citizens which allow us to come together in warm and affectionate brotherhood.

We have in this center something for everyone. I will mention a few: we sing, we dance, and we exchange experiences. We acquire knowledge and skills that we had no time for in previous years. Classes in English, Hebrew, Spanish, ceramics and outings. We enjoy old friends with warmth and affection, and we gain new friends with respect and gratitude.

Centers like this one *must* be built all over the city so that others can find what we have found here.

In conclusion, I say to all you dear friends that Senior Citizen Centers are God's very own blessing because it makes each day exciting, meaningful, and free from time waste (Ribikoff).

Center members have developed a high degree of sensitivity and skill in socialization. Some are ready to share their knowledge with staff, as the following two examples illustrate. The first is entitled, "Involvement: Observations by Visiting Social Worker."

The most memorable and undoubtedly the most helpful observation of the day came in the form of a statement made by a member of the Senior Center.

She was making paper flowers by herself, when I walked over and asked if I could watch. She asked if I would make one with her, and I said that I would just watch. As she worked her glue bottle became clogged. I voluntarily picked it up to open it. As if she had been waiting for me to make such a move, she said, "See you became involved whether you wanted to or not, so you might as well work with me."

I worked with her and became involved (Barnfield, 1968).

The following record of a group meeting was entitled, "Conflict in the Group." As we shall see it was not the group members who were in conflict with each other, but rather the group members were in conflict with the worker who had inadvertently interfered with their relationship with a new group member. The group worker wrote:

> Mrs. White attended today's meeting for the first time. She was greeted politely by the other group members, several of whom knew her. She was rather quiet for the first half hour or so, while the worker commented that we had a new group member and that, perhaps, the others would like to tell Mrs. W. something about the group.
>
> Practically all said that they were glad to have her and she responded with a smile and a slight gesture of recognition by tilting her head slightly forward. After group members had told Mrs. W. at some length what "we" were doing, the worker commented that it is difficult to come into a group anew as well as to accept a new member.
>
> The initial response was heated denial coupled with anger directed at the worker. Mrs. W. said she was glad to be here. The worker looked at her. Mrs. W. said somewhat uncertainly that perhaps it wasn't so easy after all. At this the group members turned on the worker, complaining that they were angry—not at Mrs. W.—but at the worker who had put them and Mrs. W. in an embarrassing position (Falek, 1964).

As can be seen, the worker had introduced his valid point at a most inappropriate time when the group was gently integrating the new lady into their ranks. The worker's action increased the anxiety of the newcomer and made the group's job more difficult. The group members expressed their justifiable anger at him. To the worker's credit the group members felt free enough to express their anger, and the worker felt free enough to write it up so that it could be used to help both himself and others.

Providing Mental Stimulation

Centers have developed a wide variety of educational and cultural programs. These include both formal classes and formal special interest and discussion groups. In New York City community colleges have established an Institute of Study for the Older Adult, financed under the Older American Act. Its goal is succinctly stated as "a project in continuing education as a life-long process, highlighting the sense of potential growth throughout life." Classes were held at senior centers. At the participating centers members could enroll in nine session courses in the following subjects: basic Spanish conversation, techniques of social action, current events, written and verbal expression in English, appreciation of music and art, and home gardening. One elderly English student exclaimed, "I never realized I was imprisoned until I learned to read! Now I am free to travel all over the world, from my own chair!"

Center visits to plays, ballets, operas, and concerts are part of some cultural programs. Centers have formed their own glee clubs, orchestras, folk dance, and drama groups. A theatre production can lend itself to involving the skills of a center's craft, art, woodworking, music, and sewing groups in enhancing the production and building center cohesiveness. Very creative art work has been produced by center artists—both by people returning to old hobbies and those involved for the first time. What is particularly impressive is that a good many seniors create bold works, with daring use of color and form. The author strongly recommends not placing the artist's age next to his work, which is the practice with the art work of children to indicate the extent of their youth handicap, but is demeaning for adult artists, whose work should be judged on its merit alone. Cultural activities do not have to involve large groups of participants to have value. Some staff time should be allotted for small group activities.

Center magazines and newsletters provide outlets for writers and artists, opportunities for members to express their views and help keep the members and the community informed of center services. The editor in the first issue of one center magazine wrote about its goals as follows:

> With this first issue of the community journal, the Goddard-Riverside Center for older people sets out to bring to the outside world a running series of the goings-on in the Center regarding the benefit of the members. Retired from the exacting demands of daily paid-employment the senior citizen has ample time to do considerable thinking. This journal titled *"Senior Commentator"* now offers to them, leisure groups, a place where they can give expression to their moods of joy and sorrow, and voice their opinions regarding the social

order in which we all live. They can air their grievances, present their immediate needs, make practical suggestions to the authorities concerning the improvements of their day-by-day living, and in general be heard from as a potential growing body of the public as a whole.

Among other projected ideas which should emerge in subsequent issues the *Senior Commentator* proposes from the start to act as a creative writing workshop where would-be writers of the member body shall be given a place to tell in their own words of personal experiences, both amusing and trying, for the education and entertainment of the readers; discuss personal problems confronted with in the past and present and, most important, how they did or didn't solve them.

Then the *Senior Commentator* shall as a matter of course and for the benefit of the foreign born include a page each in Yiddish and Spanish writing. Another section shall be given to writers who stirred by emotional rise would rather express their feelings and impressions in rhymes or in free verse. If there are some members who find in themselves an itching talent for sketching satirical cartoons mirroring unreasonable characters or funny situations, the *Senior Commentator* shall consider these efforts as welcome subject matter. In short every type of original creative expression shall find a home in the pages of this publication (Himmel, 1971).

An excellent educational resource is the life experiences of the members themselves. Programs built around the many national and religious holidays offer excellent opportunities for cultural interchanges. An example of one such event was an "Ethnic Day Program" featuring the cultural contributions of the Center's various ethnic groups. Other good educational resources are guest lecturers from educational institutions, professional societies, and government agencies.

A proven method to stimulate the intellects and often the emotions of the seniors is to present opposing views on a controversial topic. The author visited a senior center at the time Medicare was being voted upon by Congress. The members related with pride how their director had insisted on inviting a representative of the American Medical Association to speak on its opposition to Medicare. Mr. Leo Laks was the director. The A.M.A. had at first expressed its uneasiness in sending a representative into the heart of Medicare territory, until they were given repeated assurances by the director that no injury would befall their emissary. Before the visit the director spoke to the membership about the value of hearing all sides on an issue, and the need for courtesy to their guest. The director stayed at the speaker's side throughout his visit, and although the doctor was sharply challenged during the question period, he left the center in good health.

Providing Physical Stimulation

At a time of life when physical strength is faltering, older people need to be stimulated into using their muscles. Disuse only hastens deterioration. Seniors can still compete enthusiastically in a variety of athletics. Games can be adapted to reduce bending. For example, table-top tossing games (ring toss or tossing objects into concentric circles) have been effectively used. In addition to the physical benefits accrued, competitive sports are an excellent outlet for the discharge of aggressive energies. Such outlets are sorely needed by older people whose stage of life makes them depression prone.

Swimming is an excellent sport at any age. Pool, bowling, and bocci contests are also popular. (It is a little difficult to make an athletic case for card playing, although the occasional loud arguments do exercise the vocal cords.) A fine activity both for its physical and psychological benefits is gardening. Raised flower beds can eliminate the need for bending. Old-fashioned walking can also help tone up sagging muscles. More formal exercise groups are also of value, but members should not be pressured unduly into joining them.

Providing Food

Food is one of the essential ingredients for successful programming. Added to the importance of its nutritional value, food service provides opportunities for center members to become involved in its purchase, preparation, and serving. Much status is attached to the food services roles of center refreshment committees. Many centers make their noon meal a substantial one because they have learned that a large number of seniors cannot or will not do much cooking at home.

The cost of meals to the members should be subsidized to the greatest extent possible. Senior centers may be able to utilize the federal Nutrition for Elderly legislation, which calls for 90 percent federal reimbursement for group meals. Unfortunately, the first nutrition appropriation bill was vetoed by President Nixon.

Food programs often are the fulcrum around which new centers build their services. Mealtime can be made a festive occasion where a relaxed atmosphere makes for informal socializing. The staff's positive involvement in meeting this many-faceted need is proof to the seniors that they are truly interested in them.

Securing Medical Care

Centers have been taking an increasingly active role in helping seniors secure medical care. One approach has been to seek the aid of hospitals and clinics in conducting medical examinations at the centers. A pioneer in this area has been the Adult Health and Recreation center in Philadelphia, Pennsylvania. At the center, the examinations and tests were entirely free of charge. More than 85 percent of the members availed themselves of the annual birthday check-up. They considered it as a right of center membership. The center reported that they had been a real pay off to the recognition of the need to establish a positive and trusting climate before people would feel secure enough to make use of preventive, rather than just emergency health services (Brannick and Scheiner, 1969).

In New York City a delegation of center members met with the hospital administrator in their community. They spoke of the difficulties in obtaining comprehensive medical care at the hospital many separate out-patient clinics. This discussion resulted in the establishment of a special geriatric out-patient service. Other centers have obtained the services of public health nurses to counsel individuals and groups on health problems. Lectures on prevention and treatment also were obtained from medical societies. Mass flu inoculations and screening for glaucoma and tuberculosis were conducted at many centers. At the height of a recent flu epidemic there was a temporary shortage of serum. Rather than postpone their immunization, the members voted to have their center purchase the serum, which was administered by a doctor from the public health service. Another enterprising center worked out an interesting exchange with a home and hospital for the aged. The center provided regular volunteer services to the home; in return the home provided free medical treatment to center members (Hacker, 1971).

Preventing Crime

The fear of becoming a crime victim is a very real one for the aged, urban poor. Their low incomes force them to live in the high crime areas, where they are regarded as inviting targets by desperate drug addicts. The seniors not only are concerned over having their money stolen but fear bodily injury. Senior Centers have had to do what little they could to help their members secure better protection. Frequent social action campaigns have demanded more police protection. In a few areas, technical improvements, such as the use of scooter patrols and walkie-talkies have been introduced.

An innovative approach has been the use of a youth escort service to accompany seniors. One such escort service, funded by the Office of Economic Opportunity, was established in New York City. Thirty young men from a poverty area, all high school drop-outs, received four months of training at the Police Academy. The service, which could be obtained by telephoning, was available from 9:00 a.m. to 11:00 p.m. One center director wrote the following about its use by her center members:

> Before the inception of the Community Escort Service, the elderly of Bedford-Stuyvesant lived in constant fear of muggings and physical assaults. Sharply constricted in their mobility within the community, for the most part they remained in their apartments and experienced feelings of alienation, mistrust, and social isolation.

> This report deals with community change of a positive nature and describes a program which is 1) providing physical safety for the elderly residents of Bedford-Stuyvesant, 2) creating job opportunities for high school drop-outs of minority groups, 3) fostering communi-

cation and understanding between the youth and senior citizens of the area, and 4) introducing a vitally needed service to improve the quality of life for the entire community.

Services to the Maria Lawton Center members have included escort services to local banks so that members can cash their checks; to and from the bus so that members can visit friends and relatives; to the housing office so that members can pay their rent; and to and from stores in the area so that members can shop. Escorts are trained also to provide emergency first aid and to patrol playgrounds, streets and parks in the Model Cities area. For those who have called upon the escorts, the service is highly supportive (Staton, 1971).

Establishing a Role in the Community

Society has not established a meaningful contributory role for retired people. Centers can help in this important area. Most of the deprived elderly, however, will need to have their more immediate personal needs satisfied, before they are ready to serve others. Centers have developed a variety of service projects serving both their fellow members in the center, and people of all ages outside the center. We discussed earlier the telephone reassurance service, an excellent service to those unable to reach the center. A number of centers have developed programs in which geriatric state hospital patients visit centers and participate as members on a regular basis. Careful planning by staff and members was the secret ingredient for success. At one center preparation for this service project included visits by center staff to the state hospital, careful screening of patients by the hospital staff, center planning meetings by the membership executive, refreshment, and reception committees (Thebner, 1968).

Visits to nursing homes and homes for the aged by center glee clubs, dance groups, and orchestras have lifted the spirits of patients who previously "had never budged from their rooms." The director of one nursing home said: "Many of our patients stated that the senior center members made them feel as though there are many things to accomplish in old age. Our patients now are enthusiastic to form their own glee club." Another wrote: "Our people had a ball! One ninty-three-year-old performed by singing with the orchestra.

An aphasic patient of ours jumped to his feet when he was asked by one of the women to dance" (Wolf) .

Service to young people has been an important aspect of community service. Toys were made by center craftsmen for hospitalized children. The author has witnessed the enthusiastic response of elementary school children to a center assembly program on "Old New York." They were delighted to hear the songs and stories of life in New York City in the early 1900's. Center members also have developed good relationships with college students and recent graduates. Before long hair had become commonplace with young men, the seniors were more ready to accept this style than middle-aged people. The elderly men, at any rate, offered few complaints when the young staff women came to work in mini-skirts. In New York City a series of visits were arranged with college students to exchange views with center members. The program was appropriately called "Project: Bridge the Gap." Several visits were made to each of the centers, and views were exchanged on many subjects. The seniors were generally sympathetic to the views of the students, but expressed their anger at college radicals who ridiculed the flag and other patriotic symbols. One student commented to a member, "It's amazing, I can talk to you, but not to my parents!" (Hacker, 1971) .

In summary, community service projects enable older people to continue to make a concrete contribution to society. Besides helping those served, such projects enhance the senior's own image of himself and raise his status in the eyes of his adult children.

Helping Alleviate Financial Stringency

Earlier chapters have discussed the difficult financial plight of old people. They are the lowest level economic minority in the country. The following steps have been taken by a number of centers to make attendance possible for the aged poor. No fees are charged. Publicly made member money contributions to the center are discouraged. Costs to the members are kept at a bare minimum. Information on discount stores is publicized. A center culture is fostered in which money is not a hidden requirement for acceptance.

There are a number of seniors who want employment (particularly part-time work) and who most certainly could use added income. In conjunction with the Food Stamp Program, center members in New York City were hired as part-time food stamp application clerks. Assigned to some forty senior centers, the clerks processed applications of fellow seniors. At the Hodson Senior Center seniors have been working twenty hours weekly in the Thrift Shop and as Community Aides. They are hired and paid by an antipoverty agency. It is important that center employment be clearly differentiated from the voluntary self-help roles which are the heart of center life. Paid employment at a center should approximate salaries in the community. If funding is available it may be preferable to rotate paid assignments among a larger number of seniors. For example, a different senior food staff corps could be assigned for each day of the week.

For a variety of reasons many older people are fearful of asking for help to which they are entitled. This is particularly true in regard to any form of public assistance. Centers have been helpful in assisting their clients to secure needed financial assistance. They have discovered numerous poverty-stricken seniors who were literally starving to death, but who refused to seek public financial help without a great deal of support from center staff.

Obtaining a Voice in Decision-Making

For many seniors, obtaining a voice in decision-making is the most valuable benefit they can receive from their center relationship. Participation by members in their center's decision-making apparatus is essential if the center is to have real meaning to them. To meet this vital need centers have developed a range of committees and special interest groups, with both elected small group chairmen and center-wide officers.

The author's viewpoint is that the decision-making process should encompass the contributions of both members and staff, each having some exclusive areas, but in the main involving the input of both groups. Older people, as is true of people of all ages, want to have control over their own destiny. The aged have fewer opportunities to exercise such control. They sorely miss it. As one of the members said at a joint meeting with staff, "When decisions are made, I want to be your partner! Make me your partner!" Staff should heed this request. They should, however, also avoid moving too far in the opposite direction and abrogating their responsibilities in the decision-making process. Such a retreat would not be in the best interest of the center's members. In addition, an agency sponsoring a center has a responsibility for the unserved elderly, as well as to those now receiving the benefits of center services. Staff must maintain a strong voice in investing resources to bring the hard-to-reach under the center's umbrella of services.

Staff, as well as members, can make important contributions in the following areas:

1. *Upholding democratic concepts in the decision-making process.*
2. *Protecting minority interests from being ignored by by an overpowering majority.*
3. *Providing opportunities for leadership by many participants.*

The following case record summary of a center entertainment committee illustrates the worker's role in helping the committee members make some progress in achieving the above goals.

The committee was a prestigious one; it prepared entertainment programs and selected the performers for special events. Its status was dependent upon how well the audience received its offerings. Almost all the committee members could sing, dance or act, and they performed at the special events.

The committee was dominated by Mrs. Donalds, a stately, autocratic woman, and her close friend, Mrs. Roberts. Both women cruelly critized a third committee member, Mrs. Johnson, for her inability to perform due to a speech defect. The two leaders repeatedly sought to force her to leave the committee. She stubbornly refused and asserted her right to remain and help plan programs, even if she did not perform. There seemed to be some sympathy for her on the part of the others, but no one dared to openly support her. This unhealthy situation led to tension and verbal battling which reduced the effectiveness of the committee's work.

The worker groped for a method acceptable to the group which would break up the rigidity of the group's structure. The following approach was employed. It was the custom for small groups of committee members to meet separately with the worker to prepare skits which were previewed at full committee meetings. The worker developed a sure-fire humorous skit about a husband and wife with the wife's role almost wholly pantomime. The skit was rehearsed with Mrs. Johnson, the lady with the speech defect, and the one male member of the committee, Mr. Smith.

At its full committee try-out the skit was received with approving laughter by the committee; but was subjected to adverse criticism by the unrelenting Mrs. Donalds. To the astonishment of all, Mr. Smith, heretofore timid and retiring, turned on the redoubtable matriarch and attacked her treatment of Mrs. Johnson with such vigor and tenacity that she would have left the group in tears, had not the worker motioned her to remain.

The committee was never the same after that. Its leadership became more diverse, the atmosphere more relaxed, and the committee members were able to utilize their energies in achieving agreed upon goals (Hacker, 1963).

In regard to providing opportunities for leadership, it is suggested that center constitutions limit the president's term of office to two one-year terms. This helps to prevent an entrenched president from freezing out potential rivals and permits the incumbent to graciously transfer his power after two years in office.

4. *Bringing out hidden leadership qualities in members.*

A rich, varied program calls for many leaders. A constricted program, on the other hand, has few outlets for leadership. The worker can offer his support to a potential leader to accent the challenge of a leadership role which is within his capacity.

5. *Aiding member leaders to carry out their roles effectively as judged by their fellow members.*

Member leaders should not be used as front men for staff, but rather staff should help the member leaders to be effective in playing their roles. Such help can take the form of providing time for the leader to try out his ideas on the worker before presenting them to his constituents, if he so chooses. The sharing of current information and community contacts are other ways to assist the leader. An alert staff will look for opportunities to enhance the status of a center's elected officers, e.g. member officers, rather than staff, should introduce status guests at center functions.

6. *Suggesting alternatives and new approaches to solving a given problem, and helping the group to examine the positives and negatives of each proposed solution.*

7. *Challenging restrictive and narrow thinking by appealing to the better instincts of the participants.*

In summary, substantial member involvement in decision-making helps make each member's center relationship more meaningful, as well as making the work of staff more interesting.

In most decision-making situations the worker should contribute his input, without the implication, of course, that he expects the group to accept his contribution without critical analysis. There are situations, however, where the worker should not voice his views. For example, decisions where individual personal preferences are involved should be left entirely to the members.

Staff training on a sustained basis is essential in helping staff to obtain a clear understanding of their role in the decision-making process. Unless the delicate balance of role differentiation between staff and member is understood by both parties, the results can be disastrous for all, as can be seen from the following incident: A center director related to a group of her colleagues that in order to foster member decision-making she had appointed a membership executive committee. The committee's first order of business, she woe-fully reported, was to unanimously vote for her impeachment! She in turn, retaliated by dissolving the executive committee!

How should a worker respond when he feels the group's decision is a mistake? Unless the carrying out of the decision will endanger life and limb or violate basic agency policy, the worker should respect the group's decision. It may well turn out to have been the right one, and if not, it can be re-viewed and used as a learning experience. The group must do the primary evaluation of its work. It must develop its own standards to measure success or failure. The members should judge their own efforts, rather than look to staff for approval. The larger membership also evaluates the work of many center groups. This is particularly true when the membership as a whole is directly affected by a group's prod-uct, such as in the case of a refreshment committee.

There will be times when members strongly disagree with agency policy. All policy should not be regarded as sacred; outmoded aspects should be modified. On the other hand, sound agency policies should be upheld and not abandoned under pressure from a vocal minority or even a majority. In such cases staff must be prepared to take a firm stand at the risk of being "unpopular." The following three examples illustrate the above:

The policy of Center A is to provide services to any person sixty years of age or over. Slightly younger people with spe-cial needs can be granted membership following a confidential interview and evaluation by the director of the center. Only a few such exceptions have been made for applicants in their late fifties, and these people have been absorbed into the center without difficulty. The membership's executive com-mittee, however, seeks to secure the authority to ratify or reject any prospective new member under sixty.

This demand should be rejected by staff for the following reasons. In order to intelligently consider the case of a new applicant under sixty, the executive committee would have to be given the confidential social service history of the applicant. Secondly, the right of veto would give the executive committee the power to blackball applicants under sixty who seek and may sorely need the services of the center. Thirdly, this precedent could be the first step in extending the authority of executive committee veto to encompass all new applicants. In essence, the granting of this demand would move the center along the road to becoming a private club, rather than a social agency.

In Center B the entrenched member leaders feel threatened by the influx of a different socioeconomic group of newcomers. To protect their present hegemony they are pushing to held a membership vote on a constitutional amendment which would require a full year's membership as a prerequisite for holding center office.

Staff should not permit a vote on this proposed amendment because if it were adopted it would make second-class members of the newcomers and deny them equal opportunity to hold office. Staff should not make the serious mistake of sanctioning a member vote on an agency policy over which they should not exercise authority in the hope that the vote will go the "right way." It is much more honest for staff to explain to members why they cannot abrogate a particular policy.

It is the policy of Center C to serve the poorest seniors in the community, and therefore no membership fees of any kind are charged. Recently, faced with a depleted treasury, some center leaders have proposed that members pay for the use of arts and crafts materials.

In this situation, staff should explain how such action would in effect constitute the imposition of a fee scale, which would bar the poorer members from fully utilizing the center. As an alternate solution to the center's financial problem, the staff should suggest more creative methods to raise money.

When members and staff have a clear concept of their roles, each can concentrate on perfecting the playing of their respective roles. Thus as members develop their decision-making expertise, they will assume more of the organizational tasks which staff initially carried. This in turn will free staff to invest more time in such specialized functions as counseling and outreach. In centers where members are hired as part-time staff, or are on the boards of directors, they must play the unique roles which these positions call for. Their playing of these roles can in fact be strengthened by their intimate knowledge of the needs and aspirations of older people.

SUPPORTING SOCIAL ACTION

The most exciting recent development in the senior center movement has been a sharp increase in social action. One social action campaign recently conducted in New York State had national ramifications. In April, 1971 it was learned that all senior centers sponsored by New York City's Department of Social Services would be required shortly to impose an individual means test and monthly fee scale on every senior who received services. These requirements were mandated by both the State and Federal governments as a prerequisite for funding under Title XVI of the Social Security Act. (New York City had been paying 95 percent of the cost of its senior centers, and was in dire need of financial help.) The U.S. Department of H.E.W. said that it had to have an individual means test in order to be certain that federal monies would be allocated only for center services to low-income seniors. The New York State Department of Social Services said that it had to obey a fee requirement which had been included in an otherwise progressive state law to fund senior center programs.

The first step in the uphill battle to stop the implementation of these destructive measures was to create public awareness of the problem. In May of 1971 this was successfully achieved when over 2,000 seniors picketed the Governor's Conference for the Aging. They carried eye-catching signs protesting the means tests and fees, while hundreds more demonstrated inside the hotel where the conference was being held. The protests were extensively covered by the news media, with such headlines as, "New York senior citizens are proving they still have enough pep to protest" (Channel 5

News, NYC, May 7, 1971). Television newsmen interviewed the articulate protesters.

But protests alone were not enough. The seniors needed something positive to offer. They got it in the form of identical bills to repeal the fee and means test requirements introduced in both houses of the state legislature. With only a few days to adjournment a statewide telephone campaign was mounted to get the bills out of committee and voted upon. The assembly voted yes, and a day before adjournment the senate passed its bill. Other calls and letters had been directed to U.S. Department of H.E.W. Scores of influential people, including Dr. Arthur Flemming, Special Consultant to the President on Aging, offered help. The U.S. Department of H.E.W. was sympathetic to the plight of the seniors, and agreed to accept a 10 percent sampling in place of a person by person financial investigation. H.E.W. also agreed to include food program costs in federal reimbursements, which it had originally excluded.

Much progress had been made, but the battle was not yet over. Governor Rockefeller's signature to the state bill was needed, or all would have been lost. The seniors and their supporters directed their appeals to the Governor. The United Senior Centers of Greater New York, led by its dynamic president, Mr. David Miller, organized a well-attended "Tribute to the Friends of the Senior Center," on June 29, 1971 in which city, state, and federal officials, agency executives, unions, and volunteers were presented with certificates of appreciation for their help in the campaign. Special recognition was given to New York City Councilman Theodore Silverman, New York State Senator Jeremiah Bloom, and Congressman James Scheuer and Walter Newburger, Pres. of the Congress of Senior Citizens, for their outstanding support of the seniors. Three days later Governor Rockefeller signed the bill to repeal the fees and means test requirements.

EVALUATING CENTER SERVICES

How effective are senior center services in meeting the needs of the elderly? How best can we measure their effectiveness? Those working in the field offer much evidence of their value, but few objective studies have been made. One recent study of a union-sponsored center in Philadelphia reported that retired workers who attended the center had better physical and mental health than those who did not. There is always the factor of self-selection, however, which must be taken into account.

The goals of a center have to be spelled out precisely before its progress toward these goals can be measured. Unfortunately, centers are too ready to accept good attendance as conclusive proof of their excellence. Attendance figures by themselves do not tell the whole story. It is possible for a high attendance rate to be due to a lack of other options open to the elderly poor, rather than to the attractiveness of a center's program. It should be kept in mind that centers are patronized primarily by satisfied customers. The absent dropout and the hard-to-reach who never came are apt to be overlooked. These people's judgments also must be included in any fair measure of center effectiveness.

One constructive step that can be taken is the building of an on-going evaluation component into center programs. Member participants, as well as staff, can evaluate their work at regular intervals, i.e. at every tenth program session. As part of the preparation for such evaluation, staff should be reassured by their superiors that the critical comments which they elicit from members will not be used to the detriment of staff. Members, in turn, need to be reassured by their center staff that the center will be helped by their forthright participation in evaluating center services. The hurdle was skillfully handled by the chairman of a senior citizen panel on evaluating center services. She said to her large staff audience: "Don't be frightened, staff, we won't be too hard on you, although we have some criticisms."

THE FUTURE

The future of the vast majority of the senior centers and millions of seniors is tied to the future of our nation's cities. These centers cannot prosper when life in the neglected cities is steadily eroding. The older people bear a heavy burden of this erosion. They become the hapless victims of increased crime, are locked into substantial housing, and are the recipients of inadequate medical care. Once again they face the danger of a means test at the doors of their senior centers which would deal a crippling blow to their pride and dignity.

Basic priorities must be reordered in order to offer hope to the poor of all ages. Hungry children as well as hungry old people must be fed. Jobs which pay a living wage must be created for the unemployed. Unless this is done the future will be a sad one.

The voting power of organized seniors is fighting to force all levels of government to respond positively to the needs of the poor of all ages. Organizations such as the National Council of Senior Citizens are in the forefront of this battle. All of us must unite in this common effort, if we are to have any hope of success.

REFERENCES

Administration on Aging, *Let's End Isolation*. Washington, D.C.: U.S. Department of Health, Education, and Welfare, June, 1971.

Barnfield, L. S.: *LaGuardia Downtown Senior Center*. New York City (Unpublished), January 2, 1968.

Booth, Estelle F.: The neighborhood center: effective instrument of outreach. *Challenges Facing Senior Centers in the 1970's*. New York City, NCOA, pp. 90–113. 1969.

Brannick, Zachary, and Scheiner, Sam: The physician in the center. *Challenges Facing Senior Centers in the 1970's*. New York City, NCOA, 1969.

Falek, Hans: Elements of group experience. *Social Group Work: A New Dimension in V. A. Social Work*, Missouri, Veterans Administration Hospital, Reprinted, December, 1964.

Hacker, Abbe: *Report on Entertainment Committee, Day Center, Neponsit Home For The Aged*. 1963 (Uupublished).

Hacker, Abbe: The role of senior centers in a public welfare agency. *Public Welfare, 29* (4), Fall, 1971.

Himmel, Philip: Introducing the senior commentator. *Senior Commentator,* 1 (1), Spring, 1971, Goddard Riverside Senior Center, New York City, pg. 2.

Hunt, John: *Report of the Chairman of the Social Action Committee of the Sirovich Senior Center*. New York City, July 26, 1971 (Unpublished).

National Council on the Aging, *Project: FIND*. Washington, D.C., New York City, NCOA, January, 1966.

Pattie, Alice Young: The diversified center, *Centers for Older People Newsletter*, 2 (1), NCOA, November, 1968.

Pollak, Otto; Sagi, Philip, and Friedman, Edward P.: *Utilization Study of Senior Citizens Center*. April, 1970.

Rachlis, David: *How to Obtain Grants for the Aging Poor*. Washington, D.C., NCOA, 1968.

Ribikoff, William: The president's installation address, *Staff Newsletter*, Division of Senior Centers, Special Services for Adults, New York City, Department of Social Services, p. 27.

Russell, Alice D.: *Text of Broadcast on Radio Station WQXR*. New York City, mimeographed, July, 1971.

Service Programs for Aged, Blind, or Disabled Persons, Rules and Regulation. Washington, D.C.: Department of Health, Education and Welfare, Social and Rehabilitation Service, Federal Register, 35 (230), II, November, 1970.

South Jamaica Senior Center, Queens, New York: *Highlights of The Year*. 1970 (Unpublished).

Spier, Edwin: mimeographed, April, 1968.

Staton, Mildred: *Bedford Stuyvesant and Community Change, Community Escort Service*. (Unpublished), March, 1971.

Thebner, Leah: *A Well Planned Day At Our Center or A Big Event*. (Unpublished), November, 1968.

Tiven, Marjorie Bloomberg: *Older Americans: Special Handling Required*. Washington, D.C., NCOA, 56, June, 1971.

Wolf, Roland, Linkage: *Stac Newsletter*. Division of Senior Centers, Special Services for Adults, New York City, Department of Social Services, pp. 4–5.

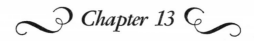
NURSING HOME CARE

Donovan J. Perkins

INTRODUCTION

Nursing homes, like other social institutions, are the result of society's demands. Their history has been molded by social and cultural change which, of course, continues even as these words are written. In introducing this chapter, a brief social history is given as ground work for discussing nursing home definitions, standards and licensing, operations, community relationships, patient/resident placement, and financing of care.

Nursing home history is heavily influenced by the history of hospitals and medicine as well as by society's attitudes towards welfare and the aged. In large measure, the history of nursing homes is one of filling voids left by hospitals as the role of the hospital changes.

Today's hospital can trace its direct lineage at least back

to the English and European hospitals of the 17th and 18th Centuries when they were primarily for the sick, homeless poor. Care was little more than room and board with religious hospitals adding prayer for the repose of the immortal soul. There is some evidence which suggests that these hospitals were more public health and sanitation institutions than they were health care institutions. The sick poor and homeless were kept off the streets and concentrated in one place where they could be cared for economically, out of the sight and conscience of the community and where they would not otherwise contaminate the community.

The early history of hospitals is not unlike the history of welfare domiciliary institutions dating back to the alms house of the same period and forward to the poor farm era, some of which still exists in this country today.

Even in its earlier history in this country, the hospital was a place of last resort; a place to go only if one could not be treated at home. One of the reasons for the initiation of the Boston Dispensary Home Care Program in 1796 was to provide care at home for the indigent sick person. Hospitalization had been only for the sick poor or homeless, but now some indigent sick patients could receive care at home as did their more well-to-do neighbors.

The trend towards the hospital as a place of preference for care is a phenomena of the 20th Century. The beginning of this trend can probably be placed near the close of World War I. With advances in hospital care, hospitalization became more acceptable and in some cases desirable during the 1920's.

As the hospital became the place of preference for care, long hospital stays for care and recovery were not uncommon. As medicine advanced, the length of hospital stay shortened. The trend toward shorter hospital stay was related not only to scientific advances in medicine, but to the need for more effective utilization of hospital beds and to the availability of appropriate patient care elsewhere for prolonged illness and extended recovery.

The hospital is emerging as the medical center of the community. An acute general hospital represents probably the most comprehensive collection of diagnostic and treatment facilities available in the community. The beds in hospitals are needed for housing and care of patients whose conditions require use of the hospital's diagnostic and treatment facilities. Obviously, beds are needed in hospitals so that the patient can be close to these facilities and can be under comprehensive nursing care. Hospitals are expensive to build and to operate. It follows that the patient should be moved from the hospital bed as soon as he no longer requires comprehensive nursing or close proximity to diagnostic and treatment facilities.

The role of the hospital just described is comparatively new in terms of the history of hospitals. It is within recent history that the hospital has become a place for the artful practice of the science of medicine. Medical historians tell us that it has been little more than fifty years since the physician has been able to effectively change the course of human illness. In the last fifty years there have been great scientific advancements in medicine focusing on hospitals.

Physicians are also changing from the opinion that the patient is too ill to leave the hospital until he is well enough to go home. The cardinal exception to this statement has been the patient who has been chronically ill, was not making progress, and required nursing care that was not available at home. In such circumstances, the patient would be transferred to a nursing home.

As the nature of the hospital changes from an emphasis on bed care with treatment facilities attached, to that of a community health center with beds as a necessary adjunct of its diagnostic and treatment capabilities, other facilities must be made available for extended convalescence, nursing care, etc. when these cannot be accomplished independently at home. This, then, is the role of nursing home care in the total spectrum of patient care.

From this point of view it should be emphasized that the key issue is the physician, his treatment of his patients, his utilization of hospital diagnostic and treatment facilities, his transfer of the patient to nursing home care and his utilization of nursing home facilities for continuing care of the patient. The introduction of the nursing home as an important care facility for the physician's utilization requires a change in thinking on the part of the physician as well as a change in his value system. Advances in medicine have conquered most of the acute illnesses enabling the physician to more fully turn his attention toward chronic disease. Chronic disease now represents a new horizon for the physician to conquer and a new challenge for medical leadership.

In the past, many chronically-ill patients were placed in nursing homes because they could not be cared for at home, or perhaps their care at home was not convenient and they were placed "out of the way." They were also "out of the way" of the hospital and "out of the way" of the physician whose prime concern was acute care. Physicians traditionally have been minimally motivated to attend patients with chronic disease whose conditions were essentially static; reluctant to travel out of their normal path to office and hospital to visit nursing home patients; and very concerned about placing their patients where the capability of staff to follow their orders might be in doubt. The patient was therefore essentially left to the nursing care of the nursing home; care which differed widely. Differences depended on motivation, preparation, and capability of the staff. However, the biggest variable was the amount the public was willing to pay for nursing home care. For those who could afford to pay for the care they needed, there was of course no problem. Physicians have been reluctant to transfer patients out of hospitals where insurance coverage or tax dollars pay for care and into nursing homes which are not covered. This has resulted in a higher than necessary utilization of hospitals and a lower than desirable utilization of nursing home facilities.

Parallel with the hospital's giving up its role in long-term care to the nursing home, a welfare trend was occurring. Alms house, poor house and poor farm were some of the terms used for the domiciliary institutions for the indigent well aged. They were predominately public institutions, although some religious and fraternal sponsored institutions provided care for their indigent members as well as for those who could pay for their own care. Special housing has been provided by government for military veterans and merchant seamen. While some of these institutions still exist, many of them have changed in nature and in so doing have more fully recognized the dignity of man. A major contribution to this movement was the original Social Security Act and its subsequent amendments over the past thirty-five years. The old age assistance amendment which provided a welfare cash grant for subsistence of a person over age sixty-five, was a significant step forward in the concept of the recipient's right to make his own decision of where and how he would spend his monthly cash grant for housing and care. He was no longer forced to enter a government operated poor house as virtually the only method of receiving public assistance with the necessities of life. This freedom of choice contributed greatly to the development of nongovernmental homes for the aged, both tax exempt and profit-making facilities. It appears that the decline in number of local, state, and federal domiciliary institutions is related to this cash grant freedom of decision program in old age assistance as well as to the straight social security benefits program which provides minimum retirement income for those who are retired wage earners. Of course, the cardinal exception has been the domiciliary program of the Veteran's Administration at the federal level.

Medical progress has been spectacular, resulting in longer life and a larger number of aged persons, only some of whom are ill with a significant chronic disease. Our culture, which traditionally pays greatest attention to youth, was faced with a geriatric problem which had grown so large that it could no longer be ignored. Those over age sixty-five now comprise approximately 10 percent of the total population, whereas at the beginning of this century, they made up only 4 percent of the total population. As with other facilities for caring for aged indigent persons, the poor farm generally existed on a meager budget in a place away from the attention and conscience of the community. One example of such a facility was the Los Angeles County Poor Farm which, at its origin in the late 1800's and up to the post World War II era when the Southern California population explosion occurred, was well away from the center of Los Angeles in an agricultural area. It was indeed out of sight and out of mind. Through the efforts of a concerned administrator, the facility's name was changed to Rancho Los Amigos. The facility's mailing address remained Los Angeles County Farm until that same administrator prevailed upon the United States Postal Service and obtained a post office substation titled Hondo, California. The primary motivation for this man's effort to disguise the address of the facility was to reduce the stigma and guilt of relatives which was caused by sending mail to or receiving mail from relatives at a county poor farm.

The two trends of health care of the chronic diseased aged and the domiciliary care of the well aged have amalgamated to form an industry of facilities providing long-term health and personal or domiciliary care of aged persons, operating under a large variety of names but generically referred to as nursing homes. Welfare trends have added their importance because, as statistics provided by the 1971 White House Conference on Aging show, over 70 percent of those over age sixty-five have no source of income other than Social Security. The increase in numbers of persons living beyond age sixty-five, as well as the increase in their percentage of total population has served to add emphasis and importance to this growing industry. Added emphasis is caused by the shift from government operated facilities to those which are proprietary and nonprofit operations.

NURSING HOME DEFINITIONS

Convalescent hospital, sanitarium, sanatorium, convalarium, convalorium, rest home, guest home, home for the aged, senior citizen's home, retirement home, residential care home, boarding home for the aged, and other such names have been used to denote facilities which care for aged persons. The generic term for such facilities has been "nursing home."

Nursing homes are expected to provide two types of care.

They are health care (physiologic care) and personal care (psychosocial care). There has been, however, a wide range of individual differences in nursing homes. Some have been heavily oriented towards providing health care and minimizing personal care, while others, generally referred to as homes for the aged, have concentrated more fully on the personal care aspects. Individual differences in nursing homes include such factors as size of facility, location, cost of care, staffing patterns, care service mix, patient/resident orientation and financial motivations. The different mixtures of kinds of care in institutions is graphically presented on the following chart.

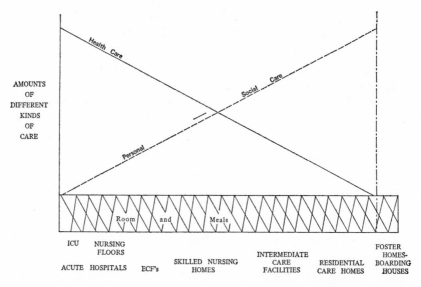

Various types of institutions are arranged according to their diminishing amounts of health care in the mixture of care services provided. All institutions on the chart from Extended Care facilities (ECF's) through residential care homes fall within the generic term of "nursing home."

Until 1970 there was no acceptable definition of the term nursing home, although several agencies had attempted to make some definition. In 1970 the National Advisory Council on Nursing Home Administration, fulfilling part of its charge from Congress, advised the Secretary of Health, Education, and Welfare and the States of their recommended definition of the term "nursing home." The American College of Nursing Home Administrators, the professional society for the field, adopted essentially the same definition and these definitions have since been endorsed by other national figures and agencies. The definitions as they have been adopted and presented for use across the nation by the American College of Nursing Home Administrators are as follows:

A *Nursing Home or its equivalent* is a facility, institution or an identifiable unit of an acute hospital or other care service facility or institution licensed for:

1. Care for persons who because of physical or mental conditions, or both, require or desire living accommodations and care which as a practical matter, can best be made available to them through institutional facilities, other than acute care units of hospitals, providing a protective and/or supervised environment, and

2. Care of persons and patients who require a combination of health care service and personal care services which are in addition to the above and may include, but are not necessarily restricted to one or more of the following care services.

   a. Therapeutic diets,

   b. Regular observation of the patient's physical and mental condition,

   c. Personal assistance including bathing, dressing, grooming, ambulation, transportation, housekeeping (such as bed making, dusting, etc.) or living quarters,

   d. A program of social and recreational activities,

   e. Assistance with self-administered medications,

   f. Emergency medical care including bedside nursing during temporary periods of illness,

   g. Professional nursing supervision,

   h. Skilled nursing care,

   i. Medical care and services by a licensed practitioner,

j. Other special medical and social care services for diagnostic and treatment purposes of rehabilitative. restorative, or maintenance nature, designed to restore and/or maintain the person in the most normal phys· ical and social condition attainable.

Care is defined as the assumption of responsibility for the custody, safety, and physical well-being of unrelated persons who are not fully capable of providing for their own needs because of physical, mental, social and/or emotional disabilities to the extent that they are dependent on the competency or training of another person to assist them with daily living.

NURSING HOME STANDARDS AND LICENSING

Society in many ways establishes minimum acceptable standards and enforces those standards through various means. Society draws on a variety of resources for reimbursement of care provided under those standards. There are social and cultural means by which standards are set and enforced, and there are many resources including voluntary contributions which pay for care. Generally, payment for care requires adherence to the payor's standards. Currently, the most typical means of establishing standards is through licensing; enforcement of standards through inspection and verification of compliance and conformance with licensing requirements; and reimbursement from government tax sources with its attendant verification of compliance with government standards as a condition of payment.

There were very few programs for licensing nursing homes prior to 1947. Since that time, there has been a growth of standard-setting programs in state government as well as standards imposed through federal programs such as Medicare and Medicaid. Standards have been constantly moving to higher levels. In earlier days, well within adult memories, society permitted care of the aged in many settings with few restrictions so long as the care programs remained out of the public eye and public attention, preferably remaining on the edge of town where the conscience of the relatives and the community could not be confronted with their existence. Nursing homes were allowed to function so long as they raised no attention nor demanded no more funds than the public was willing to pay for whatever meager care they provided to the aging. The beginning of change was the Hill-Burton Program for federal grant-in-aid to hospital planning and construction. A requirement for a state to receive Hill-Burton funds was that a licensing program be in existence and this licensing program included nursing homes. No great emphasis was placed on nursing home standards until the population of persons over age sixty-five reached seventeen million in 1965. This was too large a political voting population to ignore and government responded to their demands by enacting Medicare and Medicaid with their attendant standards and regulations.

Now that the population of senior citizens has grown to over twenty million, the demand for higher standards is heard in an even louder voice. In former years, the fact that nursing homes were allowed to function without a great deal of restriction only provided for a wide range of individual differences between facilities. Some of them were very good and some of them were very bad. Through licensing, the elevation of society's minimum standards to a higher and higher level has served to decrease the range of differences between facilities by forcing the low standard facilities to come up to a higher minimum standard. The Medicare and Medicaid laws have mandated that extended care facilities, certified nursing homes, and skilled nursing homes become full and equal partners with hospitals in the provision of care appropriate to the patient's needs. To insure this, utilization review committees have been required to validate the appropriateness of care. Transfer agreements between hospitals and nursing homes have been required to facilitate placement of the patient according to his needs. In increasing the minimum standards for nursing home care to its highest level in history, there has been a considerable narrowing of the range of differences between nursing homes. These high standards of

Medicare have set the norm of most nursing home care regardless of who pays for that care because there is such a large percentage of all nursing home patients who are Medicare or Medicaid elegible. Any private party or third party payor must therefore be prepared to purchase nursing home care at a standard not less than that set by Medicare and Medicaid.

Even though there is room for improvement in standards, reimbursement for care is not yet equal to the standards of the state of California that now exist. In the Department of Health Care Services there has been a Standards and Rates Unit which to this point has never been successful in equating government standards and government reimbursement rates for care. One can assume that the failure to report to the public the effort of the Standards and Rates Unit is mute testimony to the fact that their investigation showed clearly that reimbursement was inadequate to meet present government standards.

Nursing homes are part of the health delivery system. Two of the determinants of any system are *inputs to* and *constraints on* the system. Minimum standards in the form of enforced regulations represent a constraint on the health delivery system. Reimbursement represents an input to the system, but, if amounts of reimbursement are too low, it can represent a constraint on it.

If any system, especially a health delivery system is to function properly, its determinants cannot be in conflict. That is to say, the regulations which form a constraint on minimum performance of the system cannot be in conflict with the financial input to the system which must serve to pay for performance at a minimum standard. If reimbursement as an input is inadequate to meet standards of care required by the regulations, then reimbursement changes its position as an input and becomes a constraint limiting the system's ability to meet minimum standards. In such an instance, a conflict of determinants has arisen.

While government has been talking health delivery systems, government has at the same time failed to recognize this elementary requirement of any system—that its determinants may not be in conflict. It further serves to highlight the fact that government as a third party payor has failed to realize that all third party payors are inputs or constraints on the system and *not a part of* the system itself.

Unfortunately, Medicare standards neglected to consider the long-term patient whose nursing care needs were minimal and who did not need the continuous nursing required by Medicare. In like manner, their needs for the services for all of the paramedical specialties required by Medicare were minimal. For that matter, Medicare and Medicaid did not recognize that some persons admitted to nursing homes were in need only of personal care services in a protective environment and found the nursing home the most desirable or perhaps the only facility in the community available to meet their needs. For this type of patient, the standards for care are inappropriate and unnecessarily costly.

A further result of this oversight has been an amendment to the Social Security Law creating a new level of care called Intermediate Care. It was the intention of Congress that Intermediate Care cover the range of services from something more than board and room to skilled nursing home care. However, the implementation of this program has been found difficult and long delayed. What its impact will be ulitmately on the standards of long-term care is difficult to tell. It is further difficult to tell how this level of care will fit into the total spectrum of care; how it will relate to existing state licensing regulations, etc.

Residential care homes for the aged are sometimes referred to as nonskilled nursing homes. States deal with this type of facility in differing ways. Some states have not licensed nonskilled nursing homes at all. Some states have licensed some nonskilled nursing homes but not all of them. Some states license these facilities as residential care homes for the aged while others license them as adult group care facilities. Still others establish nursing home license categories as skilled, nonskilled, levels a, b, and c, or levels 1, 2, and 3, etc.

The enticement of more federal dollars or the threat of withholding federal dollars are strong motivators for a state to accede to the will of the federal government in establishing standards and licensing programs. The flow of federal dollars tends to predict what services and standards will be included or required for each particular level of care.

Despite this standardizing force, there is still a wide range of differences in how the fifty states license nursing homes, particularly the nonskilled nursing homes. Until there is a single set of definitions and standards, universally accepted, and in practice in all of the states, one can count on confusion and misunderstanding on the part of local, state, and federal governments, as well as by the public at large. Sadly, it is all too common that cities and counties have local regulations relative to the zoning and building, fire and safety standards which are not consistent with the licensing requirements of the state government or reimbursement requirements of the federal government.

Misunderstandings lead to false expectations as to nursing homes services to be provided. When one makes the assumption that all long-term care facilities, predominately caring for aged persons are called nursing homes, and one further assumes that the term nursing home implies that the facility is staffed with registered nurses, then one would expect to see registered nurses in attendance in every nursing home. Visiting a nursing home without registered nurses would then lead one to assume that proper nursing home standards of care were not being met. In reality, the nursing home visited might very well be a nonskilled nursing home or residential care home for aged, which perhaps is in fact prohibited by law from employing registered nurses. At the same time, the nonskilled nursing home might be providing the highest possible standards of care within its license category.

False expectations born of misunderstanding represent a terrible disservice to older people who are in need of nursing home services and who, at the same time, perhaps have concerns or fears for the future. Attempting to select the proper facility and the proper licensing category to meet his needs may be an insurmountable task for the older person.

It does not appear that a useful purpose would be served by giving examples of different licensing regulations. On the other hand, the reader is advised to make himself fully aware of the licensing regulations of each state in which he expects to have dealings with long-term care. He should know how many categories of facility licenses there are and what each category of licensing requires, permits, and prohibits. Only in this way can one begin to intelligently match level of care service with the specific needs of older persons.

In the meantime, on a voluntary basis, the field itself has attempted to set standards higher than those required by facility licensing. Institutional associations have established codes of ethics or guiding principles and the Joint Commission on Accreditation of Hospitals has entered the field of long-term-care facility accreditation. Unfortunately, a problem exists with the Joint Commission on Accreditation of Hospitals in that their classification of long-term care facilities does not properly relate to the licensing categories for long-term-care facilities used in all of the states. This fact again highlights the need for uniform definitions that have been adopted by the National Advisory Council on Nursing Home Administration and the American College of Nursing Home Administrators.

Several groups of physicians have introduced plans for accrediting the medical staff of nursing homes. This kind of program is desirable and helpful to nursing homes in maintaining higher standards through the medical profession reviewing and accrediting its peers and their performance within the facility. An organized medical staff exists in only a limited number of nursing homes. This is in contrast to the prevalence of organized medical staffs in acute hospitals. A medical staff organization is primarily controlled by the economic factor of the physician's need for medical staff privileges in the hospital in order to conduct his practice. His need for staff privileges in nursing homes does not have the same kind of economic mandate. Because of the lack of either professional or economic incentive, physicians' interest in medical staff activities for a nursing home is at a very low ebb and not a worthy competitor for priority attention of his time. Such things as medical staff accreditation that would make the concept of a medical staff or medical staff equivalents more viable and useful would be of great help. Once this concept were in operation, the idea of nursing home medical staff accreditation through the medical society would be highly desirable.

Standards are meaningless without inspection and enforcement mechanisms. The enforcement mechanisms are generally the responsibility of state agencies that inspect licensed facilities. Inspection requires trained observers who can understand what they see and properly interpret their observations. For the most part, the inspectors from the various state agencies who inspect the functions of long-term care are knowledgeable and experienced. While they may have their own biases, they are usually well prepared to perform their function of observation and enforcement. This is not to say that they could not be better prepared through further training, and additional training is being required by new regulations of the Medicare program. Such higher level of preparation of inspectors is a great step forward and it should be followed by the further step of requiring that inspectors of long-term-care facilities, themselves, be licensed nursing home administrators. They should be professionally responsible for their decisions in the same fashion that the administrator is responsible for his decisions. Further, the status and authority of the inspector would become more potent when he is licensed and speaks not only authoritatively but responsibly as a licensed professional.

Disciplinary action continues to be a long and difficult path. It will probably always be difficult because it is heavily laden with the responsibility of protecting each citizen's rights. The judicial and administrative procedures to afford such protection mandate a careful review of charges of wrong doing before a judgment of guilty is handed down and discipline is handed out. This problem is by no means confined to the field of long-term care. Rather, it is one which has attracted the attention of many people who are giving serious attention to the improvement of administrative and judicial review of disciplinary systems and procedures.

Many laymen to the field of long-term care have observed and then delivered themselves of opinions relative to nursing homes and nursing home care. Some of their observations have been complementary and some have been the opposite. No matter how well motivated the opinions may be, the validity of the statement is open to challenge purely on the basis of the lay observer's ability to properly interpret what he sees in a nursing home care program. Some newspaper reporters, not bothering to properly prepare themselves, have looked for sensational stories. Relatives, reacting from a guilt feeling, indeed even the patients reacting against their own infirmities and age, are not reliable observers and interpreters. Other well-meaning persons concerned with their fellow man have also attempted to function as observers, but their inexperience has caused the same lack of reliability. The problem, of course, has been further complicated by the confusion of definitions and misunderstanding as to the proper role and function of each license category of long-term-care facilities. The use of such observations may be very damaging to all persons concerned with long-term care. Damage results from unfounded statements magnified by sensational reporting in public news media in the form of loss of confidence in nursing homes on the part of the general public, community resentment and perhaps pressure for regulatory agencies to be more restrictive.

Still greater damage can occur to older people already fearful of care available to them, who, because of misinformation, generate greater and unwarranted fear of admission to nursing homes for care. Their adjustment to a nursing home, when their needs require admission, may be monumental and in some cases impossible. Certainly, it can create a delay in seeking admission well beyond indications of need, thereby making a debilitating condition more severe, less tractable and requiring of more care. The end result can be that life for the older person, in or out of a nursing home, is less satisfying and perhaps shortened.

On the other hand, the need for public understanding and concern over care in nursing homes cannot be underestimated. It is an essential factor in upgrading standards of care through social pressure. For too long, the nursing home has remained on the outskirts of town, out of sight, out of mind, and out of public concern. The important issue is how lay public observations and concerns can best be used. It is preferable that such concerns be expressed to the administration of nursing homes, to the organizations representing nursing homes and/or to the governmental agencies which license them. Through this means, misunderstandings may be clarified or legitimate concerns may be placed more quickly in the hands of those responsible for correcting problems which may exist. It is also incumbent on the nursing home industry, its profession, and government to reduce confusion and make a clear understanding of the nature of nursing homes and what the public has a right to expect in the way of care, as a means of bringing legitimate social pressure on nursing homes to improve standards.

NURSING HOME ADMINISTRATOR AND OPERATIONS

On January 2, 1968, Public Law 90–248 was signed by President Johnson. In part, this law required that each state wishing to continue receiving medicaid funds, enact a state law to professionally license nursing home administrators. Most of the states complied with the federal requirement and had an administrator licensing law in effect by July 1, 1972. PL 90–248, Section 1908 states, "Nursing home means any institution or facility defined as such for licensing purposes under state law or if state law does not employ the term nursing home, the equivalent term or terms as determined by the Secretary." Secretary in this case refers to the Secretary of Health, Education, and Welfare.

As mentioned earlier, this has left a wide divergence among the states as to those administrators who must be licensed. The National Advisory Council on Nursing Home

Administration, also created by Public Law 90–248, for the purposes of advising the Secretary and the States on licensing of nursing home administrators, recommended that, for the Secretary's purposes, the definitions as stated earlier in this chapter be used. Further, definitions of nursing home administrator and practice of nursing home administration have been recommended and adopted by the American College of Nursing Home Administrators and others. Those definitions are as follows:

> *Nursing Home Administrator* means any individual, who by training and experience, is qualified to assume the responsibility for planning, organizing, directing and/or controlling the operations of a nursing home or its equivalent.

> *Practice of Nursing Home Administration* means the performance of any act or the making of any decision involved in the planning, organizing, directing, and/or control of the operation of a nursing home or its equivalent.

The definition of the practice of nursing home administration is a functional definition and provides a broad framework which must be filled-in with additional description. As with all professions, one means of setting the limits of professional practice is to say "that which is the usual and customary prevailing practice in the community is regarded as a standard of practice." Another means is to identify those subject areas that are tested on the professional licensing examination and assume that by passing the examination, the professional has demonstrated his knowledge, skill, and ability in the subject areas at the depth to which the examination has tested him. He is therefore accountable before the law to properly use that knowledge, skill, and ability. In the case of the professional licensing of nursing home administrators, the core of knowledge used as the subject areas for professional licensing examinations has been developed by both the Professional Examination Service and the National Advisory Council on Nursing Home Administration and further adopted by the federal government in regulations. It has also been generally accepted and used for examinations in the majority of states. The nine basic areas of that core of knowledge is as follows:

(1) Applicable standards of environmental health and safety:
    (i) Hygiene and sanitation.
    (ii) Communicable diseases.
    (iii) Management of isolation.
    (iv) The total environment (noise, color, orientation, stimulation, temperature, lighting, air circulation).
    (v) Elements of accident prevention.
    (vi) Special architectural needs of nursing home patients.
    (vii) Drug handling and control.
    (viii) Safety factors in oxygen usage.

(2) Local health and safety regulations: Guidelines vary according to local provisions.

(3) General administration:
    (i) Institutional administration.
    (ii) Planning, organizing, directing, controlling, staffing, coordinating, and budgeting.
    (iii) Human relations:
        (a) Management/employee interrelationships.
        (b) Employee/employee interrelationships.
        (c) Employee/patient interrelationships.
        (d) Employee/family interrelationships.
    (iv) Training of personnel:
        (a) Training of employees to become sensitive to patient needs.
        (b) Ongoing in-service training/education.

(4) Psychology of patient care:
    (i) Anxiety.
    (ii) Depression.
    (iii) Drugs, alcohol, and their effect.
    (iv) Motivation.
    (v) Separation reaction.

(5) Principles of medical care:
    (i) Anatomy and physiology.
    (ii) Psychology.
    (iii) Disease recognition.
    (iv) Disease process.
    (v) Nutrition.
    (vi) Aging processes.
    (vii) Medical terminology.
    (viii) Materia Medica.
    (ix) Medical Social Service.
    (x) Utilization review.
    (xi) Professional and Medical Ethics.

(6) Personal and social care:
    (i) Resident and patient care planning.
    (ii) Activity programming:
      (a) Patient participation.
      (b) Recreation.
    (iii) Environmental adjustment: interrelationships between patient and:
      (a) Patient.
      (b) Staff (staff sensitivity to patient needs as a therapeutic function).
      (c) Family and friends.
      (d) Administrator.
      (e) Management (self-government/patient council).
    (iv) Rehabilitation and restorative activities:
      (a) Training in activities of daily living.
      (b) Techniques of group therapy.
    (v) Interdisciplinary interpretation of patient care to:
      (a) The patient.
      (b) The staff.
      (c) The family.

(7) Therapeutic and supportive care and services in long-term care:
    (i) Individual care planning as it embraces all therapeutic care and supportive services.

   (ii) Meaningful observations of patient behavior as related to total patient care.

  (iii) Interdisciplinary evaluation and revision of patient care plans and procedures.

  (iv) Unique aspects and requirements of geriatric patient care.

   (v) Professional staff interrelationships with patient's physician.

  (vi) Professional ethics and conduct.

 (vii) Rehabilitative and remotivational role of individual therapeutic and supportive services.

(viii) Psychological, social, and religious needs, in addition to physical needs of patient.

  (ix) Needs for dental service.

(8) Departmental organization and management:

   (i) Criteria for coordinating establishment of departmental and unit objectives.

  (ii) Reporting and accountability of individual departments to administrator.

  (iii) Criteria for departmental evaluation (nursing, food service, therapeutic services, maintenance, housekeeping).

  (iv) Techniques of providing adequate professional, therapeutic, supportive, and administrative services.

   (v) The following departments may be used in relating matters of organization and management:

    (*a*) Nursing.

    (*b*) Housekeeping.

    (*c*) Dietary.

    (*d*) Laundry.

    (*e*) Pharmaceutical services.

    (*f*) Social service.

    (*g*) Business office.

    (*h*) Recreation.

    (*i*) Medical records.

    (*j*) Admitting.

(*k*) Physical therapy.
(*l*) Occupational therapy.
(*m*) Medical and dental services.
(*n*) Laboratories.
(*o*) X-ray.
(*p*) Maintenance.

(9) Community interrelationships:
    (i) Community medical care, rehabilitative and social services resources.
    (ii) Other community resources:
        (*a*) Religious institutions.
        (*b*) Schools.
        (*c*) Service agencies.
        (*d*) Government agencies.
    (iii) Third party payment organizations.
    (iv) Comprehensive health planning agencies.
    (v) Volunteers and auxiliaries.

[FR Doc. 71—13213 Filed 9-8-71; 8:46 am]

In effect, the licensing of nursing home administrators has created a new set of standards. These standards are so new that their effectiveness in terms of influence on nursing home care has yet to be tried. On the other hand, one can predict that they will have an impact on care since the administrator must meet some minimum standards; and because of his professional licensing, his relationship with other professionals such as physicians or RN's will change. It can be seen from the core of knowledge which the administrator is held accountable for knowing and using, that he is in effect professionally licensed to manage a care program. Since an administrator's continued permission to practice his profession rests with his newly obtained professional license, he is less likely to jeopardize his ability to continue functioning than might have been the case before. For this reason, administrators are likely to demand that other professionals perform to a higher standard so that the total care program under the administrator's jurisdiction will be of a sufficiently high standard to safeguard against any malpractice or license revocation proceedings against him. In addition, there will be a change in responsibilities in that the licensed administrator and not the owner of the facility, unless he too is licensed, will have the ultimate responsibility for the care program. In this sense there is a break between ownership and administration in the chain of command.

In essence, the nursing home administrator is charged with the responsibility to know and apply basic concepts of management especially in the particular area of care institution administration, as well as have a knowledge of the elements of health care and personal care. He is responsible for the operations of the nursing home which involve the departmental functions listed above in the core of knowledge. The resultant care program of a nursing home should be based on preplanning as well as the three M's of management, men, money, and materials.

Preplanning should include a feasibility study that determines the needs of the community. This should include not only an identification of the care services but also the number of potential patients or residents which can be expected to be admitted to the nursing home. As described in the definition, a nursing home provides living accommodations plus one or more care services which are listed in the definition. The list of potential care services may be categorized as health care services and personal care services. The quantity and quality of mixtures of health and personal care services planned for the nursing home should be consistent with the needs of the community for such services. Further, licensing requirements must be considered as to services allowed, services required, and services specifically prohibited by the licensing category contemplated. Local requirements must be met in terms of land use such as zoning or conditional use permits, life safety, fire safety regulations, as well as all other requirements of regulatory agencies.

No matter how great the community need may be or how large the market of potential patients or residents, the development of a nursing home must be financially sound. If there are not funds to pay for the quantity and quality of services needed in the community, then the project should be determined not to be feasible. The lack of funding can result only in great disappointment and failure to meet expectations of high standards of care, and in the long run, result in poor quality of care and failure of the facility to provide a needed service. Part of preplanning must be capital financing for the development of the physical facility itself as well as operating capital reserve. The initial expense of opening a new nursing home can be anticipated to greatly exceed income realized until the occupancy of the nursing home has reached approximately 80 percent of capacity. Failure to provide for reserves to meet a negative cash flow resulting from more start up expenses than there is income can spell doom to the nursing home before it really begins to provide a community service.

The administrator is responsible for determining needs for staffing, recruiting, organizing, and supervising the staff of the nursing home which provides services to its patients or residents. Within the framework of the plan for a mix of personal and health care services, a staff of full-time, part-time, and consulting specialists must be provided. Provisions for landscape and facility maintenance, housekeeping, and food service are basic to all nursing homes. In addition, especially for skilled nursing homes, arrangements must be made for RN's, social workers, dietary consultation, medical direction, medical records supervision, etc. The level of care and mixture of care services will predict the staffing required. However, for those facilities that are to be Medicare and/or Medicaid certified, there are basic staff requirements that are necessary for participation in those reimbursement programs. This of course is in addition to the basic requirements which may be included in the separate state licensing laws.

The administrator has the added responsibility of effectively organizing the staff so that there is integration of their functions. This is not only done by a plan of organization which may include for larger facilities a departmentalization of the organization, but it also involves the development of the institution's policies, and the procedures for the implementation of those policies. Even though specialized departmental policies and procedures such as nursing procedure manuals or dietary manuals may be left to the department head to develop, it is still incumbent upon the administrator to make sure that the procedures are in fact developed, that they contribute to the proper standard of care and that the departmental procedures integrate with all other procedures so that there is an effective, smooth, total program of care services to the patients or residents. It can be seen that the roll of the administrator is far more than the usual and routine management of men, money, and materials since he assumes the responsibility for the custody, safety, and physical well-being of the patients or residents.

The function of managing a care program involves a continuing process which is subject to change because of licensing requirements, community needs, and patient needs. It is therefore the administrator's responsibility to continually observe, change, and adjust the care program to meet changing needs.

In addition to the administration of a care program, the nursing home administrator must be a business manager and deal with the more common issues of insurance, taxes, licenses, plant maintenance and planned maintenance and repair programs, landscaping maintenance, and financial management. Financial management goes well beyond bookkeeping, billing, accounting, and indeed includes financial reporting and the analysis of financial reports for both financial and operations management purposes.

Information from financial reports may often be the first indication of a troublesome area of operations. Not only the increase in costs, but the decrease in costs may flag a problem. If there is a decline in the housekeeping supplies expense category, this may be an indication that not enough attention is being paid to housekeeping. An increase in raw food costs may be an indication of waste, theft, or inefficient operation of the kitchen. Increasing salary costs may be the first indicator of a high turnover of staff and a problem in departmental supervision.

Financial reports for financial management are equally important since it is essential to maintain a balance between income and expense as well as to maintain a positive cash flow.

It is extremely rare that a nursing home is developed and operated without borrowing capital. Before loaning money, a lender wants to be assured that his money is safe and that it will be repaid. In part the answer to his questions are found in a feasibility study as mentioned above. In part the answers to his concerns depend upon the projection of income and expense of the nursing home. There must be a margin of income over expense, that margin being called profit in propritary nursing homes and surplus in nonprofit homes. In both cases, the margin of net income over expense is essential to assure the lender that funds will be available to repay his loan. Without the anticipation of a reasonable margin of profit, it is extremely difficult to obtain a loan for the development of a nursing home and certainly it is a factor in obtaining a loan at reasonable interest rates since the margin of profit anticipated is an indicator of the degree of risk the lender is taking in making the loan.

Without a positive cash flow and balance of income over expense, an administrator could find himself in a position of being forced to cut services. This can be a vicious circle of reducing services, quantity, and quality of care until the nursing home is found substandard and closed. The administrator, therefore, must be in a position to exercise sound judgment in fiscal matters in order to protect the higher standards of patient care desired.

The nursing home administrator has an important role in public relations and community involvement as well as planning to meet the changing needs of the community. He must not only let the community know of the services which his nursing home provides, but he must also make sure that his care program is well integrated with the other care facilities of the community. This in part is the reason for the Medicare requirement that there be a transfer agreement between community acute hospitals and skilled nursing homes that are certified under Medicare as extended care facilities.

By the same token, the skilled nursing home should be very familiar with the services provided by nonskilled nursing homes or homes for the aged in his community so that when a patient's needs shift from a predominance of health care services to a predominance of personal care services, the patient can be transferred to a status of residency in a residential care home or home for the aged. In each case the reverse is true. When a resident in a home for the aged is judged to need greater health care than can be provided, the administrator should be alert to this fact and help to arrange transfer to an appropriate facility that does provide for a greater component of health care. In like fashion the nursing home administrator must be alert to needs for greater care than his facility may be equipped to provide and encourage the physician to order a transfer of his patient to an acute hospital.

As the demographic, social, and cultural aspects of the community change, so also does the role of the nursing home in the community. Many of these changes result in changes in licensing requirements, reimbursement programs, etc. Some recent changes nationally are the federal interest in new programs of intermediate care, of health maintenance organizations, and in the inclusion of nursing homes at all levels in local and state comprehensive health planning organizations. Indeed, it is incumbent upon the licensed administrator to play an active role in the community, especially in agencies and organizations which influence the changing nature of health and personal care delivery systems as well as reimbursement for care. It is important for the administrator to keep himself well informed of changes. Because of this, most state laws professionally licensing the nursing home administrator require some continuing education for reregistration of his license. It is therefore evident that the administrator must, if he is fully accomplishing his role, arrange the internal operations of his nursing home, through patterns of delegation, so that he is free to spend a considerable amount of time outside of the four walls of the home itself and in the community at large.

One indicator of the standards of a nursing home is evidence that the administrator is participating in the community. Evidence of membership in the nursing home associations, in the American College of Nursing Home Administrators, participation in various community health or welfare-related organizations are all positive indicators. At the same time, one must certainly take advantage of the sense of sight and smell in observing a nursing home. Its odors, its appearance of cleanliness, the cleanliness and neatness of residents and patients all reflect the standards of the nursing home.

PATIENT/RESIDENT PLACEMENT AND FINANCING CARE

Since its beginning, social security coverage has expanded until nine out of ten workers are contributing to social security. More workers are retiring with social security benefits and more beneficiaries are approaching full benefits. In addition, there are more nongovernmental retirement plans over and above social security, all of which make financial consideration less of a restriction for skilled nursing care. However, recent reports indicate that more than 70 percent of all persons over age sixty-five have no source of income other than social security. Nursing homes on the average find that more than 70 percent (in some areas 80 to 90 percent) of their patients have government as a third party payor for care. In addition to social security and other personal financial resources for daily living, Medicare and other private coinsurance plans for health and medical care, old age assistance and other state welfare programs exist for those who find themselves totally indigent. In most states Medicaid (grants to states for medical assistance) is available for those who are totally indigent or for those who are partially indigent with respect to resources for paying health care expenses (medically indigent).

While government programs for financing subsistence and health care exist, they are not adequately funded. This presents a considerable problem since the vast majority of nursing home patients and residents are dependent on financial assistance from those government programs. Inadequate funding may make it virtually impossible to provide services at the standards required and in the quantity and quality consistent with the person's needs. Inadequate funding and therefore inadequate return can make lenders more fearful of loaning the money necessary for capital financing of needed beds to replace substandard physical facilities as well as to meet the needs in communities where bed shortages exist. Inadequate funding can also be a deterrent to attracting well qualified staff for service in the nursing home. In addition, attempts to compensate for the inadequacies of government financing can put an unnecessarily high drain on the personal resources of private paying patients or residents.

Equally restrictive and categorized are the requirements, restrictions, and constraints on providers of service, especially where the requirements of third party payors, predominately government, are added to the requirements of professional and facility licensing.

Discussions of specific regulations would be of little value since they would be immediately outdated by the rapidly changing nature of regulations, and in addition, such a discussion would not be universally applicable to the situations in all states.

Unfortunately, people do not fit neatly into well-constructed categories and there are few if any well-defined dividing lines with respect to human needs for care. The result is a difficult job in identifying each person's individual needs for care. A person's needs for personal care, the social or cultural setting in which he functions best, his needs for physical health care and mental health care must all be considered.

The individual's social situation must also be considered. For example, if there is a spouse living whose needs for care are different, would placement in a skilled or nonskilled nursing home mean separation from the spouse to the detriment of both husband and wife? The financial situation must be considered; that is the availability of personal and community resources to pay for the care needed as well as to meet related financial needs. Again, the example of a living spouse, will he or she have enough money to meet living and care needs? In all cases it is most important to preserve and improve if possible the person's physical, mental, social, and financial condition. Any placement for care should maximize the person's human dignity, human individuality, and right to independence and self-determination. In this sense, providing more care than is needed by the patient or resident, can be as detrimental as not providing enough care.

If the patient's need is for more than personal care, a physician must determine the extent of need for health care. A physician's order will be necessary to admit a patient to a skilled nursing home and to subsequently direct medical care for his patient. If the mental condition of the person is one of the factors requiring care, there may be legal questions relating to conservatorship or legal right to prevent the person from leaving the facility. Conversely, it is also of concern to the facility that they have the legal right to care for such persons and to prevent them from leaving.

A second part of the problem must be dealt with, that being the location of a facility qualified to give the care needed, with the legal authority to provide that care and to receive payment from the financial sources planned for payment.

In all cases of placing a patient or resident, whether it be into one care setting from another care setting, or a new placement from the person's own home, such change in environment should be planned well in advance and the person prepared as much as possible for the change. Any change, particularly a sudden change in the living arrangements of older people can be very traumatic. In some cases it is life threatening. In all cases it is potentially detrimental to the person's adjustment to his new life style. Failure to adjust to the living arrangements of a nursing home may mean that care services are less effective than they would be had the patient more fully adjusted to his circumstances.

THOUGHTS ON THE FUTURE OF LONG-TERM CARE OF THE ELDERLY

The population of the country has been increasing. Improvements in health care have resulted in longer life. The net effect is a larger population of persons over the age of sixty-five years. This age group represents a larger percentage of the total population. Over twenty million persons sixty-five years or older, representing nearly 10 percent of the total population is too large a population segment to overlook, even for a western culture which has historically overlooked the aging in favor of greater concern for its youth.

The trend of our culture has been away from care of the aged in the family home, away from the pattern of more than two generations in the same household. Where institutions for the health and personal care of the elderly primarily served persons who had no family to care for them, the trend has been towards caring for elderly persons without regard to their family status.

Our nation has been described as one obsessed with health, and it is certainly true that health problems are of major importance to the elderly. Health care costs, particulary for the aged, have a significant economic influence.

The merging of these trends has resulted in a trend of higher care standards reflected in licensing and certification regulations; more emphasis on inspection and enforcement mechanisms; and greater concern over reducing the ever-increasing demand for allocation of tax dollars for care of the aged.

The principle thrust of this trend has been a concern for health care. The result has been: (1) an increase in new, larger facilities designed to meet newer and higher health care standards, (2) a decrease in the small, old facilities, generally converted houses, licensable only through grandfather clauses of regulations, (3) an emphasis on meeting health and safety requirements, and (4) a secondary emphasis on the social and cultural elements of care including psychological and mental health aspects, social status, impact of the environment (milieu), etc.

While one would hope for a better balance between the social and health elements of care in the future, the game of "catch-up" which the social elements of care must play is a difficult one.

Health care, especially care of life threatening conditions commands first priority. Budgets and tax dollars as well as assignment of manpower and standards for public safety follow that priority.

High standards are of positive value in protecting the public; however, they also have a negative influence in that they tend to place restrictions on planning new and innovative approaches to care!

Even though social change may be slow, it is nonetheless worth pursuing. In an effort to stimulate innovative thinking which may lead to future action resulting in improvements in care of the aged, the following thoughts are offered. Consider:

1. The trend towards more and better retirement incomes among those reaching the age of sixty-five years.

2. That retirement income may be a family income upon which more than one person is dependent: i.e. a spouse and/ or other family members.

3. The impact on both the social and financial circumstances of the family if one of its members must be separated from the family for care purposes. As an example, a husband and wife living independently, who must be separated because one of them must be admitted to a nursing home for care of a chronic disease while the other one is not sick enough to be admitted.

4. The continuing decline often with small daily exacerbations and remissions of mental health functions, social status and resources, financial status and resources, as well as physical health and functions.

5. The different rates of decline for elderly persons, especially in a family unit. For one, physical health and function may decline rapidly and at an early age leaving an alert mind, while the spouse may remain physically active but suffer a slowly progressing decrement in mental function.

6. That, given proper circumstances, family members of all ages may tend to care for each other more: i.e. an elderly husband may be able to care for his chronically-ill wife in part but is not able to provide full care. He may wish to provide the care he is able to. The offspring of a widowed parent may be able to provide partial care but not full care. Even neighbors on occasion become members of an "extended" family and are eager to give that help which they are able to give. Current practice seems to create dichotomies. One must be responsible for giving all care or give no care at all because the responsibility has shifted exclusively to the staff of a care institution.

7. The possibility of replacing dichotomies with continued which not only permit but encourage family care to its fullest potential.

8. The value of family care, not only in terms of its tangible value to the recipient, but its intangible value of strengthening family ties; the recipient's sense of someone caring, of not being forgotten; the sense of worth on the part of the giver of care, that he or she is needed by someone else and can do something worth while; the contribution to the sense of worth, dignity, self-determination and social status that can be made to both family members giving and receiving care; the reduction of financial impact offered by the family caring for itself and supplemented by paid staff giving support and services only to the degree necessary.

9. The current trend of retired persons moving to mobile home parks apparently because the parks represent an environment offering some physical, social, and economic protection. The mobile home parks may not offer all the protection desired, needed, or anticipated, but they provide more protection than former living arrangements offered and are considered preferable to surrendering to the status of inmate in an institution for aging in order to obtain all the protective environment needed or desired.

With these considerations in mind, and with some innovative thinking, new approaches to design of facilities for care of the elderly can be proposed. The reader is encouraged in this direction and it is the author's profound hope that the considerations above and the suggested planning criteria below will serve as a stimulus to thinking, a mere beginning to planning care settings for the elderly that in the future will meet their total needs better than the facilities which are generally found today.

Proposed planning criteria for facilities to care for the aged might include:

1. Plan care facilities for the total person who has a full spectrum of needs, only one of which is a health need. Other needs are a sense of worth, dignity, self-determination, financial protection, and social, cultural, and psychological protection.

2. Plan for the older person who may be a member of a family unit and may have needs related to protecting his status as an integral part of a family unit.

3. Plan facility for multiple levels of care, anticipating decline at varying rates of physical, mental, and social functions of one or more members of a family unit admitted for care.

4. Adapt to the degree feasible the design concepts from the past of the cottage hospital. Combine them with design concepts of the modern mobile home parks to design a care institution with a noninstitutional milieu, a garden park care institution, recognizing current life styles, small social group living arrangements (constitution of a new "foster" family unit for those who have no family) perhaps where neighbor helps neighbor.

5. Design facilities with maximum flexibility for convenient and economical adaption to changing needs of the resident/patient population.

6. Avoid overbuilding or over design, but do design for efficiency and a strong position in a competitive market, as well as to meet the needs of patient/residents.

7. Design facilities which compensate for functional decline of eyesight, endurance and strength of legs for walking, hands and arms for opening doors and drawers, etc.

8. Design facilities to use environmental stimuli for orientation to compensate for loss of mental function.

9. Locate facilities in areas planned for residential use, and integrate the facility into the residential life rather than the commercial life of the community.

10. Locate facilities in areas where community facilities and services are accessible. These should include churches, libraries, other public buildings, medical and other health services, shopping facilities, social, recreation and entertainment facilities especially for participation as a spectator, senior citizen's centers and services, public health and social services, and public transportation.

11. Locate facilities in areas of social mix with respect to ages, social activities, etc. so as to accommodate the patient resident's desire and capability to participate in the mainstream of community life, observe it and/or conveniently retreat from it when energy and interest wane.

12. Plan for the resident/patients to live in dignity, self-determination and independence, to do as much for themselves and for each other as is feasible as well as for other family members, to assist in care as is common practice in other cultures and countries.

13. Plan for trained staff to observe and assist patient/residents and their families to achieve a proper balance between not enough self-help and too much self-help as well as to efficiently provide needed care services.

14. Plan for the tempo of activities to be consistent with the needs of patients/residents. People tend to slow down in all types of functions as they grow older.

15. Plan for economic impacts, such as keep the family income intact. It costs too much to separate spouses. It is an uneconomical use of family income and/or tax money. It is less costly to allow patient/residents to do as much as possible for themselves instead of requiring paid staff to do everything. Continuing the current practice of staffing with predominantly minimum wage employees may be false economy corrected by fewer, better trained and better paid staff members. Proliforation of tax-exempt care institutions

may be a false economy with respect to tax base, shifting and incidence of taxation, and motivations for cost reduction considerations. Multiple licensing and certification programs, each with its own regulations for standards, inspection, and enforcement may result in duplication of effort, poor utilization of limited professional man power, and excessive administrative costs as compared to results.

Old age can be a difficult time of declining physical, mental, social, and financial resources complicated by increasing needs for more costly care to preserve all of the person's remaining resources. All of society should be concerned and involved. The professionals in long-term care of the aging should provide leadership in reducing despair and increasing recognition of the challenge offered in providing for the needs of older people.

APPENDIX

Listing of Agencies with Transportation Projects in Rural Areas

Alabama

Pickens Community Action   (205) 367-8388
    Committee, Inc.
P.O. Box 348
Carrollton, Alabama 35477

Arkansas

Arkansas Mid-Delta Office of   (501) 338-6408
    Economic Opportunity, Inc.
Third Floor, Court House
Helena, Arkansas 72342

East Central Arkansas Economic   (501) 633-7686
    Opportunity Corporation
P.O. Box 709
Forest City, Arkansas 72335

Bradley County Community Action   (501) 226-5715
    Corporation
P.O. Drawer 312
117 Scotta
Warren, Arkansas 71671

California

Economic Opportunity Commission of   (714) 352-8521
    Imperial County, Inc.
143 South Sixty Street
El Centro, California 92243

Mountain Transportation Cooperative   (916) 652-7247
3500 Midas Avenue
Rocklin, California 95677

Marin Senior Coordinating Council, Inc. (415) 456-9062
"The Depot" 930 Tamalpais Avenue
San Rafael, California 94901

Florida

Lake County Economic Opportunity, Inc. (904) 357-5550
1224 Hazzard Avenue
P.O. Box 687
Eustis, Florida 32726

Gadsden County Community Action, Inc. (904) 627-3872
P.O. Box 389
Quincy, Florida 32351

Putnam County Community Action   (904) 324-1482
    Agency, Inc.
P.O. Box 728
Palatka, Florida 32077

Georgia

Twilight Improvement Association, Inc. (404) 359-5844
P.O. Box 426
Lincolnton, Georgia 30817

Economic Opportunity Atlanta, Inc.   (404) 525-4262
101 Marietta Street, N.W.
Atlanta, Georgia 30303

Illinois

Kankaleeland Community Action   (815) 939-4401
    Program, Inc.
185 North Joseph Street
Kankakee, Illinois 60901

Indiana

Lake County Economic Opportunity   (219) 885-6273
   Council, Inc.
708 Broadway
Gary, Indiana 46402

Trans-Op   (317) 966-2801
908 North 12th Street
Richmond, Indiana 47374

Iowa

MATURA Action Corp.   (515) 782-5208
Over 110 West Montgomery
Creston, Iowa 50801

Kansas

NEK-CAP, Inc.   (913) 486-2156
113 East 8th Street
Horton, Kansas 66439

SEK-CAP, Inc.   (316) 724-8204
110 North Ozark
Girard, Kansas 66743

Mid-Kansas Community Action   (316) 321-6373
   Program, Inc.
P.O. Box 1034
El Dorado, Kansas 67042

Louisiana

Jefferson-Davis Community Action   (318) 824-0519
   Association, Inc.
P.O. Box 1106
Jennings, Louisiana 70546

Tri-Parish Progress, Inc.   (318) 783-7491
P.O. Box 1404
Crowley, Louisiana 70526

Beauregard Community Action   (318) 463-7895
    Association, Inc.
P.O. Box 573
DeRidder, Louisiana 70634

Maine

Northern Kennebec Valley   (207) 872-9292
    Community Action Council
60 Main Street
Waterville, Maine 04901

York County Community Action Council   (207) 324-5762
County Courthouse Annex
Alfred, Maine 05002

Southern Kennebec Valley   (207) 623-3871
    Community Action Council
City Hall
Augusta, Maine 04330

Maryland

Rural Community Bus Lines, Inc.   (301) 268-4800
c/o Anne Arundel Economic Opportunity
    Committee
126 West Street
Annapolis, Maryland 21401

Michigan

Gogebic-Ontonagon Community   (906) 932-4200
    Action Agency, Inc.
216 West Ayer Street
P.O. Box 188
Ironwood, Michigan 49938

Missouri

Green Hills Human Resources Corp.   (816) 359-3907
P.O. Box 151
Trenton, Missouri 64683

Montana

Northern Cheyenne Cooperative   (406) 477-6381
    Association
c/o Northern Cheyenne Tribal Council
P.O. Box 337
Lame Deer, Montana 59043

Nebraska

Southeast Nebraska Community   (402) 862-2881
    Action Council, Inc.
P.O. Box 646
Humboldt, Nebraska 68376

New Hampshire

Rockingham County Community   (603) 436-3896
    Action Program, Inc.
50 South School Street
Portsmouth, New Hampshire 03801

New Jersey

Progress on Wheels   (201) 454-7000
Northwest New Jersey Community Action
    Program, Inc.
Phillipsburg Municipal Building
Phillipsburg, New Jersey 08865

New Mexico

Taos-Rio Arriba Counties   (505) 758-4486
    Community Action Program Inc.
P.O. Box 1215
Taos, New Mexico 87571

New York

Sullivan Community Action   (914) 292-5821
    Commission to Help the Economy, Inc.
10 Church Street
Liberty, New York 12754

Commission on Economic   (518) 272-6012
    Opportunity for Rensselaer County
    Area, Inc.
346 Fuller Street
Troy, New York 12180

North Carolina
    Choanoke Area Development   (919) 398-4131
        Association, Inc.
    P.O. Box 280
    Murfreesboro, North Carolina 27855

    Johnston County Community   (919) 934-2145
        Action, Inc.
    P.O. Drawer 1435
    Smithfield, North Carolina 27577

    Wake County Opportunities, Inc.   (919) 833-2886
    P.O. Box 726
    Raleigh, North Carolina 27601

    Anson-Union Community   (704) 289-2521
        Action Commission, Inc.
    200 East Windsor Street
    Monroe, North Carolina 28110

    Nash-Edgecombe Economic   (919) 442-8081
        Development, Inc.
    P.O. Box 307
    Rocky Mount, North Carolina 27801

    Green Eagle Rural Community   (704) 264-2421
        Transportation Cooperative
    c/o WAMY Community Action, Inc.
    P.O. Box 552
    Boone, North Carolina 28607

    Onslow County Fund, Inc.   (919) 347-2151
    823 Court Street
    P.O. Drawer X
    Jacksonville, North Carolina 28540

Oregon

Jackson County Community   (503) 779-5911
    Action Council, Inc.
P.O. Box 1151
Medford, Oregon 97601

Pennsylvania

Warren-Forrest Counties   (814) 723-1712
    Economic Opportunity Council, Inc.
225 Pennsylvania Avenue, West
Warren, Pennsylvania 16365

Venango Action Corp.   (814) 437-6821
P.O. Box 231
Franklin, Pennsylvania 16323

Texas

South Plains Community   (806) 894-3649
    Action Association, Inc.
City Part Post Office Box 610
Levelland, Texas 79336

Harrison-Panola Community   (214) 935-9952
    Action Association, Inc.
P.O. Box 1343
Marshall, Texas 75670

The Community Council of Cass,   (214) 756-5596
    Marion and Morrison Counties, Inc.
P.O. Box 666
Lindon, Texas 75563

Vermont

Champlain Valley   (802) 655-2300
    Transportation Company, Inc.
110 East Spring Street
Winooski, Vermont 05404

West Virginia

Mercer County Economic   (304) 589-5451
    Opportunity Council
P.O. Box 3185
Bluewell, West Virginia 24701

Raleigh County Community   (304) 252-6396
    Action Association, Inc.
P.O. Box 922
Beckley, West Virginia 25801

Laurel Valley Transportation   (304) 682-6913
    Cooperative
c/o Wyoming County Community Action
P.O. Box 567
Oceana, West Virginia 24874

Wisconsin

Indianhead Community   (715) 532-3719
    Action Agency, Inc.
Rusk County Court House
Ladysmith, Wisconsin 54848

INDEX